S0-BRZ-494

ECONOMIC CAUSES OF THE REFORMATION IN ENGLAND

THE MACMILLAN COMPANY
NEW YORK · BOSTON · CHICAGO · DALLAS
ATLANTA · SAN FRANCISCO

MACMILLAN & CO., LIMITED
LONDON · BOMBAY · CALCUTTA
MELBOURNE

THE MACMILLAN COMPANY
OF CANADA, LIMITED
TORONTO

ECONOMIC CAUSES OF

THE REFORMATION
IN ENGLAND

By Oscar Albert Marti Ph.D.

Professor of History,
Central Missouri State Teachers College

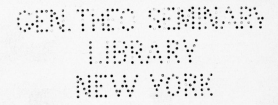

GEN. THEO. SEMINARY
LIBRARY
NEW YORK

New York
THE MACMILLAN COMPANY
1929

283.04 S
M 362
87712

Copyright, 1929.
By THE MACMILLAN COMPANY

All rights reserved, including the
right of reproduction in whole or
in part in any form.

Set up and printed.
Published October, 1929.

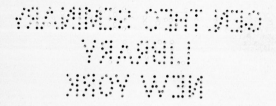

GENERAL THEOLOGICAL
LIBRARY
NEW YORK

PRINTED IN THE UNITED STATES OF AMERICA
BY THE STRATFORD PRESS, INC., NEW YORK

DEDICATED TO

HILARY E. MELTON MARTI

INTRODUCTION

THE founder of Christianity is reputed to have said that one cannot serve God and mammon. Nevertheless the church has been a diligent conservator of this world's goods. At a very early date it stressed ideals of frugality and industry for its members which insured it an enviable economic stability even during the years of declining prosperity experienced by the society of the later Roman Empire. When finally admitted to the privileges of a state religion, Christianity itself became an extensive holder of property. During the Middle Ages its incomes, relatively speaking, were enormous. Prior to the Reformation bishoprics and monasteries controlled a large proportion of Europe's wealth, which at that time consisted chiefly in land. When the new nations of Europe began to emerge out of the chaos of feudalism, princes frequently found themselves seriously embarrassed on account of the immunity from taxation enjoyed by the large estates of the church. Hence the agitation of governments for disendowment, especially of the monasteries.

The importance of the economic situation for an understanding of the Reformation, particularly in England, is fully appreciated by Dr. Marti, whose extended researches in this field are now made available for the public. We bespeak a hearty reception and a wide usefulness for this timely and scholarly volume.

SHIRLEY JACKSON CASE,
University of Chicago.

CONTENTS

ix

CHAPTER III

*Motives and Movements toward the Disendowment
of the English Clergy*

CHAPTER IV

Revolt of the Reformation Parliament against Ecclesiastical Exactions in England, 1529-1536

CHAPTER V

Economic Factors Tending toward the Final Secularization of Church Property in England, 1533-1539

CONTENTS

PRELIMINARY SURVEY

PRELIMINARY SURVEY

THE reformation in the church of England has three distinct phases the course of which it took a century and a quarter to consummate. The first phase had to do with the severance of ecclesiastical jurisdiction from the papal court in the time of Henry VIII. The second phase was marked by a nascent doctrinal and liturgical change in the reign of Edward VI. The third phase, embraced in the century of Puritanism, witnessed the emergence and partial triumph of new doctrinal, ritualistic, and administrative ideals beginning in the Elizabethan Era and ending with the Commonwealth. With the last two phases of the reformation this study has nothing to do. They are developments that grew out of the first phase and a mere continuation of the earlier movement.

The Henrican phase of the English reformation can thus be isolated for purposes of analysis by its peculiar marks and limitations. The first decade of ecclesiastical change in England had paramountly neither a doctrinal nor a ceremonial nor an administrative emphasis. There was an abrupt doctrinal shift manifest in the appearance of the Ten Articles, but the movement quickly reverted back to type. The initial phase of the English reformation involved primarily a break with the papal see. What were the motives giving rise to that rupture between England and Rome? The motives were no doubt mixed—political, legal, religious, dynastic, personal—but it must be borne in mind that the decade immediately following the breach with the papacy was marked by the emergence of a set of revolutionary eco-

nomic changes affecting the church. Many of the changes
were manifest in a series of legislative acts passed by the
Reformation Parliament that began its sessions in 1529.
Among such measures were acts for restraint of the annates, an act for the restraint of appeals to Rome, the Ecclesiastical Appointments Act, an act forbidding papal dispensations and the payment of Peter's pence, the acts for
the suppression of the smaller and greater monasteries. Besides these parliamentary provisions for relief from economic burdens, petitions of protest against economic abuses
were showered upon the king from both parliamentary and
extra-parliamentary sources. Such were the Petition of the
Commons, the Petition of the Convocation, and the Supplication of the Beggars. These essential facts challenge investigation. They give rise to the problem as to just what
part economic factors played in bringing about the ecclesiastical breach between England and Rome during that
period.

That economic forces assumed a leading rôle in consummating the rupture in the church is apparent when the
abuses with which laws of the Reformation Parliament
had to do are investigated in their genetic aspect. Many of
the financial irregularities involved can be traced back at
least three centuries in English history. When so traced
they are seen as disturbing factors long before the final
breach with the papacy in the sixteenth century. Moreover,
a number of financial abuses emerged and spent their
force long before the Reformation period. The latter, together with the abuses that persisted until Reformation
times, gave rise to loud protests, acts of violence, and even
threats of secession; and to a great extent they undermined
the prestige of the papacy and prepared the way for the
final split. Difficulties involving economic interests were by
no means limited to England, but they were common to the

was particularly rapid after the end of the Hundred Years War and of the Wars of the Roses. A national consciousness emerged and developed that resented the idea of allegiance to Rome and the tribute sent there yearly in the form of annates, Peter's pence, provisors, appeals, and papal dues in general. Political centralization and a program of power called for additional and new forms of taxation. The decay of the manor and consequent decline in feudal dues changed the basis of taxation from land to personal property and to imposts on commercial commodities. In this way the church seemed no longer to bear its share of the burden of taxation. Moreover, the clergy resented the new methods of taxation so that the result was a number of acute crises between clergy and monarch long before the breach of the sixteenth century. A notable case in point was that of Edward I in connection with the papal bull, Clericis Laicos.

The underlying cause of opposition to papal taxation, one may almost say, was a conflict between two well defined ideals. The papacy clung to a vision of ecclesiastical imperialism over against which sprung up the spirit of English nationality. After the surrender of King John, England was looked upon as a fief of the Roman See. The popes succeeding Innocent III openly claimed all the churches of England as rightfully belonging to them. They assumed to do with these churches as they saw fit. Particularly did the papacy assert the privilege to impose feudal dues of several sorts. The spirit of nationality resented all papal claims. The friction between these two ideals may be noticed from the time of Henry III to that of Henry VIII. As a whole, the aims, ideals and institutions of the English people tended to nationality and political independence, while the Roman court, by its financial and feudal demands, appeared as a foreign power bent on enriching its coffers at the expense of a state it regarded as tributary.

Finally, the wealth of the church gave rise to internal corruption leading to a long and bitter protest that ultimately ended in the overthrow of the economic sway of the clergy. The continuous calls for money disgusted the nation with the whole papal system, undermined faith in the teaching of the church, and gradually prepared the way for casting aside ecclesiastical authority. Faith in the prayers of priests and prelates was weakened because the clergy prayed only before an open purse. Belief in Purgatory, for instance, was refuted and abandoned by thinking men because it appeared to be a clever device framed by ecclesiastics to exact payment for praying men out of it. "If there be any purgatory," said Simon Fish, a contemporary of Luther, "and the pope with his pardons delivereth one soul thence, then he may deliver as well without money, and if he deliver one then he may deliver a thousand, then all, and thus destroy purgatory. And then he is a tyrant without charity if he keeps them within prison until men give him money. . . . But many men of great literature declare there is no purgatory, but it is a thing invented by the covetousness of the spirituality." Likewise the selling of indulgences at a fixed price in an open market led men to conclude that papal bulls could not be extremely efficacious in the power to absolve sinners from transgression. The church opposed the circulation of Tyndal's New Testament principally because that set of writings tended to confirm the new teaching that absolution came directly through grace "for the sure faith men have in Christ, and not through the pope's pardons." The clergy well understood that such a discovery once accepted by the masses would cut off a prolific source of papal revenues.

In the Petition of the Clergy, in the Petition of the Commons, in the Supplication of the Beggars, in the Act Suspending the Payment of the Annates to Rome, in document after document the cry against excessive fees, unjust ecclesiastical taxation, and against the impoverishment of the realm by means of papal dues was continually reiterated. This was true not only at the time immediately antecedent to the break with Rome but the protest was heard back as far as Wyclif and Grosseteste. The system, adverse in its operations, had been functioning so long and the patience of the English people had been so tried in the past that only the occasion of the king's divorce was required to effect the utter collapse of papal power. The time was ripe for a break with the past and for a new ecclesiastical régime that would promise relief from financial burdens and insure a better investment of ecclesiastical wealth.

The ecclesiastical revolt of the sixteenth century had its roots deeply embedded in the past. No revolution had ever been more carefully prepared and longer delayed than this one that separated almost half of Europe from the communion of Rome. No factors seem clearer in the foundation and development of the movement than the economic. As far as England was concerned, certainly that rebellion was much more than a domestic incident in the career of one of its kings. There were motives back of the revolution much more important than the desire of Henry the Eighth to rid himself of one wife to marry another. The sources of the revolt go deeper than the dynastic hopes of the monarch and disputes about the supremacy. The roots of the reformation reached deep down into a subsoil of money matters and of fundamental economic changes that were taking place. It is only in the added light that such facts furnish that the reformation in England may be clearly understood.

ECONOMIC CAUSES OF THE REFORMATION IN ENGLAND

Economic Causes of the Reformation in England

CHAPTER I

THE WEALTH OF THE ENGLISH CLERGY

THE object of this chapter is not to compile statistics in order to approximate, much less to determine accurately in pounds and shillings, the value of the property and the income derived from it on the part of the clergy of England before the reformation of the sixteenth century. There are at least two good reasons for this limitation. In the first place exhaustive statistics are lacking and in the second place an accurate statistical computation is unnecessary for the purposes of this study. At best an idea of the ramifying reach of ecclesiastical wealth and tenure, and its bearing on the daily life of the people can be determined. And this is important only insofar as it reflected popular disapproval and discontent. The proportion of wealth controlled by the English clergy at the time of its confiscation has been variously estimated by contemporary and subsequent writers to include all the way from a fifth to a half of the wealth of the entire realm. The great majority of authorities, however, give an estimate midway between these extremes by stating that the church controlled a third of the wealth of the kingdom. This conservative approximation perhaps represents most accurately the real proportion of property tenure on the part of the church.

I

Popular attitudes, however, far outweigh the question of figures and exact estimates in ascertaining the causes for revolt against the tyranny, excessive tenure, and abuses of ecclesiastical property. If accurate figures cannot be produced, at least a descriptive account of the economic interests of the clergy can be rendered. Outstanding examples of church holdings can be given; the ramifying tenures of prelates and priors can be shown; the appeal of clerical wealth to the popular imagination can be indicated; and various estimates by outstanding writers can be cited. This will be done to serve as a basis for the reason of popular feeling and of popular opinion against the tenure of the church.

I. The Evolution of Ecclesiastical Endowment

Before the problem of the extent of church property is examined, it may be well to look into the subject of ecclesiastical wealth from a genetic point of view. A summary survey of the process of endowment is necessary to understand the position of the clergy, moral and legal, at times when the confiscation of their property has been threatened. Centuries of custom and tradition rendered the right of ecclesiastical tenure almost immune from attack. In fact had it not been for corresponding spirited protests and sporadic attempts at disendowment running parallel with the growth of wealth, the position of the church as possessor, when finally assailed in earnest, would have been impregnable. As matters stood, the ultimate sequestration of church property was consummated only after a long, slow, and checkered process.

Going back to the very beginning of the evolution of endowment, it may be pointed out that Jesus himself seemed to be wholly without worldly possessions. The foxes, he said, have holes, and the birds of the heavens nests, but the

Son of Man hath not a place to lay his head. This doubtless was literally true, and he seems to have inculcated the same spirit and practice of renunciation in his immediate followers. He made the tenure of property a bar to discipleship.[1] He inspired his fellows with such a personal and direct devotion that they sold their goods in order to aid in the propagation of his teachings.[2]

The early church accumulated little property.[3] This was possibly due to the decided chiliastic attitude that prevailed in the first few centuries.[4] The church looking for a second advent was absorbed in spreading the new message to the ends of the earth. However, Clement of Alexandria in the late second century not only justified the institution of private property, but asserted that it was not wrong for Christians to amass large fortunes.[5] There was a law dating from A.D. 321, allowing anyone at death to leave whatever property he wished to "the most holy catholic church."[6] Statutes like this favoring the incipient state church of Constantine proved in the end the articles of incorporation of the church. They were a first step in laying the foundation for the patrimony of St. Peter. Abuses immediately set in. Exactly a half century later a civic check had to be put on the cupidity of the clergy, for in A.D. 371 there appeared a statute warning religious men against taking possession of widows' houses. The law threatened interference on the part of the imperial officials in regard to "property acquired under the cloak of religion."[7] Thus before the fourth century had spent itself civil laws were necessary to correct ecclesiastical abuses in respect to land grabbing.

But the evil was by no means mitigated. On the contrary, it increased and gained strength in spite of legal barriers. This was made clear by Jerome who intimated that the vision of other-worldliness among churchmen early began to be displaced by a crass materialism. St. Jerome drew from direct information and observation an interesting picture of ecclesiastics full of feigned sorrow watching at the deathbed of the heirless pious rich.[8] Quick in outward ministering these holy men inwardly desired death to quicken his pace, since they knew the church to be the beneficiary in a testament already legally drawn up, sealed, and safely filed away. Possibly Jerome touched up the scene slightly, yet he wanted it understood as representing a tendency of the time. For referring to the statute mentioned above, he said: "I do not complain at the law, but I grieve that we need a statute so harsh. The law is strict and far seeing, but even so the rapacity goes on unchecked." [9] Some eight centuries later Grosseteste, Bishop of Lincoln, was forced to paint a somewhat similar picture,[10] and later still John Wyclif was also found engaged in work along the same line.[11]

Although the so-called Donation of Constantine has proven a forgery and his reputed liberality much of a myth, he gave some property to the church. His example was followed later by many leading Roman families.[12] The donation of Pipin was by no means a fiction. He made possible the enrichment of a church already immensely wealthy, and by his defeat of the Lombards rendered a far greater service by making secure holdings that the papacy already claimed. The time of Leo the Isaurian saw the church possessed of vast holdings.[13] There were large patrimonies in Sicily, in Italy, and in the adjacent islands. The landed estates of the papacy already in the age of Gregory the Great made the pope the richest landlord in Italy. The minimum estimates of one authority gives 1360 square miles of territory with an annual income of about $600,000.[14] The correspondence of Gregory was full of allusions concerning the administration of these vast revenues.[15] Much of the stimulus given to accumulating wealth on the part of the clergy during this period and after was due to the philosophy of Augustine. His theory of history was that the visible church militant was ordained of God to take the place of the old imperial order then rapidly decaying. If the church was to inherit and dominate the earth, it surely had the right of laying claim to its wealth.

Under the Franks in Western Europe the church early took advantage of a Roman practice by acquiring land through the "praecarium" method or tenure. In the Carolingian period the church vastly increased its possessions by this means. Already in the time of Charles Martel the lands of the Franks had been appropriated by the ecclesiastics to such an extent that the state had to resort to a system of confiscation. As the imperial régime of Charlemagne fell to pieces, the bishops and abbots owing to their wealth and powers of protection developed into great feudal lords.[16]

A modified form of continental feudalism was made operative in England after the conquest of 1066. William the Conqueror reorganized the possessions of the English clergy in such a manner as to make their revenues contribute to the defense and maintenance of the realm. Bishops, abbots, and priors were made vassals of the king and were forced to render service the same as the lay lords.[17] Some idea of the wealth of the higher clergy of that time may be gained by noticing the service ecclesiastical lords had to render. The Archbishop of Canterbury furnished William the Conqueror with eighty horses and fully equipped knights in military service, and the rest of the clergy—the bishops, abbots, and priors—also supplied contingents in proportion to their tenures. Walsingham was authority for the statement that

in the early fifteenth century the king derived as many
soldiers from church fees as he did from lay fees.[18] It is
a fact that the clergy supplied a very large force in time
of war.[19] Going back to the Doomsday Survey there is
revealed a great portion of wealth owned and controlled
by the church. In the county of Kent only four knights were
land owners, the others were the king, the Archbishop of
Canterbury, the suffragan bishops, the abbots, and the
priors. Other counties of England show similar figures.[20]
In the middle of the thirteenth century the Earl of Cornwall had an annual income of 36,500 marks, a sum fabulous for that time; yet almost twice that amount was
sent yearly to the pope by the English clergy.[21] In the days
of Henry VIII, the Duke of Buckingham was regarded
as the richest peer in the realm. He had an annual stipend
of about 6000 pounds sterling. But the Archbishop of
Canterbury was rated at approximately the same amount
of revenues.[22]

The period of the Crusades had given a powerful impetus to the enrichment of the clergy. In those days the
church proved a veritable bank from which prospective
crusaders could borrow ready money. For this money they
gave their lands and what property they had in security.
The case of Robert of Normandy illustrated this method
of getting cash and credit, but even kings lacked immediate money.[23] The clergy, on the other hand, could be
depended on for ready cash and as a consequence they
came into possession of mortgages on land and of pledges
on personal property. Notice the following case in point: [24]

> In this year (1250) Roger of Montalt, one of the
> higher rank of the nobles in the kingdom of Eng-
> land, assumed the cross, and let the share which is
> held in the woods and other revenues in Coventry to
> the prior and convent of that place in fee-farm for a

large sum of money in order to provide himself with travelling expenses; he also alienated much of his other property, as did also other nobles both on the continent and on this side of the channel.

Many of the crusaders failed to return, and most of the ones that did come back were financially unable to redeem their lands and pledges. As a result the lands and goods reverted to the church. This process went on for approximately two centuries.[25]

From what has been pointed out it may be seen that the Christian church very early in its career began to be an important economic power in that part of the world where it originated and developed its institutions. The course of endowment started almost at the beginning of organized Christianity and went on for centuries, gradually gaining momentum. The movement did not stop with the Crusades which accentuated it. The Act of Mortmain and the continual evasion of that measure shows that the church was bent on acquiring more land up to the sixteenth century. Again, for two centuries previous to the reformation the pious rich heaped up treasure for the clergy by the erection and endowment of chantries and free chapels.[26] During the same period and somewhat before it began the mendicant orders, having lost the ideal of apostolic poverty, became immensely wealthy.[27] This tendency of accumulating worldly wealth coupled with the policy of never alienating any of it made the church a powerful economic factor in Western Europe up to the end of the Middle Ages.

II. The Nature, Proportion, and Ramification of Ecclesiastical Wealth in England

Not only did the church come to be an outstanding economic factor in Western Europe, but its very opulence gave it an unusual social and political prestige which made its position almost invulnerable. The church emerged in the Middle Ages as a rich ecclesiastical corporation buttressed by precedents and traditions that gave a peculiar moral and legal sanction to its vast holdings. Moral and legal approval was strengthened by the fact that a deference verging on superstition prevailed as to the sacredness of religious property, adding a religious sanction. Such a superstitious sentimentality was strong already in the days of Gregory of Tours, and added further to immunity of church property from seizure.[28] The attitude persisted unbrokenly until the rise of the anti-churchly sects of the eleventh century when by those sects organized agitation was launched for a return of the church to its original ideal of apostolic poverty. The system of tenure of the Roman type was introduced into England in the late sixth century by the missionary monk Augustine. From Anglo-Saxon times to the reformation the English clergy came into possession of a large proportion of the property of the realm, and were fortified in that claim by moral, legal, and religious sanctions.

The proportion of the wealth of England controlled by the clergy at the time of the revolt in the sixteenth century has been estimated by the majority of authorities as being about a third of the entire realm.[29] This appears to be a conservative opinion when compared with some of the others that range from a half to a fifth. But the conservatism marking this computation perhaps makes it in the end the one to be accepted.

The survey of the realm made in the reign of Edward I in the late thirteenth century presented data that showed the number of knights' fees to be 67,000.[30] The church controlled 28,000 of these.[31] In the following century the figures given by one writer placed the number of knights' fees at 75,000, and the number of these under men of religion was put at 27,005.[32] Capello, the Venetian envoy at the court of Henry VII, stated that there were 96,230 knights' fees and that the church possessed 28,015 of them.[33] The three sets of figures represent different periods of time and different ratio, and they certainly warrant no generalization being made. They are at best vaguely descriptive of the proportion of ecclesiastical wealth at different times and possibly from decided differences in point of view.

One of the barons whom Wyclif introduced as opposing the papal tribute money being sent to Rome in the reign of Edward III spoke of the lands of the clergy as equaling a third of those of the entire realm.[34] Lord Herbert of Cherbury who wrote in the seventeenth century gave the same estimate.[35] In another connection the last-named authority inserted a quotation of what is set down as part of a speech delivered before the king, Henry VIII, in privy council: [36]

> But what proportion doth the clergy now hold, when the fourth part of the revenues of the kingdom are employed in that way. For, Sir, when the tenth we pay them in one kind, and the land they hold in another, is estimated, it amounts to this rate and more, as I am informed.

The speech as a whole, however, was strongly biased and sounded like an echo from the Supplication of the Beggars. This note of disparagement against the clergy Henry VIII delighted to hear, and such speeches easily lent themselves to exaggeration.

The Supplication of the Beggers was an incendiary phamphlet that appeared in 1527. It pointed out the proportion of the wealth of England controlled by the church, but what was of much more importance bearing on the reformation it showed the attitude and the propaganda of the time toward the wealth of the clergy. In spite of its deep prejudice it was therefore of great significance. It asserted that the clergy possessed a third of the land of England, and that when the tithes, fees, annates, offerings and alms were added to this a half of the wealth of the kingdom was in their hands. Both the regular and the secular clergy were denounced by it: [37]

> These are not the herds but ravenous wolves going in herd's clothing and devouring the flock; the bishops, abbots, friars, canons, pardoners, somners, priors, deacons, archdeacons, suffragans, priests, monks, and who is able to number this idle, ravenous sort, which setting all labor aside have begged so importunately that they have gotten into their hands one third of all your realm. The goodliest lordships, manors, lands, territories are theirs. Besides they have a tenth part of the corn, meadows, pasture, grass, wool, colts, calves, lambs, pigs, geese, and chickens. Over and besides these they have the tenth of every servant's wages, the tenth part of honey, wax, milk, cheese, and butter. Yea, and so narrowly look they at their profits that the poor wives must be accountable to them for every tenth egg, or else she getteth not her rights at Easter, and shall be taken as a heratic.

The tirade went on along this line indicating gross discontent over the unequal distribution of wealth in that day. If the dissatisfaction was not general, the attitude of a party was at least revealed. The king strongly sympathized with this attitude, reading the pamphlet with avidity and protecting the author of it. [38]

In getting at the extent and ramifications of the tenures of the English clergy one should avoid the common habit of regarding the wealth of the church in a dual relation, namely as regular and secular. In the large the classification was a right one, but it was also largely imaginary and for the purposes of this study it is misleading. The line of demarcation was not clear cut. This was due to two movements. First, the practice of "appropriations" brought many secular prebends and livings under monastic control.[39] Likewise a bishop could also be an abbot, or control vast monastic revenues remote from his diocese.[40] Secondly, the amalgamation of the two types of property was due to the historical development of the church in Britain. England had been invaded in the seventh century almost simultaneously by two groups of missionary monks approaching from two geographical extremeties. From the South the Roman type of ecclesiastical ideal and organization advanced with its two well marked orders of clergy, regular and secular. From the North came the Celtic type with its single order of clergy. In the latter the head of a monastery was also a sort of bishop with jurisdiction over the whole community adjacent to the monastery. Contacts ensued, and the inevitable conflict was finally settled at the Council of Whitby in 664. Now while the Roman form apparently triumphed, Celtic ideals and forms were absorbed by it and survived. Other factors, not necessary to mention, made the separation of the two types on an economic basis into two distinct classes a more or less artificial one.

However classified, the wealth of the English church powerfully appealed to the imagination of contemporaries. Capello, the Venetian ambassador, writing about the year 1500, spoke of England as the richest country of Europe. He commented on its great natural resources, its rich soil, its deposits of tin and lead, its herds of cattle and sheep, and its abundance of fine wool. He also described the

luxury displayed in the inns and the homes of the well
to do, and finally remarked: [41]

> But above all these things are their riches displayed
> in the church treasuries. . . . Nor is there a convent
> of mendicant friars so poor as not to have all these
> articles (candlesticks, censers, cups, etc.) in silver, be-
> sides many other ornaments of the same metal worthy
> of a cathedral church. . . . Imagine what the decora-
> tions of those enormously rich Benedictine, Carthusian,
> and Cistercian monasteries must be. These are in-
> deed more like baronial palaces than religious houses.

Capello incidentally mentioned the two convents of Glastonbury and Shaftsbury as yielding annual incomes to the
amount of 25,000 crowns and 10,000 crowns respectively.[42]
Such sums were large fortunes in that period.

What played on the imagination was verified by actual
fact when a survey of the monasteries was made at the
time of their suppression. The vast wealth of the church
as a whole was also shown in the records of the "Valor
Ecclesiasticus" of Henry VIII. The silver plate, ornaments,
and personal property alone of some of the religious
houses was enormous in value, while the extent of their
lands seems in some cases without limits.

An inventory of the silver and gold plate, and of the
jewels in the cathedral church and convent of St. Swithins
in Winchester sent to Cromwell by the commission to in-
vestigate the status of the monasteries at the time of their
suppression has been preserved.[43] The value of the altar
furniture alone was fabulous. The high altar of the church
was plated with gold and studded with precious stones.
Its whole front was bordered with pearls. A table support-
ing the silver images was finished in silver garnished with
precious stones. The large crucifix was plated with gold and
decked with gems. There was a smaller cross, an image

of the Christ, one of the Virgin, and one of St. John the Apostle all wrought in silver and gold. There was finally the shrine of St. Swithins itself made of silver.

The shrine of Thomas à Becket, dismantled at this time was made of pure gold and studded with precious stones. Speed described it as follows: [44]

> It did abound in more than Princely riches. . . . The Timber worke of this Shrine was coured with plates of gold, damasked and embossed with wires of gold, garnished with broches, images, angels, precious stones, and greate Orient Pearls. All these defaced filled two Chests, and were for price of vnestimable value.

Evidently the special Court of Augmentation which passed upon the confiscated property of the monasteries kept an accurate and itemized account of every piece of property involved. It was weighed or valued in some manner and turned over to the king. It might be sold on the spot, its value recorded, and the proceeds sent to the royal exchequer.[45] For instance, the exact weight of the gold and silver taken from the shrine of the priory at Bridlington was given at 3470 ounces.[46] The accounts of Speed and Strype cited above seem to have come from the records of this court.

A monastic chronicle has recently been discovered containing some records of Christ's Church Priory at Canterbury.[47] During the incumbency of Thomas Chillenden as prior from 1391 to 1411, within eight years the institution spent the sum of 13,056 pounds and 11 shillings in building operations exclusive of repairs. This it could afford to do only because the annual income of the priory amounted to 2400 pounds sterling. Details given in this record reveal the extravagant and unstinted use of money for materials and workmanship. The silver table that stood before the high altar weighed 903 pounds, and the cost of the work upon it was given at 1204 pounds sterling. The carvers, painters, and gilders were paid 1020 pounds sterling for work upon the altar screen which it took them four years to finish.

The hired personnel of some of the religious houses gives some indication of their wealth and the division of labor by reason of it. The household of Buttley was an instance. It was by no means one of the largest monasteries yet there were eighty-four persons on its household staff. Among the skilled workers were a barber, a butcher, two sheep reeves, three shepherds, two horsekeepers, a brewer, two maltsters, six laundresses, two candlemakers, two cartwrights, five carters, and two woodmakers. There was also a cooper, a smith, two warreners, and three bakers.[48]

The broad local extension of monastic land and the far reaching ramifications of ecclesiastical tenures in distant places made the oppressions due to clerical wealth more keenly felt. It also aroused the jealousy of ambitious nobles and the competing new middle classes. The commission for confiscation writing to Cromwell vividly described the territorial extent of the estates of Glastonbury thus: [49]

> The house is greate, goodly, and so pryncely as we have not seen the lyke, with foure parkes adjoynyng, the furthermost of them but foure myles distaunte from the house: a greate mere (lake) whyche ys 5 myles cumpas well replenished wyth greate pykis, bremes, perche, and coche; foure faire manors placis, beyng goodly mansions and also one in Dorsettshire 20 myles distaunte from the late house.

Deerhurst priory near Gloucester had in its possession eight rich manors. Merton priory had lands in twenty counties, Battle Abbey in twelve, and Kenilworth Abbey in seven.[50] These cases are typical rather than unusual. The following reports of the commissioners cover what might be said of most of the monasteries they investigated during this time: "Surveyed the demeans of the late monastery of Whalle & granges of the same, but as yet not all the lands, for hyt lyyth fer assunder yn dyvers shires." [51] "Surrender of the monastery (Stratford Langthorne Abbey) with all its possessions in Sussex, Kent, City of London, and elsewhere in England and Wales and the marches thereof." [52]

The deed of the surrender of Westminster Abbey in 1540 illustrated pretty well the diverse, involved, and expanded interests of some of the greater monasteries. The document turned over unconditionally to the king the monastery itself, and its intricate rights, privileges and possessions in nineteen different counties: [53]

> William . . . abbot of the monastery of St. Peter, Westminster, in the county of Middlesex, and the convent of the same place, greeting: Know ye that we, the aforesaid abbot and convent, by our unanimous consent and assent and free will, have given, granted, and by this our present charter confirmed to our most excellent prince and lord, the lord Henry VIII . . . all our monastery aforesaid, and the church, cloister, site, ambit, circuit, and precincts of the said monastery, as well as all and singular our lordships, manors, hundreds, granges, messuages, lands, tenements, meadows, marshes, feedings, pastures, woods, parks, warrens, commons, wastes, furze and heath lands, waters, fisheries, rents, reversions, services, annuities, fee farms, churches, chapels, chantries, and rights of patronage of churches, chapels, chantries, hospitals, pensions, portions, tithes, obligations, knights' fees, escheats, reliefs, courtsleet, views of frankpledge, fairs, markets, and other rights, juris-

dictions, franchises, liberties, privileges, possessions, and hereditaments whatsoever, as well spiritual as temporal, of whatsoever kind, nature, or sort they be, or by whatsoever names they be called, known, or recognized, situate, lying, or being, as well in the county of Middlesex, Hertford, Essex, Cambridge, Lincoln, Norfolk, Suffolk, Berks, Oxford, Bucks, Bedford, Kent, Sussex, Surrey, Somerset, Dorset, Southampton, Wilts, and Gloucester, and in the city of London as elsewhere wheresoever within the kingdom of England and in Wales, and the marches of the same.

It will be noticed that many of these rights, jurisdictions, and privileges were mere forms and feudal survivals, but even as such they indicate the control of the church over economic resources in the earlier period when discontent and schism threatened.

Such was the nature and extent of the monastic wealth of the church in England at the outbreak of the reformation. The monks had settled on waste lands and brought them under cultivation by almost superhuman effort. The community grew up about them and thus increased their value. The monasteries became first outposts then centers of civilization and culture, industry and wealth, and remained so until the commercial revolution in the fifteenth century when they were forced to take second place. Their history was marked by cycles of spiritual and moral decline and revival. But on the economic side this fluctuation was not so much in evidence. In fact their wealth was bound to increase in the long run since it was the policy of the religious houses ever to acquire and never to alienate property. With the exception of a few illy directed attempts at confiscation, monastic wealth never decreased in content. Wyclif likened the monasteries to whirlpools that sucked in all and gave out nothing: "Swolwis of the see and helle that receyven all that they maye, and gelden not agen." [54]

III. Income and Evaluation of Ecclesiastical Wealth

The total number of monasteries in England at the time of their suppression has been variously estimated all the way from 600 to 1000.[55] The wide range of difference between these two figures indicates two extreme tendencies, one including too few and the other too many. The number of religious houses included in the first confiscation, the smaller monasteries in 1536, was exactly 376. This figure is beyond dispute. A conservative estimate of the larger houses would approximate 300, so that the entire number of religious houses throughout the realm ought not exceed 700 at the highest.

None of the group of the 376 smaller monasteries yielded an annual income above 200 pounds sterling. This was not true of the greater monasteries included in the second confiscation. Many of the latter group yielded immense incomes at the time of their suppression and had been doing so for centuries. In the time of Henry III sixty abbots and thirty priors were classed as "summoniti" of the kingdom. The "summoniti" were subjects ranking as peers with the option of attending the councils of the king.[56] Out of the purses of these mitered abbots came a substantial portion of the financial maintenance of the realm. Edward III fixed the number of these monastic peers at twenty-six, but one was added by Henry VIII making twenty-seven at the time of the break with the papacy.[57] These mitered prelates had enormous incomes in terms of values for the times. Two of them had revenues amounting to 3500 pounds sterling each per annum, six received over 2000 pounds apiece per annum, two others got 1000 pounds, five got 1200 pounds, and the remaining twelve ranged in incomes from 429 to 987 pounds. Multiplying these figures by twenty, and even by thirty would probably bring them up to present day values.[58]

The four abbesses of Shaftsbury, Barking, Wilton, and St. Mary's were rich enough for each to supply the full quota of knights required for baronial rank. The accident of sex alone barred them from the peerage. Shaftsbury possessed revenues valued at over 1300 pounds sterling a year, and Barking at nearly 1000 pounds.[59] There was a current saying among country wits, and the more sophisticated delighted to repeat it also at the court, that should the abbot of Glastonbury wed the abbess of Shaftsbury the heir would come into possession of more land than the demesne of the king.[60]

The combined annual revenues of the 376 lesser monasteries suppressed in 1536 approximated 32,000 pounds sterling.[61] But there were various appraisals. The figure just given included only houses with an income of 200 pounds, or less, a year. The personal property of these smaller houses yielded to the king 100,000 pounds sterling in spite of the fact that the goods were sold at "Robin Hood pennie worthes" prices.[62] This amount included the proceeds from the silver and gold plate. But everything was sold for which a market could be found; including stained glass, iron work, altar cloths, candle spits, basins, frying pans, etc., etc.[63] Items sold as low as four pence are on the list of sale. The lead on the roofs of the houses was specially coveted, and the documents are full of references to it.[64] The lead from Barlinger and Kirkstead was rated at the high figure of 4000 pounds sterling, that from Buttley at 1000 pounds, and that of Boxley at 400 to 500 pounds. The demand for it and the high price it commanded was doubtless due to the fast increasing use of gunpowder.

Only an approximation of the aggregate value of the monasteries has been possible. There are, however, many conscientious and painstaking estimates based on the precarious data compiled in the Valor Ecclesiasticus of Henry VIII and on that found in records of the Court of Augmentation. Speed, an early seventeenth century writer, reckoned the annual revenues of all the religious houses to be £171,313, 4s., 5d. He inserted in his history a carefully compiled catalogue of "their names, their orders, and the true valuation, as in the original Booke thereof taken by the commissioners." [65] Herbert of Cherbury, a later seventeenth century biographer of Henry VIII, put the aggregate annual income of the monasteries at £161,100. [66] Later investigators like Stevens found that the gross annual revenues were £152,517; Tanner £140,785, 16s., 3d.; and Bishop Burnet £131,609. [67] All these authorities claim to have aimed at accuracy and to have investigated in detail, but their results show a wide range of differences. It goes to show how difficult it is to determine the exact wealth of the monasteries because the essential data are wanting in the form of an unbiased and disinterested survey of the religious houses.

In accepting the foregoing estimates of monastic income much leeway has to be allowed for the cupidity and dishonesty of the appraisers, on the one hand, and for the benevolence of the monks, on the other. The royal commissioners often slashed the appraisal of rents and personal property with the view of personal purchases later. [68] The monks had long been in the habit of letting out their lands at rates of rental much lower than secular owners. This was true in particular, when the monks were courting popular favor to stay the course of suppression.[69] One writer stated that the lands were scarcely let at a tenth of their real value since the pious proprietors were the best of landlords, letting their lands at the same rates that were in vogue two, three, and four hundred years in the past.[70] Bishop Burnet's estimate given above was qualified by the statement that it represented at best only a fraction of the annual yield of the monasteries, and Thorold Rogers stated that the very highest estimates ought to be taken at only a half of the actual value of the religious houses.[71]

Cardinal Gasquet, a more recent investigator, has perhaps approached the problem from a somewhat different angle and his conclusions are for that reason both interesting and unique.[72] Taking the records of the Court of Augmentation as a basis, Gasquet demonstrated that in the decade between 1536 and 1546 there was turned over to this court the sum of £315,005, 6s., 10.5d. Taking the receipts of this special tribunal as a whole, he concluded:

> In round numbers the money received by Henry VIII was 1,338,500 pounds sterling. To this must be added 85,000 pounds sterling, the value of the plate, making a total of 1,423,500 pounds sterling; or making between 14,000,000 and 15,000,000 pounds sterling of present day (prewar) money. Besides this the worth of the vestments and ecclesiastical furniture, and . . . countless precious stones and jewels from all the churches of England, the money value of which it is impossible to guess.

According to the Valor Ecclesiasticus of Henry VIII the value of all livings, regular and secular, in England was £320,180, 10s. per annum.[73] Of this vast sum the higher prelates, owing to the practice of "appropriation," of pluralities, and of non-residence, received a great share. The number of secular livings alone, in the time of Henry VIII,

of both England and Wales was 9407, and the revenues
from them was 113,270 pounds sterling per annum. Nearly
one half of these prebends were valued under ten pounds
sterling a year, but it must be understood that five pounds
per annum in this period was considered a good living;
the remainder ranged in value from ten to fifty pounds
sterling per annum.[74]

The overlapping interests of the regular and secular clergy, the devious ramifications of the ecclesiastical economic
system, and the definite organization of church revenues
may best be studied in the light of the data and detail compiled in the Valor Ecclesiasticus of Henry VIII. This
Doomsday Book of the church was an immense amalgam
of statistics resulting from an exhaustive survey of church
property at the time that the annates were diverted from
Rome to the royal exchequer. Its purpose was to furnish a
new basis for computing the annates and tithes. It was in
fact a revised edition of the taxation lists of Nicholas IV
made in the late thirteenth century, and it served the interests of the royal court like the earlier work of the pope
served the papal curia.

The entire field covered by this far reaching survey
cannot be and need not be gone over here in order to
understand the ecclesiastical economic system in England.
A study of the county of Kent and the diocese of Canterbury will serve to illustrate the point. Kent was the oldest
seat of Roman Christianity on the Island, and the ecclesiastical capital of the realm. It embraced an area of 1550
square miles, about one thirtieth that of the whole kingdom,
and although mediocre in natural resources it produced an
abundance of wheat, oats, and beans and was well adapted
to grazing.[75] The annual returns from church property
in Kent, according to the taxation lists of Nicholas IV,
was 12,260 pounds sterling, which had increased only by

about 1000 pounds sterling according to the Valor Ecclesiasticus.[76] In ecclesiastical organization Kent was divided
into two dioceses, Canterbury and Rochester. Canterbury
was divided into eleven deaneries, and Rochester into four.
The deaneries varied in geographical extent and their limits
followed no natural boundaries such as river or seaboard,
but gerrymandered in a wholly arbitrary manner.[77]

The sources of income of the Archbishop of Canterbury were not confined to the diocese of Canterbury nor
to the county of Kent, although a great proportion of it
came thence. The extent of his livings as a secular clergy-
man was far flung, and his financial interests were well
organized and managed. The whole range of his holdings
were divided into seven stewardships, three of which were
outside the county of Kent. From these three extraneous
fiscal districts alone there flowed annually into the archiepiscopal treasury the sum of £1255, 16s., 1d., clear of
expenditures.[78] A fourth stewardship yielded the see £378,
10s., 2d., in clear annual profits. The three remaining districts produced revenues to the amount of £1421, 4s., 9d.
From these seven sources involving secular livings the
primate of England received annually £3093, 18s., 8d.[79]

In addition to these possessions directly at his disposal,
the Archbishop of Canterbury controlled the revenues of
Christ's Church Priory of which he was ex officio head.
The income from this monastery was almost equal to the
revenues already mentioned. Most of it was made up of
farms, rents, pensions, and various other returns from
interests located in Kent. It had, however, like most rich
monasteries, holdings in numerous parts of England. In
Surrey five manors were under its control, two of which
paid £8 each in annual rents; a third paid £20; a fourth
£22; and a fifth £11. Southwark and London contributed
£89 in farms, pensions, and other returns. Eight manors in

Essex paid £47. Money came also from Suffolk, Norfolk, Berkshire, Oxfordshire, and Devonshire.[80] Even from Ireland revenues were forwarded to the coffers of this powerful monastery.[81] The clear annual revenues of Christ's Church Priory according to this survey of Henry VIII totalled £2349, 8s., 5d.[82] Altogether from these two types of sources, regular and secular, the archbishop of Canterbury received, according to the Valor Ecclesiasticus, the total sum of £5443, 7s., 1d.; an income that made him next to the Duke of Buckingham the richest peer of the realm.[83]

The survey of Henry VIII not only reveals the extent of the wealth of the church, but it also implies an intimate economic contact between clergy and people. The record is full of allusions and items regarding pigs, cows, sheep, and all kinds of livestock. It indicates that the church was in possession of manor houses, lands and tenements, and that it controlled tenants. Mention of the church taking in tithes and dues is made everywhere on its pages. The church was a great business as well as a religious corporation, its interest touched the whole economic life of the people, and its power was felt at every turn. It meant that a very small minority of the population was in possession of a large proportion of the wealth of the country—always a grave cause of unrest. The poll tax lists of 1377 and 1381 indicated that the clergy comprised less than two per centum of the population.[84]

To understand the meaning of the foregoing figures it should be pointed out that the value of the pound sterling in terms of wages and commodities differed in the early Tudor period from that of the present day. The purchasing power of the pound fluctuated from time to time, but the general tendency has been a decreasing scale of value since the beginning of the Commercial Revolution of the sixteenth century. Less and less was to be purchased with the same unit of money. The result has been a constant rise in prices, so that a pound sterling in the time of Henry VIII would represent as much value in work and commodities as twenty pounds does at the present time. The increase of prices seemed to be stimulated at the start by the influx of precious metals from the New World, but many factors incident to the rise and expansion of commerce and industry played a part. The process cannot be discussed here, and the fact alone must be pointed out.

From the year 1400 to 1540 the average price of wheat per quarter was about five and a half shillings, but during the succeeding forty years it soared to thirteen shillings. Barley, oats, rye, peas, beans, and malt as well as other foods showed a proportional increase.[85] A seventeenth century writer mentioned that five shillings in his day would buy as much as one shilling in the time of Henry VIII.[86] Stow made mention of the fact that an act of Parliament passed in 1533 forced the following regulations. It showed the disparity between that time and the present in prices of meat; the act provided:[87]

> Butchers sell Beef and Mutton by Weight: Beef at a half penny the Pound; and Mutton for Three Farthings. . . . For at that time fat Oxen were sold for 26 s, 8 d; Fat Wethers for 3 s, 4 d; fat Calves for the same price; a fat Lamb for 12 d. The Butchers sold Penny Pieces of Beef for the Relief of the Poor; every Piece two Pounds and a half and sometimes three Pounds. And thirteen and sometimes fourteen of these Pieces for 12 d. Mutton 3 d the Quarter and 100 Weight of Beef for 4 s, 8 d. What price it has grown to since, it needeth not be set down.

Hugh Latimer, the court preacher of Henry VIII, stated in a sermon that his father had been a yeoman who paid at most three or four pounds annual rental for his tenure.

Yet upon this holding he employed six men, grazed a hundred sheep, and milked thirty cows. He also served the king in war, furnishing a horse and coat of mail. He gave his son a university education, and provided a marriage dowry of five pounds sterling for each of his daughters. In addition to this he held open house for his poor neighbors at intervals, and gave much alms.[88] No doubt a great deal should be allowed in this particular case for good management, but placing efficiency at one hundred per cent this was an extraordinary outlay of labor and livestock on a holding of four or less pounds a year. It illustrates vividly the amazing change in money value.

The case of Latimer was representative rather than unique. A catalogue of strips of land owned by the abbey of Durford in Sussex showed the rentals on a list of fields ranging from two to forty acres. In this, a two-acre plot, including orchard and garden, was valued at a shilling an acre; five fields of meadow land were given at two shillings an acre; one field of thirteen acres rented at six and a half shillings. According to the catalogue the average rental of land on the monastery was a shilling an acre. The 255 acres of demesne land of the abbey were rented for twelve pounds per annum; that is, slightly less than a shilling an acre.[89] Leicester, the home county of Hugh Latimer, was somewhat richer than Sussex county,[90] but rentals of land in the latter could not have exceeded a shilling an acre. It is safe to conclude that the father of Hugh Latimer, for an annual rental of three or four pounds, must have cultivated a tract of seventy or one hundred acres.

In way of summary, the church in England before the Protestant Revolt was possessed of an undue proportion of the national resources controlled by a small minority of the population. Papal provisors, absenteeism, pluralities, and appropriations of smaller livings by abbey and cathedral church tended to centralize this wealth more and more, making it a menace to the political power. This situation invited foreign interference, jeopardized the national defense, and made trouble in the matter of taxation. The wealth of the clergy was inefficiently managed and put to abusive uses. Discontent over ecclesiastical abuses in the thirteenth century followed by a propaganda for disendowment in the fourteenth century were but steps that led to the ultimate attack on church property in the sixteenth century.

CHAPTER II

THE middle period of the reign of King Henry III marked a protest against papal taxation in England that was of vital significance in relation to the ecclesiastical revolt of the sixteenth century.[1] Between the years 1226 and 1258 issues arose over papal finances that at times threatened to end in schism, and although an actual split was avoided, certainly a definite decline of papal prestige was marked.[2] The storm of bitter protest and dangerous discontent was never quite wholly calmed, but either worked in an undercurrent or broke forth openly, at times, until the ultimate breach with the Roman See in 1533. The interim between 1226 and 1258 was the critical period of papal finance.

The year 1216 marked both the accession of Henry III and the demise of the masterful Pope Innocent III. At that time deference to the papal authority was at its zenith throughout Western Europe. Its decline now set in. Decay of the papal prestige in England during the reign of Henry III was only a phase of the general tendency in the same direction on the Continent, and it was due to the same cause—trouble over taxation.[3] In England two centuries intervened between the deaths of Becket and of Sudbury as Archbishops of Canterbury. Within that interim there was a complete cycle of change in popular attitude toward ecclesiastical institutions. Becket, looked upon as champion of the populace, was canonized through mass opinion; Sudbury, symbol for exploitation of the masses, was torn in pieces by the mob.[4] The reign of Henry III, coming midway between these events, marked an epoch for this diametrical change of attitude. There was a twofold phase of protest and revolt against papal abuses and ecclesiastical tyranny, one external and the other internal, from the time of Henry III to Henry VIII. There was discontent over the impositions of the papal exchequer and there was dissent over the economic abuses of the English clergy.

I. A Clash between Two Ideals

As was stated in the preliminary survey, a contributing cause of this thirteenth century opposition to papal taxation was the conflict between two well defined ideals, one of which was long standing and the other just emerging. On the one hand, the papacy clung tenaciously to the vision of ecclesiastical imperialism. Especially after the submission of King John in 1213, England, according to the current feudal interpretation, was looked upon as a fief of the papacy. Innocent III and succeeding popes openly claimed all the churches of England as papal property and England itself as a province of the Roman See.[5] Innocent IV insolently alluded to Henry III as his vassal. When the English delegation protested over papal abuses at the Council of Lyons in 1245, he said: [6]

> It is desirable that we should put the king of England on the same level (excommunication) with that prince (Frederick II), so as to crush him, since he is our vassal and is now resisting us.

On another occasion he spoke of the English king not only as a vassal but as his slave.[7] As far as Henry himself was concerned, he virtually agreed to fulfill his father's engagements, assuming this attitude with few exceptions throughout his long reign; but this was certainly not the case with some of his subjects.[8] With such an attitude the papacy assumed the right to collect the annual tribute money promised by King John and to impose dues and feudal obligations of various sorts. It was the attempt on the part of the papacy to exercise this assumed privilege that made the danger of schism loom up, and that permanently crippled papal prestige in England.

Over against the vision of papal imperialism was rapidly developing the incipient ideal of English nationality. The feeling of insular isolation and territorial compactness of Englishmen, to be sure, had its greatest impulse later during the Hundred Years War; but the ideal was forming as early as the reign of Henry II and that of John.[9] The process was stimulated by the twelfth century revival of Roman law and the administrative centralization of Henry II. It was intensified during the reign of King John by the loss of the Angevin feudal inheritance in the victories of Philip Augustus. The loss of these continental possessions dissipated a dream of imperialism abroad and centered political interests of Englishmen within the Island itself. All this helped the growth of nationalism. A consciousness of isolation was plainly in evidence in the time of Henry III.[10] Speed, referring to this thirteenth century tendency, used a very suggestive word to express the attitude. It is the king, Henry III, whom he represents as commenting on papal taxation:[11]

> The things which the pope would perswade us to doe stretch themselves as farre as the Christian world is wide. And because England is but an *out-angle* thereof, when we shall see other kingdoms give us an example he shall finde us more forward to obey.

The crusading movement had given a powerful impulse to commerce, and the growth of commerce in turn stimulated national integration and concentration. The social and economic by-products of commerce—industry, the towns, and the middle classes—all militated against feudalism in favor of the national monarchy. Capital invested both at home and abroad needed protection and the smaller feudal political unit was inadequate. Profitable trade and uninterrupted industry required institutions that made for law and order, and the monarchy lent itself powerfully to this end. Unity, uniformity, centralization of the administration became the order of the day, and this movement was strong by the middle of the thirteenth century. This tendency reacted against ecclesiastical cosmopolitanism. The parliament of Edward I boldly asserted to the pope: [12]

> The kings of England have never pleaded, nor been bound to plead respecting their rights in the kingdom of Scotland, or any other temporal rights, before any judge, ecclesiastical or secular. . . . Our lord, the king, shall not plead before you nor submit in any manner to your judgment, nor suffer his rights to be brought into question.

It was the growing spirit of nationality with which the papal court came into contact in trying to impose its authority as a suzerain power over a vassal territory such as England was regarded to be in the thirteenth century.

The result of this awakening national consciousness, then, was a tendency to resent foreign interference of every kind. This included the intermeddling of the papacy. Such intermeddling asserted itself during the period in question, that is from 1226 to 1258, in three distinct ways; namely, the operations of the Italian bankers, the practice of papal provisions, and direct papal taxation. These things re-

sulted in grievous oppression giving rise to grave consequences. They had their rise during the reign of Henry
III and became seriously aggravated within the same period. In fact, the situation was so menacing a number of
times that the reign of that monarch marked a distinct
crisis in papal finance because of the protest and revolt that
was staged. This was true not in that the evils were eradicated, or even mitigated, through the crucial development,
but in that there was prolonged and coöperative resistance
offered. The noxious practices continued until the final
religious revolution of the sixteenth century, [13] but an attitude developed toward these abuses that branded them as
intolerable and illegitimate.

II. The Operations of the Italian Bankers

The coursines, as the Italian bankers were called, seem to
have made their initial appearance in England about
1235.[14] They came, evidently, as papal agents, but if they
were not the official promoters of the papal court, their
presence was at least connived at by Rome and the papacy
was looked upon as a participant in their nefarious business.[15] They were in fact popularly spoken of as "merchants of the pope," though the only "merchandise" with
which they dealt was bills of exchange and ready bullion
by which they carried on a disguised usury and an illicit
banking system.[16] One writer alluded to them as pests,
merciless debtors, the bane of the English people, who
brought great sums of money into the kingdom and loaned
it usuriously contrary to the canon law.[17] Long tradition
had, in fact, made the taking of interest both an unethical
and an irreligious practice; the civil law, also, had made
it a crime to be penalized by confiscation, and the canon

law reckoned it as a deadly sin;[18] yet these alien money mongers had the temerity to charge exorbitant rates of usury.

The particular business of the Italian bankers was to furnish ready money, especially on the occasion of a papal levy or tax, to whosoever would be forced to borrow from them. Priests, laymen, monks, and prelates were time and again compelled to resort to them for the payment of tithes, dispensations, commutation of vows, and other ecclesiastical obligations.[19] The king himself was at times heavily in their debt.[20] At a later time this matter of royal indebtedness to the Italian bankers, indirectly at least, proved a factor in promulgating the Provisions of Oxford and in precipitating the contest between king and barons finally decided at the battle of Lewes in 1264.[21] The king had borrowed largely through the agency of these bankers to carry on a foreign project that involved the exchequer in a huge debt and the nation in entangling alien alliances deeply resented by the barons.

These alien money lenders bound their victims by an iron clad contract meant to hold the borrower in abject dependence permanently, or at least for a long protracted period. The form of contract used by them in conducting business was binding not only because of the gilt edged security involved, but also because of the prestige and papal authority back of it.[22] An exceedingly high rate of interest was assured the lender by the nature of the legal document drawn up in the transaction. For each mark loaned, according to the contract, a pound sterling would be due at the end of a twelvemonth.[23] If one reckons the old Anglo-Saxon mark of account at $3.23 in present day value and the pound sterling at $4.86—which was perhaps the true relative ratio—an interest rate of about 50 per cent was charged. In a number of instances when the amount

borrowed was 100 marks the bond stipulated that 104 marks
were due at maturity. This was to be in good "lawful
money sterling, each mark being computed at 13 shillings
and four pence sterling." [24] Thus a sort of premium,
amounting to 4 per cent, was attached to the transaction
and had to come ultimately out of the borrower's pocket.
Payment of principal and release from the contract was
practically impossible until the bond was due. This was to
assure a continuity of interest over a definite period of
time. For instance, a loan of 100 marks demanded the payment of 100 pounds sterling at the end of a year.[25] If
the borrower wanted to redeem the contract say at the
end of a month or two months, the full 100 pounds would
have to be paid. This may have lent stability and dependence to the banking business, but it worked an injustice
to the borrowing public. This made the Italian bankers
appear more extortionate than the Jews, and the New
Temple in London, the home of these foreign financiers,
became a symbol of oppression.[26]

In case a loan became overdue, at the end of each bi-
monthly period one mark for every ten marks of the
original debt was due the lenders.[27] This would make an
interest rate of sixty per cent, so that overdue notes automatically increased in the rate of interest. All expenses involved in collecting overdue installments had to be borne
by the debtor.[28] Risk on the part of the money lenders was
reduced to a minimum for the two reasons already mentioned. In the first place, the prestige and fear of the
papal authority guaranteed the utmost effort of the borrower to pay, and in the second place, a gilt edged collateral was provided. In regard to the latter, the churches
and monasteries which did business with the papal money
lenders were bound by the following agreement: [29]

We bind ourselves and our church, and our successors, and all our goods and those of our church, moveable and unmovable, ecclesiastical and temporal, in possession and hereafter to be in possession, wheresoever they shall be found, to the said merchants and their heirs, until the full payment of the aforesaid; which goods we hereby recognize we possess from them by a precarious tenure.

The Italian bankers were an important factor in the manifest discontent, protest, and revolt of the period. They clutched within their grasp all the financially straitened whether king, laymen, prelates, priests, or monks. Under color of covering alleged exorbitant losses, well secured against by adequate collateral, they collected excessive rates of interest illegally imposed. Papal envoys used them to finance pledges and absolutions.[30] English noblemen used them to lend out surplus money at good interest, but by the masses they were detested, and even the king was their enemy.[31] They were present in England not to aid laymen and churchmen in times of financial straits, but apparently to exploit them in case of unusual and extraordinary papal demands. At any rate, both individuals and religious corporations were bled for that which looked like selfish gain, and the papal court seemed to enjoy an effective means of controlling the purse strings of both king and people.[32] They were thus linked in popular attitude indirectly with the Roman exchequer. They did not scruple in resorting to bribery for securing license to carry on practices that current sentiment condemned.[33] Above all, they were accused of immorality in their private life.[34] They amassed vast fortunes and kept splendid residences in London.[35] They were openly denounced by churchmen and laymen alike as schismatics, heretics, usurers, and traitors.[36] "They polluted the land with base usury." Official action was on one or two occasions taken against them, but with little success. As early as 1235 the Bishop of London pronounced an anathema against them, trying to expel them from the diocese; but they merely laughed at his efforts and successfully appealed to the papacy.[37] In 1251 a prosecution of them was undertaken by the civil courts with some success, since many were arrested and others had to seek refuge. Yet by illicit use of their wealth they saved themselves from permanent expulsion from the realm.[38]

III. The Practice of Papal Provisions—Opposition by Organized Direct Action

By the middle of the thirteenth century foreign influence was rapidly becoming a menace in England along three different lines. The French marriage of the king brought dictation of Frenchmen in political matters. The operations of the Italian bankers threatened the control of financial interests by a group of undesirable aliens. And now a third danger loomed up in the shape of papal provisions for English benefices that tended to place ecclesiastical affairs also under the power of hated foreigners. The reign of Henry III marked the beginning of a practice that reached several acute crises within this period itself, that went on until it brought about the Statutes of Provisors of Benefices in 1351 and 1390, and that, in spite of the statutes, persisted to some extent to the time of the reformation.

The practice of papal provisions presented a twofold evil as to the welfare of the realm. One was spiritual and religious while the other was economic and financial. It meant that ecclesiastical livings were being filled, through papal appointment, with foreign incumbents, chiefly Italians. Some were non-resident prelates dwelling on the Continent out of contact and out of sympathy with their charges; others were resident priests ignorant of the vernacular, adverse to English ideals, and indifferent to the welfare of the flock.[39] Papal provisions were odious to churchmen and laymen for these reasons and because they drained large sums of money from the country without adequate services rendered.[40]

Appointments of this sort were constant and involved now and then a mass displacement of English priests and prelates by the alien favorites. To say that England was infested with alien priests holding benefices great and small is the statement of a fact. Their presence, their attitude and their methods were regarded with hatred and suspicion. "The Romans and their legates lorded it in England, causing much injury to laymen as well as ecclesiastics in the matter of advowsons of churches, providing their own friends with vacant benefices at pleasure, setting themselves up in opposition to bishops, abbots, and other religious men, and involving them in sentences of excommunication."[41] In 1240 warrants came to the Archbishop of Canterbury and to the bishops of Lincoln and Salisbury to provide livings for 300 Italians at one time.[42] Rather than be responsible for carrying out such an order, the archbishop of Canterbury underwent voluntary exile.[43] When Martin, a papal nuncio, came to England in 1244, he was invested with power to suspend prelates and minor clergymen to make room for the clerks and nephews of the pope as he saw fit.[44]

These Italians held some of the richest benefices in the kingdom, and they were of "an endless number."[45] Pope Innocent IV was particularly generous in this direction for "he impoverished the universal church more than all his predecessors since the establishment of the papacy."[46] Grosseteste, Bishop of Lincoln, complained that the for-

eign clergy was drawing an annual income of 70,000
marks.[47] Others pointed out that their combined income
exceeded that of the king himself.[48] One of these Italian
prelates was Archdeacon of Richmond for fifty years,
amassing an immense fortune and keeping the papacy in-
formed regarding vacancies.[49] This encroachment on their
interests was not looked upon passively by the English
people, so that the result was a long and spirited protest
and at times open revolt against the practice. To such an
extent was public sentiment aroused against the papal intruders that riots broke out on account of them. Sometimes
their barns and storehouses were burned, and sometimes
they were opened and the goods distributed to the poor.
Such resentment was aroused over the system on the part
of men of rank that open schism loomed up and allegiance
to the papacy was threatened.[50] In this respect three instances stand out prominently; the popular demonstrations
of 1231-2, the attitude of the English party at the Council
of Lyons in 1245, and the protest of Grosseteste, Bishop of
Lincoln, in 1253.

The popular demonstrations that took place in 1231-2
were due to a general and a well organized movement directed against the alien incumbents of English benefices.[51]
They were significant as to the nature of the protest involved, the methods used, and the social standing of some
of the participants. Exasperated by the injustice and oppression of this system of papal patronage, its opponents organized into secret societies to rid the country of the foreign intruders. Such societies spread over a large part of
England.[52] The movement was organized into local group
units of as many as 100 persons and had as leaders high
officials of the church, sheriffs, knights, and other prominent laymen. Hubert de Burgh was among them and ac-
tively assisted in some of the mob methods.[53] So powerful

was the influence of these associations that the soldiers sent to interfere with their operations were usually won over to the cause of the rioters.[54]

The organization resorted to propaganda, threat, and open violence. The Italian clergy were denounced as a menace. It was pointed out that advowsons were being perverted and misused by the foreign incumbents. Appointments to benefices, it was claimed, belonged to the local bishops and not to the papacy.[55] The societies posed as the saviors of the church by attempting to rescue it from foreign patronage.[56] They addressed letters warning ecclesiastics not to interfere with them in their work. They forbade the payment of farms to the Roman incumbents, essaying to force out the Italian clergy by depriving them of their revenues. They threatened violence to property in case of all warnings not heeded and instructions not followed.[57]

But the association went even a step farther by actually seizing the goods of the foreign clergy already in possession, selling these goods and distributing the proceeds to the poor.[58] An armed band of men took possession of the church at Wingham after this fashion, opened its barns, disposed of the stuff therein, and distributed the proceeds to the wonted charities of that benefice.[59] This was not an isolated instance of such a procedure, but the work was carried on at various places and continued throughout the winter of 1231-2.[60] At times more violent methods were used; the Italian clergy were attacked, their granaries pillaged, their farms and possessions wasted, and their persons insulted so that many fled the country or went into hiding. Sometimes the alien incumbents were kidnaped, abducted to places of security, and forced under threat to promise the proper administration of the charities involved in their livings.[61] If this movement succeeded little in doing away with the evils of papal patronage, scarcely checking its growth even temporarily, it at least illustrates the spirit of the times and shows to what ends Englishmen were willing to go in opposing papal claims. At best this episode registered only the beginning of a spirited resistance which persisted until the final eradication of the evil in the dim dawn of pre-reformation times.

IV. THE PRACTICE OF PAPAL PROVISIONS—BONIFACE OF SAVOY

The demonstrations of 1231-2 came at a time when the abuses of papal patronage as to English benefices were in their earliest stages. The evil not only persisted but increased until the time of Pope Innocent IV, who ascended the papal throne in 1243, marked its richest harvest.[62] Boniface of Savoy, as Archbishop of Canterbury, was perhaps one of the most outstanding instances of the evil results of papal provisions for English church livings. Elevated to the see of Canterbury in 1240 and finally consecrated in 1245, Boniface throughout his incumbency used the archiepiscopal office as a means of plundering his ecclesiastical province to maintain a sumptuous residence abroad and to carry out his foreign schemes.[63] He was an uncle of the English queen, and the fact that his election was manipulated by the royal court aggravated the popular ill feeling, for the partiality of the king toward his wife's relations proved an ever increasing grievance until the revolt of 1258.[64] He was wholly of a secular turn of mind, unfitted for any ecclesiastical post, and hence entirely out of place in the highest office of the church in England.[65] Even the fact that he seemed at times to take a stand with the nationalist party did not tend to decrease his unpopularity.[66]

For a long time after his election Boniface aided his brother, Philip of Savoy, in prosecuting a private war in Provence. To do so, under pretext of raising money to pay

the debts left by his predecessor, Boniface cut down and
sold the wood on the lands of the see, levied heavy fines
and taxes on the people, and thus raised 15,000 marks to
carry on a war in which Englishmen had no interest except that of opposition.[67] The contemporary chronicler,
Matthew of Paris, registered public complaint on this matter thus: [68]

> Boniface of Savoy, elect archbishop of Canterbury,
> and his brother Philip Bal, gave their attention to this
> war . . . thus causing great expense and injury to the
> English church; for in order to sustain the war, they
> pleaded divers pretexts for raising money, and heaped
> together treasure upon treasure, distributing it among
> the trained knights and other men of blood.

Besides abducting vast sums of money in this irregular
manner, Philip of Savoy through the influence of Boniface
and of Innocent IV was permitted to hold remunerative
livings in England as an absentee tenant who never set
foot on English soil.[69]

Boniface obtained permission of the pope to collect the
revenues for a year of all the churches in his province falling vacant and to which reappointments were made.[70] Here
one finds for the first time the imposition of a sort of local
annates which within a decade turned itself into the practice of collecting the papal annates.[71] Thus in the decade
of 1246-1256 the foundation was laid for an abuse that
proved a paramount cause of the break with the papacy
three centuries later.[72] This "new and unheard of contribution" of Boniface had to be paid immediately on pain
of suspension, and "the bishops being unwilling as well as
unable to kick against the pope's mandate and authority,
at length consented although unwillingly and with bitterness of heart." [73] Later, when the bishops showed signs of
rebellion because of this new practice they were warned

that "all detractors, all rebukers, and all who practiced deceit in the matter would be excommunicated by him, the pope." The bishops on this occasion did persist in their protest and as a result were excommunicated throughout the province of Canterbury.[74] The episode illustrated the arbitrary methods of Boniface and the papacy, the reluctant spirit of conforming by English churchmen, and the pressure brought to bear to enforce papal authority. Throughout England men began to cherish secret malice in their hearts toward a system bold enough and hard enough to impose such an injustice.[75] Men even began to openly curse the king for tolerating the levy of such a tax upon Englishmen.[76]

In an attempt to carry out a visitation of his province, "for a greedy love for money" rather than for a desire to eradicate immorality and correct laxity in discipline and administration, Boniface was met with a spirited resistance from his clergy.[77] This he in turn met with physical force carried to a point of extreme violence.[78] At Canterbury itself the visitation was made with "great strictness and without mercy," arousing a feeling of deep resentment among the monks of Christ's Church Priory.[79] Proceeding from Canterbury he extorted thirty marks from the not overly rich priory of Rochester, fleeced likewise the abbey of Faversham, and reached London where he demanded the rights of purveyance.[80] At London he met with the first open resistance, for the canons of St. Paul's opposed his visitation and appealed to the pope.[81] When the priory of St. Bartholomew showed a similar disposition to resent the visitation, Boniface pounced upon the sub-prior, struck him a blow on the head, trampled on his prostrate body, and inflicted life-long injuries upon him.[82] He even, in his rage, cried out for a sword, evidently to finish his work at the priory with murder. In the fray, it was revealed that the archbishop, unlike Becket wearing a hair shirt next to his skin, wore a coat of mail under his vestments.[83] The incident aroused all London. When the king ignored an appeal for redressing this incident, a riot immediately threatened. A mob gathered and sought for the archbishop, crying out to cut him in pieces, and he escaped only by secretly leaving the city. The tumult proved so serious that the king, fearing sedition, ordered that none take further part in the controversy on pain of life and limb. But resentment was so strong that the archbishop fled the realm seeking consolation at the papal court.[84] The visitation proved a failure and resentment toward the practice of papal provisions became more deeply seated.

V. The Practice of Papal Provisions—Challenge at the Council of Lyons

The Council of Lyons held in 1245 marked the excommunication of Frederick II and the temporary triumph of the papal party over the German interference in Southern Italy. This has been the usual emphasis in the historical significance of that council and it has been a proper one. But in the interests of this study, it is important to notice other activities and attitudes of the assembled churchmen. In particular, the protest of the English delegation over papal provisions was significant because it ended practically in the nature of a challenge to the Roman authority. The protest was certainly firm and emphatic, though no act of violence emerged or was threatened. The whole episode sounded like an echo of another council held at Bourges nearly twenty years earlier, in 1226. At that time the papal legate, Romanus, made the attempt to acquire in behalf of the papacy a definite number of foreign ecclesiastical livings.[85] The result was a threat of schism, one of the earliest recorded, for he was frankly told: *"Moveat vos zelus universalis ecclesiae et sanctae sedis Romanae. Quia si omnium esset universalis oppressio posset timeri ne immineret generalis discessio, quod Deus avertat."* [86] Balked by the attitude of the churchmen, the papacy resorted to the more subtle method of acquiring benefices by means of provisions, and the protest of 1245 was the fruits of that policy.

Among the English prelates present at the Council of Lyons in 1245 was Robert Grosseteste, Bishop of Lincoln. It was he for one that boldly and vigorously attacked the system of provisions and the papal methods.[87] He asserted before the assembled council that the filling of English livings with alien priests was both an imposition and a crime against the English people. He said that the "cause, fountain, and source" of the corruption of the church was the Roman court itself, and that papal provisions was one of the principal means of making it corrupt. The Roman Curia, he said,[88]

> appoints not pastors, but destroyers of the flock; and that it may provide a livelihood for some one person, hands over to the jaws of the beasts of the field and to eternal death souls many, for the life of each of which the Son of God was willing to be condemned to a most shameful death.

He roundly denounced the favoritism, nepotism, and selfish patronage of the papacy. Anyone guilty of such sins made himself an apostate, *ipso facto*, from the Body of Christ which was the church. The papacy, Grosseteste alleged, had taken a long step in that direction through the practice of papal provisions, and the only way for it to retain its ancient prestige was by a reformation in that respect. "Unless it corrects itself without delay, quickly will it deprive itself of all good things." [89]

William of Poweric, addressing the Council as a layman and as the spokesman of the English people, pointed out that papal patronage of foreign clergymen was not only unjust but that it would no longer be tolerated.[90] He complained of the numerous financial exactions of the papacy which up to that time had been freely paid.[91] The matter of papal provisions, however, was a specially serious matter. The practice was not only a great annoyance and an "intolerable injury," but it involved a serious legal problem. Advowsons of churches had been provided originally by their founders for the edification of the local community and for the support of the poor. That aim was now being thwarted and perverted by the revenues of these foundations diverted abroad through an alien clergy to the neglect of the local interests.[92] After speaking at length along this line, Poweric turning to the pope directly, said:[93]

> But now by you and your predecessors having no consideration, besides the aforesaid supplies, Italians (of whom there is an endless number) are now enriched by the patronage belonging to those very religious men, who are called the rectors of the churches, thus leaving those whom they ought to defend entirely unprotected, giving no care for the souls of the people, but allowing these most rapacious wolves to devour the flock, and carry off the sheep. . . . They do not practice hospitality or the bestowal of alms enjoined by the church, but they only receive the fruits to carry them out of the kingdom, impoverishing it to no slight degree by possessing themselves of the revenues. . . . These Italians, receiving sixty thousand marks a year in England besides other receipts, carry off more clear gain in revenues from the kingdom than the king himself receives, who is the protector of the church and holds the reins of government in his hands.

But the English national party at Lyons did not end

matters with a mere protest. It warned the pope that the oppression must cease, for it would no longer be endured. The warning was couched in terms of deference but the spirit of revolt was plainly apparent. The pope giving fair promises merely played for time, but the English envoys demanded immediate redress.[94] When this was finally refused, the delegation lost its temper and threw down the gauntlet. The contemporary historian said:[95]

> They departed in great anger, giving vent to their threats and swearing with a terrible oath that they would never satisfy the detestable avarice of the Romans by paying the tribute, nor would they suffer any longer the produce and revenues of the churches to be extorted from them as heretofore.

This was the mood in which certain of the English envoys left the Council of Lyons. They had come seeking redress and returned with no assurances of relief. They were now convinced of papal indifference and even antipathy toward their grievances. Resentment was enhanced when exactions did not cease and when in the following year the papacy, angered at the attitude of the English group at Lyons, attempted an alliance with the French for the purpose of attacking England, subduing it, and forcing upon it a spirit of greater deference for the Roman court.[96] On the whole, the indignation of leaders in England, lay and ecclesiastical, was stirred to the depths, and mumblings of secession were heard. Alluding to the practice of papal provisions, a contemporary chronographer wrote:[97]

> Here is the cause, here are the reasons why people secede in heart, if not in body, from our father the pope, who is provoked to the austerity of a stepfather; and also from our mother the Roman church, who vents her fury with the persecutions of a stepmother.

VI. The Practice of Papal Provisions—Grosseteste the Belligerent Bishop of Lincoln

One of the most outstanding figures in the so-called greatest of centuries was Robert Grosseteste, Bishop of Lincoln—Oxford scholar and lecturer, medieval scientist, and eminent churchman. He was a self-made man, rising upward from the villein class to make for himself an international renown. In spite of his nickname he was an Englishman by birth, and for over twenty years after he became Bishop of Lincoln, he stood as the leader and champion of the English national party opposed to the imperialism of papal Rome. His voice was not, therefore, a solitary one, but he was merely spokesman for a large following both lay and ecclesiastical.[98] This fact alone accounts for the boldness of his utterances and the drastic nature of some of his actions. His extensive diocese of Lincoln forced leadership upon him owing to the extreme unpopularity and the protracted absence of Boniface of Savoy, Archbishop of Canterbury, whose position should have made him the natural leader of the English group. Also the fact that his incumbency of the see of Lincoln was long contemporaneous with the papal reign of Innocent IV whose financial abuses exceeded those of all his predecessors brought Grosseteste to the front as an antagonist of the papal demands.[99]

The particular fight of the Bishop of Lincoln was against the practice of papal provisions, but he was the sworn enemy of every form of papal abuse. Letters of the type given below had been coming into England thick and fast ever since the accession of Pope Innocent IV, and the evil of provisions was getting beyond the point of endurance. The following letter was written by Innocent IV to the abbot of St. Albans, dated from Lyons, December 12, 1251:[100]

Whereas our well beloved son, John of Camecave, our nephew and chaplain, holds the church of Wengrave, the right of presentation to which belongs, as we understand, to you; we in our paternal affection beg you, and by these apostolic letters order you to exchange the said church for the first in your presentation which shall become vacant, which the said chaplain, or his proctor, shall think proper to accept of, reserving Wengrave for our own gift; notwithstanding any prohibition of reservation whatever, and notwithstanding even the indulgence which is said to be granted to the English, that the benefices of Italian clerks who resign them, or die, shall not be immediately given to some other Italian clerk.

In this letter the arbitrariness of the papal system of provisors was plainly evident. The letter presented not a mere request ("beg you") but primarily a demand ("order you") in a day when papal demands could not be slighted with impunity. The demand also took precedence over all previous arrangements for the disposition of the property involved, indulgences not excepted. Again such papal appointments were indirect and cumulative; the church of John of Camecave was not released from papal provision, and John of Camecave was on the ground taking note of the richest living about to become void, ready to step into it as authorized by the letter. The writer of the period lamented over the situation: "We have inserted this letter that all may know with what sufferings and injuries the Roman church afflicted us wretched English; for whoever may consider the purport of it will find in it contempt, injury, and oppression." [10]

It was a letter written in this spirit that led Grosseteste, Bishop of Lincoln, to launch his epoch-making protest and revolt against papal inductions of foreign priests. He flatly refused to obey a papal mandate for admitting Frederick de Lavagna, a nephew of the pope, as a canon of the cathedral church of London.[102] His attitude toward this sort of papal favoritism had already been expressed several years before at the Council of Lyons where he asserted it to be a crime against the English nation. Hence, when this demand came in 1253 he opposed it almost to a point of open schism with the papacy. He justified his position by holding that a system guilty of such a demand was unworthy of obedience and that carrying out such a mandate meant the destruction of souls rather than their salvation. The system deprived souls of the proper pastors and gave them over to men "who procure their salary from the milk and wool of the flock of Christ, and do not minister to their wants." His rebellion was plainly spoken: [103]

> The most holy apostolic see cannot incline towards any sin of such a kind as to order, enjoin, or in any way attempt at anything so hateful, detestable, and abominable to our Lord Jesus Christ, so extremely pernicious to the human race. For it would evidently be a defection from, or an abuse, or a corruption of its most holy and full power, or an estrangement from the throne of glory of our Lord Jesus Christ. . . . And no faithful subject of the said see, in immaculate and sincere obedience to it can obey such mandates or precepts . . . but it is a necessary duty for him to oppose and resist them with his utmost strength. Therefore, my reverend lord, by virtue of the obedience and fidelity due from me to both fathers of the most holy apostolic see, and out of regard to my union with it in the Body of Christ; I, although with all desire for union, and in filial obedience and affection refuse to obey, and oppose, and resist the orders contained in the aforesaid letters because they tend to that which is most abominable in sin against our Lord Jesus Christ and to that which is most pernicious to the human race, and because they are contrary to the Catholic faith.

This was open rebellion to the Roman see, in spite of the guarded language used. The rest of the letter was full of similar sentiment. It placed the responsibility for provisions on the papal incumbent, Innocent IV, refusing to honor the mandate of a pope who had overstepped himself in papal authority. It did not ignore or repudiate the apostolic authority, but the protest and revolt was against the officer and not the office. Grosseteste called the incumbent pope Antichrist, Wyclif applied the term to the papacy, and thus marked a step farther in the revolt from Roman deference. By attacking the incumbent, though sparing the institution, the Bishop of Lincoln laid a foundation for rejecting the papal system three centuries later.[104] The pope was greatly angered by the refusal, but he feared to take up the challenge because it was evident that Grosseteste had a powerful national party back of him after the Council of Lyons.[105]

Grosseteste did not limit his opposition to the evils of papal provisions, but those evils seemed to be uppermost in his mind. A deathbed pronouncement gave a long list of other abuses which the bellicose churchman detested. Thus he carried on the fight to the bitter end, pointing out that the church would not be free from the galling papal bondage except by the "bloody point of the sword." Avarice, usury, simony, fiscal robberies, provisions of benefices by the Roman exchequer were all leading to the inevitable conflict.[106] The Bishop of Lincoln was one of the first to see danger in papal aggression and the need of reformation:[107]

> The church of England is now worn down and torn by so many oppressions and provisions, that while its people are thirsting, it is compelled to give its milk to the use of aliens and foreigners, and its ample patrimony is ceded to a people unknown to it.

Unless a remedy be speedily applied with all caution against it, through these reservations, provisions, and processes of the Roman court, which through the too great patience of the English people (I should say too great folly) day by day grow stronger; that church which of old was free shall be subject to perpetual tribute.

Finally he sounded the note of forcible resistance to Roman interference with English church livings, advocating a resort to arms if that was necessary, or at least to armed preparedness. Such a procedure, he pointed out, would be praiseworthy in the eyes of men and meritorious in the sight of God: [108]

Let therefore the noble knights of England, the renowned citizens of London, and the whole kingdom take heed of the injury of their exalted mother, and rise like men to repel it. Let them see and understand if it be fitting and expedient for Englishmen (like sheep and oxen which carry the fleece and bear the yoke not for themselves but for others) should behold others reap what they themselves have sown, and that thus they that labor the least should claim the food for themselves. Let the secular power be effectually armed, that excluding altogether provisions of this sort, the priesthood of the kingdom may be increased in the Lord, and the treasure of the English may be kept to supply their own land, a thing which indeed will not only tend to the unspeakable advantage of the kingdom and the people, to the glorious title of praise forever to be remembered, but to the immense accumulation of merit in the sight of God.

Thus the spirit of resistance of the English clergy, barons, and middle classes gained strength, especially after the Council of Lyons in 1245 and the increasing demands for money needed to crush Frederick II. Before the Council

of Lyons, Grosseteste looked upon disobedience to the
papacy as a heinous sin, now he looked upon it as a filial
duty to rebel.[109] A change of attitude came upon Englishmen after the papacy repudiated the promises given at the
Council of Lyons.[110] "A lukewarmness came over the devotion which used to be felt towards the pope our father,
and towards the Roman church our mother. For strange
reports were spread about him, and preconceived hopes of
the pope's sanctity were extinguished." [111] The spirit of the
age steeped in time seasoned veneration of the papacy
thwarted the consummation of an open rupture with Rome,
but the Bishop of Lincoln caught the vision of the final
outcome. In his last moments, commenting on the evils
and oppressions of the Roman court, he pointed out that
the end would be revolution.[112] The evils he had in mind
were the methods of the Italian money lenders, the med-
dling of the friars in regard to wills, the absolving of
crusaders from vows for money, prolonging vacancies to
reap the revenues, and papal provisions for benefices.

VII. Direct Papal Taxation—The Papal-Imperial Wars

Protest and revolt over papal finance in the middle thirteenth century was not confined to discontent due to the
practice of provisors, but it extended to other methods
of drawing money from the realm through direct taxation
such as the tithe or some form of it. Thousands of marks
left England annually through this means to swell the
coffers of the papal exchequer. To meet the ever-increas-
ing expenses of the Roman court vast revenues were
needed. This was due to the avarice of the popes, the extravagance of the papal curia, and the worldly ambitions
of the papacy.

Grosseteste made a visit to Rome in 1250 to make a

personal appeal against certain "unheard of oppressions."
It was on this occasion that he was forced to exclaim:
"O money, money, what a power thou hast, especially at
the Roman court." [113] On another occasion, commenting
on the enormities of the papal exchequer, he said: "to
satisfy its avarice the whole world doth not suffice, and for
its pleasures all the harlots of the world are not sufficient." [114] This was a thirteenth century attitude not only
toward the papacy but toward the clergy as a whole. Frederick II, writing to various princes in Europe after his
excommunication, complained that the clergy were rich
and proud, their great revenues made them mad, they were
continually grasping for more, they ought to be humbled
from their worldly position and pride.[115] A late thirteenth
century observer noted that: "Money does everything at
the Roman court. . . . The marvelous vanity and the detestable cupidity of that court has aroused scandal throughout the whole world." [116] The Bishop of Lincoln returned
from the Eternal City so disgusted with the maladministration of the papal court and its mercenary proclivities that
he decided to resign his diocese and retire to private life.
Only the welfare of the church caused him, on taking second thought, to yield to a better impulse.[117] Venality was
rampant at Rome, simony was openly practiced, favor and
justice came only through bribes, pluralities and absenteeism were encouraged, and provisions were freely made.[118]

The temporal ambition of the papacy manifested itself
in a contest for power with the emperor.[119] To overthrow
the Hohenstaufens in Southern Italy, the papacy was forced
to make continual demands for money and to seek new
ways of collecting it. This accounted for the presence of
so many papal agents in England, for that country felt
the weight of these constant levies perhaps more than any
other land. That kingdom was not only regarded as a

feudal appendage of the papacy, but its king was made the dupe of the pope. Henry III at the instigation of Innocent IV and Alexander IV spent thousands of marks to secure the Apulian succession for his son Edmund, which the papacy held out as an inducement to get the financial aid of the English king in the final overthrow of the Hohenstaufens.[120] Between the barons on the one hand and the clergy on the other, the period was full of revolt and revolution over the issue.[121] Clerical protests were so pronounced that there were threats of secession from Rome.[122] The barons, due largely to complications in papal finance over the Apulian Affair, finally revolted and reorganized the government under the leadership of Simon de Montfort.[123]

The writers of the time complainingly depict the condition of things that prevailed saying that the fire of true faith died away so as scarcely to emit a spark, because simony was practiced without a blush, charity expired, and usurers extorted money from minors: [124]

> The daughter of Zion became as it were a shameless harlot without a blush. Illiterate persons of the lowest class, armed with bulls from the Roman church, bursting forth into threats daily presumed, despite the sacred privileges we enjoy from our ancestors, to plunder the revenues left by pious men of old time . . . and by thundering forth sentences of excommunication, they at once obtained their demands. And if any of the injured or robbed parties resorted to appeals, they immediately suspended or excommunicated them by means of some other prelate, on the authority and warrant of the pope, and in this way not by prayers nor canonically but by imperious extortion did they rob the simple minded. . . . Hence it came to pass that where nobles and bountiful clerks, guardians and protectors of the churches, used to make themselves

renown throughout the whole of the adjacent country by entertaining travelers and the poor, these debased men devoid of morals and full of cunning, agents and farmers of the Romans, now scraped together all that was useful and valuable and transmitted it to foreign countries to their lords who lived daintily on the patrimony of Christ bragging on the possessions of others. . . . Woe is England, which once was the chief of provinces, mistress of nations, and a pattern in religion, is now laid under tribute and has fallen a prey to degenerate men.

Farther on the same writer referred to the Roman church as a common, brazen-faced strumpet exposed to the hire of everyone, which considered usury a trivial offense and simony as no crime at all.[125]

Matthew of Westminster commenting on contemporary conditions represented papal exactions as "intolerable grievances" which "incessantly inflicted vexed all men, both nobles and prelates, because they could not endure it any longer without imminent ruin and without branding themselves with cowardice." The pope, violating the promises he had made at the Council of Lyons, plundered the kingdom of its treasures in a most high-handed manner.[126] The papal agents, he said, carrying off all they could from the country turned aside the hearts of the faithful from devotion to the Roman church, "wounding them with great anguish: [127]

The hearts of all men were naturally wounded to the degree of feeling bitterness of soul. But when the stream of those days had passed by, then devotion of the faithful became lukewarm and the affection of filial love which everyone is bound to entertain towards his spiritual father, the pope, was impaired and lost not without great peril to men's souls, and was in fact turned to detestable hatred and secret maledictions.

The middle period of the reign of Henry III, then, was marked by a continuous demand for money by the Roman court which used the money primarily in carrying on the papal-imperial wars over the control of Southern Italy and Sicily. To finance these wars the papacy sent special agents to various countries in Western Europe to oversee and to organize the papal taxation. The agents were authorized by the Roman court both to increase old revenues and to impose new and unheard of taxes. Three such papal officials appeared in England during this time: Otho in 1226 and in 1237; Martin in 1244; and Rustand in 1255. These were envoys plenipotentiary from the papal see to exploit the revenues not only of the English clergy but also, if possible, those of the barons. Deep resentment, bitter agitation, and apparent schism were the results. Incidental to the operations of one of these papal agents blood was on one occasion shed, a second had to flee the country in fear of his life, and a third retired from England in disgrace.[128] In the absence of special agents sent directly from Rome, local representatives of the papacy also acted. These received little better treatment. On the situation as a whole, the pope at one time wrote the king complaining that one of his representatives had been cut in pieces, another had been left half dead, papal letters and credentials had been torn up, and papal bulls had been trodden under foot.[129]

VIII. Direct Papal Taxation—The Legate Otho

Otho came to England as cardinal-legate vested with such powers by the Roman See that he was dubbed the second pope by the English clergy.[130] Otho made two visits to England, the first of which marked a real epoch in ecclesiastical taxation.[131] A step in the direction of papal provisions may be recognized on his first coming, in 1226, when through him the Roman court attempted to systematically use English benefices as a regular and permanent source of revenue for the papal exchequer. On that occasion Otho came armed with a letter demanding two prebends out of each cathedral church and the living of one monk out of each monastery. It was a brilliant scheme on the part of Honorius III to acquire a fixed, dependable, and perpetual annual income at the expense of all the clergy of Western Europe. The pope frankly admitted that the money thus collected was to be received in lieu of bribes and presents usually accepted by the Roman court in suits of appeal. Such a subsidy would remove the stigma of avarice attached to the practices of the papal curia.[132]

When Romanus, a papal envoy, presented the proposition to an assembly of French prelates at Bourges, they raised a number of objections and warned the legate that if the plan were imposed on the French clergy schism would ensue. The French prelates objected to the demand because the papacy could not be trusted to stay within the number of livings specified; because it would place in every province a special papal collector with a staff of assistants, involving great expense; because the collector would likely be a papal agent who would unduly influence local episcopal affairs; because the tax would insure the papal treasury an annual income greater than that of the king himself; because it would render the Roman court financially independent and delay appeals; and finally it would concentrate too much wealth in the hands of the Roman curia and make it dangerous. When the legate insisted on pressing the matter the French prelates warned him that: "If these general oppressions were to be brought into effect, we fear that a general schism would be imminent." [133]

These dangers, real or imagined, could equally have been applied to the situation in England, but there the papal thrust was parried in another way. Englishmen partly ridiculed the request, partly trusted in their geographical isolation, yet at the same time took the demand more or less seriously. But both barons and prelates opposed the proposition, initiating a struggle that continued vigorously for over a quarter of a century. Stephen Langton who led the opposition at this time looked upon the scheme of Otho as the ruin of religion. The clergy as a whole evoked surprise, played for time, and were unwilling to commit themselves regarding the proposal submitted by the legate. The barons on the other hand took immediate action. They sent a delegation to the prelates holding baronies "in capite," warning them not to engage their lay fees in any such manner. These secular lords feared that churchmen alienating their revenues in any way weakened the defense of the realm. In the end the demand of the papacy utterly destroyed the influence of the legate on the Island, and Otho was recalled to Rome in haste. His summons thence came at the urgent request of the Archbishop of Canterbury. Over a decade elapsed before his return when he met with opposition of a different temper.[134]

In the meantime Stephen, a chaplain of the pope already in England, was empowered to finance papal interests in the absence of the legate. He prosecuted the work in a rather blunt but very thorough manner. At a council of prelates and barons gathered at Westminster, Stephen demanded a tithe on all movable property throughout England, Ireland and Wales. He stated that this money was needed by the pope to aid in carrying on war against the emperor, Frederick II. He argued that since the emperor was making war against the papacy he was an enemy of the church universal and therefor all Christendom ought to assist in his overthrow. The assembly at Westminster failed to see the situation in that light, and the barons flatly refused to contribute to the enterprise in the manner demanded by Stephen. They did not care to pledge their possessions for the support of the Roman cause, which was unpopular in Britain, at the expense of the German cause with which a number of the barons sympathized. On the other hand the bishops, abbots, and priors submitted to the tax after much grumbling and protest. They yielded only because they feared excommunication if they refused to honor the papal demand.[135]

Stephen victorious over the opposition of the prelates proceeded to organize efficiently the work of collecting the tax by appointing sub-agents for every county of the realm. Not content with a tithe of the net income of the prelates, Stephen based his estimate on the gross revenues of the clergy. Roger of Wendover stated that he took a tenth part of all incomes, yearly profits, produce of plowed lands, offerings, tithes, provisions for men and beasts, and of all revenues of all churches and other possessions under whatsoever name they were listed, "on no occasion deducting any debt or expenses." [136] Owing to the pressing needs of the papacy for carrying on the war, the money had to be furnished at once under pain of excommunication and interdict if delayed. The prelates were thus forced to pawn the altar furniture, borrow money at high interest of the Italian bankers, and even pledge the growing crops to meet this extraordinary demand. The effect of the new papal levy and the procedure of Stephen is best told in the exact words of a contemporary writer: [137]

> The country was filled with incessant though secret maledictions, and all prayed that such an exaction might never be productive of any advantage to their exactors.

Thus on the second advent of the legate Otho in 1237, the clouds had already gathered and the storm burst. The fact of his coming alone outraged the nationalistic feelings of the barons who severely censured the king for inviting him into the kingdom "to make alterations therein." [138] So unpopular was the mission and presence of Otho that violence against him asserted itself almost from the moment of his landing.[139] The king, however, gave him a showy reception which perhaps increased popular bitterness, though the public behavior of the legate was marked by extreme tact. But at Oxford, on the arrogant action of a member of his train, he was suddenly mobbed by the populace. In this fray the brother of Otho was killed by an arrow, and the legate himself was forced to flee for his life. He found a refuge with the king, but the attitude of the people remained ugly. The chronicler wrote: [140]

> The clerks beside themselves with rage did not cease to search for the legate in the most secret places, shouting and saying: "Where is that usurer, that simoniac, that plunderer of revenues, that thirster for money who perverts the king and subverts the kingdom to enrich foreigners with our spoil?"

At a council held in London, Otho had to be guarded by an armed band of two hundred soldiers.[141] On making a trip into Scotland he sent on ahead scouts to inform him concerning possible attempts on his life.[142] The barons regarded him as the secret enemy of the kingdom and they warned him time after time to leave England with little avail since he was under the safe conduct of the king. When he finally departed in 1241, no one saving the king regretted his leaving. During his stay he succeeded in absorbing for the papal exchequer one half of the yearly revenues of the English clergy.[143] The general purpose of Otho's second visit was to raise funds in support of the papal-imperial conflict. To that end a fifth of the revenues of the alien clergy in England was now devoted. It proved a cause of extreme discontent since the hated system of provisors was in this manner used to support an unpopular cause.[144] But not content with taxing the alien clergy, the papacy soon extended the double tithe to include the revenues of the native clergy. This was looked upon as an unbearable burden, but the clergy was forced to pay it. The legate also gathered money by absolving vows of crusaders, unable or unwilling to carry out their holy mission, by accepting payment for the cost of the crusading journey.[145] He gave to papal favorites prebends, churches, and over three hundred rich revenues. As a result of his work, Matthew of Paris wrote:[146]

> The kingdom was like a vineyard exposed to every passerby, and which the wild boar of the woods laid waste, languishing in a miserable state of desolation. He left the church of Canterbury in a state of disquietude and languishing in widowhood, as well as many other cathedral and conventual churches destitute of all comfort and consolation. And he did not strengthen any weaker part of the country, as was proved by clear evidence, because he was sent not to protect the sheep that were lost, but to gather in the money he could find.

Opposition to the exactions of the legate, manifest from the beginning of his operations, gradually came to a head but resistance on the whole was marked by failure of effective results. The collection of procuration money, arrogant and arbitrary as it proved to be, had to be silently endured.[147] The commutation of crusading vows was tolerated. The demand for the double tithe had to be met although it was stiffly resented. It was when the legate resorted to a sort of swindling and to back-handed methods that collective resistance was initiated. This manifested itself in the action of a number of groups working separately—abbots bishops, and rectors—which was usually limited to an appeal to the apathetic monarch. The groups failed to act in concert and failed even to maintain a solid front within themselves.[148] The bishops tried to turn the king against the legate by reminding him of his alliance with the emperor and by showing him that money thus collected and sent abroad weakened the defense of the kingdom.[149] The rectors of Berkshire remonstrated to the king on a point of principle stating that St. Peter had been given power to bind and not to exact.[150] The following are the main reasons for failure of effective resistance to Otho: The latter limited his demands to the revenues of the clergy and thus direct baronial opposition was eliminated; the king was in sympathy with the legate during the period of his presence;[151] opposition lacked proper organization and leadership; and concerted action when it appeared was thwarted by the legate by intrigue and bribes.[152] But if resistance failed there was at work a deep undercurrent of extreme discontent over the methods and demands of the legate that paved the way to a more successful opposition for his successor.

IX. Direct Papal Taxation—The Nuncio Martin

Otho retired from England in 1241 and an interval of three years elapsed before the coming of another special agent from Rome. But in this interim the papacy was not left without representatives, for two local clerks exacted money for the papal exchequer throughout England, Scotland, and Ireland. Their names, Peter le Rough and Peter de Supino, suggest papal incumbents in English church livings which they likely were originally, but they proved themselves worthy of the new office. They were alluded to as "two indefatigable extortioners who held a papal warrant for exaction of procurations, imposing interdicts and excommunication, and extorting money by divers methods from the wretched English . . . amassing fresh heaps of money during this time." [153]

The advent of Martin opened no new phase in the papal financial policy, but his mission was to continue the work of his predecessor in raising funds to finance the war against the emperor. His stay in England was marked by a more determined resistance to papal taxation, due to the fact that opposition had been growing and organizing itself during the past two decades of papal exactions. Besides this, Martin made the mistake of insisting on talliages, collections, and special contributions involving lay fees, which drove the barons to strong opposition against him. [154] Martin was not a papal legate although at times he posed as one, yet his powers were even greater than those of Otho. His capacity to act as papal agent exceeded all precedent in power to suspend, excommunicate, and otherwise punish any who opposed his will. The belief was current that he held an unlimited number of blank papal bulls over the seals of which he had the privilege to write "according to his own mind" any demand that suited his immediate purpose. [155]

The first demand of Martin was for a sum of 10,000 marks to be given by the English prelates as a free contribution to the papacy, a sort of donation to aid in crushing the emperor. This was refused him outrightly. [156] He next laid hold on the revenues of vacant churches, bestowing them on relatives and favorites of the pope. [157] He ordered gifts including horses, food and clothing to be brought him by the monasteries, presumably to be used in the papal wars; and he fixed a minimum allotment of these for each religious house. [158] He urged the payment of the tribute money promised by King John and by so doing stirred up a bitter protest.[159] Although the stay of Martin in England was brief, he raised issues and stirred up discontent that drove the English nation to the verge of a schism with Rome.[160] It was at this critical situation that loud and violent complaint broke out everywhere, accompanied by an unconcealed tendency to thwart the papal financial policy. "England was to the Pope as Balaam's Asse, whiche being so wronged, spurgalled, and cudgeld, it was no maruile that at length shee opened here mouth to complaine." [161] Matthew of Paris described the situation as follows: [162]

> The Roman church laying aside all sense of shame unceasingly continued to extort revenues. The discontent which had long been conceived and rankled in the hearts of the English in consequence, now broke out into open complaints, and as if in parturition they spoke out openly being able no longer to contain themselves.
>
> Whilst the stream of the time was thus flowing onward, the devotion of the Christians grew lukewarm, and the feeling of filial affection which each Christian is bound to entertain towards our spiritual father the pope, was, not without peril to our souls, wounded and died away; yea indeed, it was converted into execrable hatred and secret maledictions. For each and all saw, and seeing felt, that the pope, to the injury and impoverishment of many, was insatiably intent on the plunder of money; and many did not now believe that he held the power which was granted from Heaven to St. Peter, namely the binding and unloosing, since he proved himself to be entirely dissimilar to St. Peter. The mouth of evil speakers and rebukers was unloosed everywhere, and especially in France where many nobles conspired against the pope and the church, a circumstance we never remember the occurrence of before.

Papal exactions were carried on to such a degree and in so high-handed a manner that even the Romanophile king finally awakened to the danger of the situation. He sent envoys to Rome to protest against the gross impositions that were being made.[163] He also withdrew the royal protection from the papal agent Martin, causing him to flee the country in dreadful haste.

The manner and circumstances of Martin's exit from England were quite significant in regard to the attitude and action of Englishmen toward the papal methods. First of all, his stay on the Island was short showing that public sentiment, long preparing adversely toward papal exactions because of former agents, suddenly came to a head to force his expulsion. In the second place, the king had turned against the papal methods at least in a half-hearted way, and temporarily withdrew his support from the papal party. Again, the removal of Martin although forced by the barons was executed in the name of armed knights who had met in protest of the papal methods, and because the king could not restrain his barons from rising against him unless the exit of Martin was effected.[164] Finally, the barons were so exasperated by the work of the papal agent, and so much in earnest in getting rid of him that they made threats against his life. Before the ultimatum for the expulsion of Martin was given, there had been an attempt on the part of the nobles to render his mission inoperative by cutting him off from communication with Rome. To this end all ports were watched to intercept papal letters and to seize papal messengers, but the failure to procure the coöperation of the court in this respect caused the plan to fall through.

Finally a band of armed knights accosted Martin and his staff of assistants, and gave them three days' time for preparation to leave England or be cut in pieces at the expiration of that time. The scene of his ejection was dramatically pictured by the contemporary chronicler, given with a slight touch of humor:[165]

On coming into his presence, Fulk Fitz-Warren eying the clerk with scowling brow thus addressed him: "Depart from England at once." Master Martin then asked him: "Who orders me to do so, do you this of your own authority?" To which Fulk replied: "You are ordered to do so through me by the community of armed knights who lately met at Luton and Dunstable; and if you listen to prudent counsel you will not stay til the third day from this time lest you and your companions be cut in pieces." On the said Fulk departing in anger after heaping threat upon threat with a terrible oath, Master Martin went immediately to the king, breathless with alarm, and said to him: "My lord, I have just heard such and such things; is this done by your authority, or is it by the audacity of your subjects?" To this the king replied: "I declare that I am not the author of this proceeding; but my barons can scarcely restrain themselves rising against me because I have hitherto tolerated the depredations and injuries committed by you in this kingdom, and which exceed all measure of justice; and with difficulty I have prevented them in their fury from attacking you and tearing you limb from limb." With a trembling and low voice Martin replied: "I therefor ask your majesty out of your love for God and reverence to the pope to allow me free exit and permit me to depart safely under your conduct." To which the king said in anger: "May the devil take you and carry you through hell."

But he was given a safe conduct, and his escorts amused themselves by keeping him in constant dread of ambush throughout the danger zone. When that region was passed and his guards retired "he did not spare the sides of his horse but made all haste to the sea coast, reproaching his conductors for delay; and on his arrival at Dover he immediately embarked."

The exit of Master Martin "rejoiced the hearts of many." The spirit of revolt was so acute that the resident Italian clergy were forced into hiding and the Coursines in large numbers had to flee the realm.[166] But the attitude of the papacy was defiant. When Master Martin reported at Rome, the pope in a violent rage over the episode of his exit said to certain envoys of the emperor who happened to be present: "It is expedient for us to make terms with your prince in order to crush these petty princes; for when the dragon is crushed or pacified, the little serpents will easily be trodden under foot." [167] This utterance of the pope had a disturbing effect in England. But what proved worse in alienating the English was the fact that extortions went on apace. The Roman court, blind to the seriousness of the situation, repeated the requests for money year after year. New methods were employed, one of which was the collection of talliages. This tax not only stirred the king to opposition because it infringed on the revenues of the exchequer, but it affected the incipient new middle classes.[168] Another new means of spoliation was intestate personal property of clerks and prelates, the papacy decreeing that all such goods should revert to the papal exchequer.[169] The king forbade this decree being promulgated in England, but the pope insisted on receiving the property.

X. Direct Papal Taxation—Coördinated Protest and Submerged Revolt

Discontent and revolt over papal methods of taxation and financial oppressions have been alluded to at several places in this chapter up to this point. It was cumulative and the visit of the nuncio Martin brought it to a head. It had gathered momentum ever since the start with the first visit of Otho in 1226 augmenting, with the evil effects of papal provisions, the methods of the Italian bankers, and the work of the special papal agents. The popular demonstrations of 1231-32, the protests of Grosseteste, the challenge of the English delegation at Lyons, the mobbing of Otho at Oxford, and the threats of violence that precipitated the flight of Martin are all the outcroppings of a deep undercurrent of rebellion and submerged revolt that grew in intensity until the final revolt of the barons in 1258.

It was particularly with the visit of the nuncio Martin in England that this spirit of rebellion against Rome drew from certain groups coördinated protests and quasi-organized methods of opposition that bespeak the depths which popular discontent had reached. The exactions had been forced upon the English on a sort of increasing graduated scale; first a twentieth, then a tenth, a fifth, a third, and even a half of the yearly revenues of the clergy were at times sequestered in the way of a tax.[170] Even the vacillatory king finally wrote the pope charging that England was the nation most heavily trampled on by papal oppression, robbed of its property and of the fruits of its labor. "No one robs him (the pope) though he acts as a robber of others. . . . O Lord God of Vengeance, when wilt thou sharpen thy sword like lightening that it may be steeped in the blood of such people." [171] Under this load the English people groaned audibly and protested bitterly. [172]

> From these grievances and others of a similar kind, a murmur arose among the clergy and the people in general, so that whatever they contributed they brought unwillingly (and that I may not suppress the truth), with causes and maledictions; enumerating afresh to

the lord the pope their grievances, with complaints from
the bottom of their hearts, and representing the intolerable oppressions to which they were subjected. The
English church is intolerably oppressed in an infinite
number of ways: in the matter of the tithe of all its
goods; in that of the aid exacted in haste; in that of
money extorted for the soldiers; in that of the subsidy
lately extorted under various pretenses by the agency of
Otho the legate; in that of the subsidy of the Roman
Empire (Holy); in that of the subsidy lately granted
gratuitously; in that of the subsidies demanded on the
part of the king and the archbishop of Canterbury: all
these matters have been carried forward in an intoler-
ant manner and in a bitter spirit devoid of all affection
and devotion.

Thus in the turmoil of affairs finally stirred up with the
presence of the nuncio Martin sentiment was rife, indicative of a rupture with the papacy, coming from the country
as a whole, from assemblies of nobles, from the king, and
from various groups of churchmen.[173] One of the special
matters of complaint was the orders for knights, horses, and
arms to aid in the war of the papacy against the empire.[174]
Formal protests and articles of grievances appeared and
special letters were sent to the pope asking that injuries be
mitigated in order to avoid the danger of schism and secession.[175] An assembly of all the barons held in London
in 1246 formally complained to the king of the continual
contributions and extortions forced upon the land by the
papacy. The nobles assembled referred to these as "irregular
levies made contrary to the ancient customs, liberties, and
rights of the kingdom, without the consent or assent of the
king and in spite of all appeals." [176] In the following year a
similar complaint was launched in which papal exactions
and the arrogant spirit with which they were imposed were
alike condemned. The nobles asserted that death itself was

preferable to bearing this yoke of papal servitude any longer.[177]

The king addressed a letter directly to the pope saying that he could no longer turn a deaf ear to the unusually clamorous complaints of the nobles of England, backed by the clergy and the people as a whole, no matter how much affection and loyalty he felt toward the Roman church. He gave the reasons:[178]

> For the said nobles have become more than usually loud in their complaints, calling on us to procure their liberation from the oppressions which have been ere now brought to your notice by their special messengers; but bad as they were, the recent oppressions weigh much more heavily upon them. Wherefore, as the said nobles with good reasons send their special messengers to us, we earnestly beg your holiness to accede to their entreaties in such a way that you may render us, the sons, well wishing and devoted to our mother the church and to yourself, lest if you act otherwise, we, as well as the Roman church, may be placed in such a peril that we shall never be able to recover ourselves from it.

At the same time the king wrote to the cardinals at Rome pleading for their intercession to the pope in order that the latter might adjust matters regarding taxation and exactions in such a way as to avoid a schism. Protesting his love to the Roman church and his interest in its welfare, he said:[179]

> We cannot dissemblingly pass by the clamorous complaints of the nobles of England, clergy as well as people, who have now become more than usually loud in their outcries against the oppressions which have been brought at some former time to the notice of the pope as well as to yourselves by special messengers. Wherefore we humbly and devotedly entreat the pope

that he will condescend to listen to their reasonable entreaties, which have been made to him by repeated messengers, so that we may render them more favorable and devoted to the said church and to us, and prevent them from becoming estranged from their allegiance. We also earnestly beg you in your paternal affection to interpose your efforts, that the messengers of the said nobles now again sent may be listened to with much favor by the pope and by yourselves, that imminent peril which seems to hang over the said church may not fall on us and on it, although it is feared in no slight degree by each and all in our kingdom.

Besides the king, the abbots of England as a body addressed a letter to the papal court protesting that the English church was intent upon her loyalty to Rome, but that she was seriously grieved and troubled over the exactions, oppressions, and manifold tribulations which had been lately so heavily imposed upon her. This group of churchmen warned the pope that nobles and people alike were on now demanded immediate relief to avert open violence: [182]

For as we have heard from the assertions of the nobles and also from the cries of the people, the wind rushing in from the desert has violently attacked and agitated the four corners of the said church like the house of Job. . . . Inasmuch then as we are faithful and devoted children of the holy Roman church, we have, in order that the missel being foreseen may not hurt too much, thought right to intimate the foregoing matters to the Apostolic see, seeing that manifold perils are impending over it, and unless in many points a remedy be applied by you, there will be reason to fear that a disturbance will occur among the people, scandal will arise and manifold schisms will be produced. For the people are excited against the king and are ready to secede from their allegiance unless the impending diseases are quickly met by the royal power. May it therefore please your holiness to make provision that the kingdom and the priesthood be not separated. For if the English church were to be dragged into ruin, a division being thus made between the priesthood and the kingdom, the people as well as the priesthood would be discontented and a massacre of many people would follow without delay.

A letter sent by the bishops of England reasoned along the same line. Those prelates similarly pictured the spirit of discontent of the people as having reached a point where it no longer could be appeased by mere promises of relief. Exactions of the papacy had to actually cease at once, they said, because the danger of an uprising was imminent.[181]

But most outspoken and perhaps most significant of all was the letter written and sent to the papacy by the English barons. In plain, though guarded, language they spoke in behalf of the whole nation, threatening open revolt and resistance by force unless the papal exactions were mitigated. The barons protested their patience in the past, but they now demanded immediate relief to avert open violence: [182]

Unless relief comes speedily scandal will arise, urged on as we are ourselves as well as the king by the clamor of the people. It will be necessary for us unless the king and the kingdom are soon released from the practices by which they are oppressed to oppose ourselves as a wall for the house of the Lord and for the liberty of the kingdom. This we have, out of respect to the Apostolic See, hitherto delayed doing; but we shall not be able to dissemble after the return of our messengers who are sent on this matter to the Apostolic See, or refrain from giving succor, as far as lies in our power, to the clergy as well as to the people of the kingdom of England, who will on no account endure these proceedings. And your holiness may rest assured that unless the aforesaid matters be speedily reformed by you, there will be reasonable grounds to fear that such a peril will impend the Roman church as well as our lord the king, that it may not be easy to apply a remedy to the same; which God forbid.

This spirit of revolt at the time was not confined to England alone, for in France a conspiracy was organized against the papacy and the church because of ecclesiastical exactions.[183] A league was planned, which was to include men of various countries, for the defense of men's rights against papal impositions. Provision was made to amply finance the scheme, but the papacy apparently bribed its leaders and the plan proved abortive.[184]

In Britain the times seemed ripe for a revolt and secession from Rome, for papal prestige had declined to the extent that Englishmen began to doubt the papal claims and pretensions.[185] Popular feeling was rapidly tending toward a break in spite of the loyalty of certain groups of pro-papal leaders. The anti-papal party was looking for the king to take the initiative in severing relations with the Roman See. Had he done so and not wavered and finally drawn back altogether the rupture in the church that seemed so imminent would doubtless have been consummated.[186] Several times the vacillating monarch turned to resist the papal encroachments, but his opposition was only half-hearted, and always he desisted in the end for fear of interdict.[187] The writers of the period lamented over "this womanly fickleness of the king." [188]

> Through the hissing of some ambitious clergy and some of the bishops in the papal interest, the king abandoned like a woman the designs which he had undertaken and adopted like a man.
>
> Hence all the endeavors of the nobles as well as the bishops were of no avail, and all hope of release for the

kingdom and the English church died away, to the bitter heart-felt grief of many; and the grasping of Roman avarice was satisfied with impunity in the matter of said contributions.

XI. The Consummation of the Crisis—The Anglo-Apulian Episode and the Provisions of Oxford

Popular protest and revolt against papal finance in England during the period under consideration found final expression in the political revolt of 1258 that imposed the Provisions of Oxford upon the king. The ecclesiastical situation was so closely connected with the political crisis that the blow aimed at the papacy fell upon the king. The ultimate issue grew out of the promised crusade of the English monarch, and the attempt of the latter to procure the Apulian succession for his son. Both projects involved the expenditure of vast sums of money manipulated by the papal court. Influenced by Innocent IV, Henry III took oath to make a pilgrimage to the Holy Land in the form of a crusade. The affair soon became extremely unpopular in England, for from the start many believed that the pope was using the idea of a crusading pilgrimage as a means for exploiting the wealth of the kingdom under a pious guise. [189] The king was in no position to actually make such a holy expedition, and his vow could easily be commuted by the papacy for the payment of sums of money. Evidently it was thought that this was being done, for it aroused discontent and opposition. To make the expedition possible, the papacy had granted the king the privilege to collect tithes for three years from both clergy and laity, and it was estimated that if this was fully collected it would amount to the prodigious sum of 600,000 marks. All this was to be accumulated before the king could even think of starting on the journey.

A systematic attempt was now made to collect this money, involving a survey of the property of the entire realm somewhat on the order of the later surveys of Nicholas IV and Henry VIII. When the mandate to impose the tax was presented to an assembly of prelates at London, it created a storm of protest and opposition. The bishop of Lincoln warned the king that the measure was taking him on dangerous ground, and asserted he would not pay the "accursed contribution." He was supported by a number of other bishops. They did not waver when the king "raved against them like a madman," but boldly and frankly told him that the project for him to take the sign of the cross was a blind used by the papacy to carry off the wealth of the kingdom.[190] But a compromise was eventually effected by which the prelates agreed to pay the tax on condition that the king never again impose a like contribution and that he renew the charters of liberty.[191] Though the monarch consented to do this under oath, his vow seems to have been but slightly esteemed by the churchmen; notwithstanding it was administered with bell, book, and candle.

The Apulian episode led to far more serious consequences than did the vow of the king to undertake the pilgrimage; in fact, Henry was now absolved from the latter in order to be free to spend time and money to realize the former project. At the instigation of the papacy the English king accepted the Sicilian crown for his son, Edmund; and his credulity and gullibility recognized no bounds in this obvious intention of the papacy to use English money as a means of driving the last of the Hohenstaufens out of Southern Italy.[192] Henry III gave to the pope permission under the royal seal to borrow almost unlimited sums of money to carry out this visionary scheme.[193] To complicate matters the pope negotiated loans on the strength of

the king's action through the hated Italian bankers.[194]
With the aid of this money the papacy carried on a series
of campaigns against the German claimants of the Apulian
crown. For this purpose one or two armies were enlisted,
consisting of Italian mercenaries "idle and worthless fellows, devoid of faith, who looked not upon the advantage
of the king of England but were only intent on gorging
money." [195] The expeditions of the Italian armies proved
fiascos, but the English people in the end were held for the
payment of the money and the piously conscientious king
approved of it.[196] As a climax to the affair, the papacy got
the king to promise that he would personally lead an army
into Italy in order to retrieve, if possible, the former military disasters.[197] Of course the English king did not carry
out this design, but it gave the pope another hold on the
purse strings of the English people.

The papacy now had a tangible pretext for imposing a
tax upon the English people in order to balance the papal
deficit over the Apulian expeditions covered by the financial promises of the king. Alexander IV, the newly elected
pope, did not profit by the lesson of other popes in the
past, but sent another special agent to promote the collection of this money, commissioning the Archbishop of
Canterbury and the Bishop of Hereford, both foreigners,
to assist the agent. They were authorized to collect the
tithes in England, Scotland, and Ireland, and to obtain
money by various other means. The first act of the new
papal agent, Rustand, was to order a crusade to be preached
against Manfred, the Hohenstaufen incumbent of the Apulian throne; this scandalized the English people because
it involved the shedding of Christian blood by Christians.
The new levies of the papacy involved "immense sums of
money. . . . If this money had been collected the church
of England, indeed the whole kingdom, would have been

affected with irremediable poverty and reduced to abject slavery." [198] The bishops refused for a long time to pay anything towards the levies, and gave a long list of objections.[199] The Bishop of London protested that before he would give his consent for the church to be subjected to such an injurious state of slavery he would cut off his head to free himself from the "intolerable oppressions," and the Bishop of Rochester said that before the holy church should submit to such ruinous impositions he would condemn himself to be hung.[200]

The Apulian Affair in the end involved the English king in a debt reckoned all the way from 140,000 to 250,000 marks.[201] The interest on the debt was said to have amounted to over 100 pounds sterling a day.[202] Perhaps this was due to the exorbitant rates of usury charged by the Italian bankers. This large deficit accumulated in spite of the fact that a tithe of five years and the annates were devoted to the payment of the Apulian expedition.[203] It was estimated at the time that the king spent altogether the sum of 950,000 marks to aid in carrying out this visionary undertaking.[204] The extravagance and mismanagement regarding this financing helped bring about the political crisis that ultimately culminated with the battle of Lewes in 1264. As early as the Gascon war of 1243 the barons had demanded a closer supervision of the royal exchequer and imposed conditions on the king as to making promiscuous grants of money. This tendency to put a check on the loose financial policy of the monarch was given strength by the continual papal exactions. Three times the barons, backed by the prelates, refused to accede to the wishes of the king in subsidizing the Sicilian expedition; and on the third occasion they came to the council in armor and imposed the Provisions of Oxford upon the monarch. It was the breaking of this compact that caused the rupture between the king and the national party led by Simon de Montfort. The Provisions of Oxford and the Barons' War grew out of a financial situation in which arbitrary papal taxation was a powerful factor.

The result of the papal financial policy during this entire period that has been brought under study was the breakdown of papal prestige. The constant demand for ever increasing sums of money coupled with extreme indifference to the spiritual welfare of the country caused many doubts as to the heavenly derived mission of the popes. To the English people the Roman court appeared more and more as a worldly institution with imperialistic and purely temporal ambitions. Papal envoys appeared in England to promote not religious edification but financial interests, so that resentment was awakened and sentiment was aroused that tended to break down the time honored deference paid the Roman See. In France the immediate outcome was a conspiracy for the overthrow of the papal authority and a foundation was laid for the victory of Philip the Fair and the later Pragmatic Sanction of Bourges. In England this attitude brought forth measures such as the Act of Mortmain, of Praemunire, of Provisors, and the final statutes that effected the ultimate breach with Rome in the sixteenth century.

CHAPTER III

THE problem of placing a check on the increasing wealth of
the church and the question of the disendowment of the
clergy emerged very early in the process of ecclesiastical
acquisitiveness. Forces and movements that tended to counteract the growth of church property came into play almost
from the beginning and were active from time to time in
the course of the Christian centuries. The actual movement
toward the disendowment of the English clergy took an organized and consciously directed form about the middle of
the fourteenth century. Before that time, however, forces
serving to check and actions aiming to deprive the clergy in
the tendency to accumulate excessive wealth were operative
on the Continent. This earlier continental process of checking a materialistic expansion of the church had two phases
conveniently divided by the beginning of the crusading
movement. The basis of this analysis is the degree of opposition manifested. Before the Crusades resistance to the
idea of a richly endowed clergy was marked by sporadic
protests, occasional legislative checks, and ideals of other-
worldliness operative in the rise of monasticism. After the
beginning of the Crusades there came an unbroken chain
of movements, as well as a number of isolated individuals,
that were openly and violently opposed to an endowed
church. Since the crusading movement was a prolific means

of increasing the wealth of the church, one is tempted to attribute the new phase of opposition to it. Such a conclusion is hardly warranted by a careful study of the situation, although there may be some connection in the way of cause and effect between the two facts. After the outbreak of the Hundred Years War the disendowment of the church took a more pronounced and organized form as a measure of military defense manifest in the attitude toward the alien priories. The final confiscation of these foreign houses came in 1415, but in the meantime Wyclif and the Lollards took up and carried on a fierce fight in behalf of a general disendowment of the clergy. This in its time led to grave consequences as far as placing the wealth of the church in jeopardy was concerned, but it also paved the way for the ultimate confiscation of church property at a later time.

I. Earlier Movements Militating against the
Endowment of the Church

The legal restraints placed on religious men accumulating undue wealth in the late fourth century has already been pointed out.[1] Renewed pressure by the state regarding this matter seems to have been brought to bear again in the time of both Jerome and Ambrose.[2] Jerome complained of the necessity for such laws, but confessed that the legal barriers were impotent against the subtle rapacity of the clergy. The rapid development of monasticism after the recognition of Christianity by the state may be looked upon as a protest against the formalism, the materialistic spirit, and the worldly ideal of the church of the times. Anthony, the founder of the movement, impressed by the words of Christ to the rich young man, renounced his private fortune to live in solitude and self-denial. Pachomius, the organizer of the movement, Martin of Tours, who introduced it into Gaul, and Benedict of Nursia, who reduced it to a system, were men of the same type as the founder. The monastic movement, so quickly perverted by worldly wealth, was launched with the ideal of apostolic poverty in view. It stood out in relief against the wealth and worldly show of the bishops and city priests, the sumptuous living of whom Ammianus Marcellinus contrasts with the poor churchmen of the provinces.[3]

In the eighth century, Charles Martel, leader of the Franks, took an actual step to deprive the church of some of its wealth by an act of confiscation. The increased need of the horse to offset the cavalry of the Saracen called for additional subsidies in way of land, and Charles encroached on the domain of the churchmen. But that was not, apparently, the only motive in this act of confiscation, for Charles was becoming alarmed at the growing wealth of the clergy.[4]

From what has been said, it will appear that from very early times movements were on foot that served to check the abnormal growth of ecclesiastical property. But by the beginning of the twelfth century this tendency entered into a new phase by being increased to an unprecedented degree. At that time or soon following there emerged three types of activities militating against the idea of an endowed church; these were the preaching of outstanding individuals, the organization of anti-churchly sects, and the formation of new monastic orders within the church. These activities were decidedly anti-economic in their interests, and one of the principal tenets common to each of them was the necessity of the church to return to its original condition of apostolic poverty. The influence of the preaching individuals was largely temporary, since they left no organized following; but the anti-sacerdotal sects were powerful groups that persisted until suppressed by the crusading zeal directed against them or crushed by the machinery of the Inquisition. The new monastic orders upheld the ideal of apostolic poverty for a time, but ultimately reverted to type in becoming immensely wealthy themselves.

Henry of Lausanne was the earliest if he was not the foremost of these individual anti-ecclesiastical leaders. He had been a Benedictine monk, but had left the order and preached from 1101 until his death in 1145 to a large following in western and southern France. The test of spiritual worthiness, according to Henry, was the ascetic life and the will to live in apostolic poverty. He unsparingly condemned the worldly, wealthy, power-seeking clergy. Similar in his emphasis in condemning the idea of endowment was Peter of Bruys, also of southern France, who was burned by a mob for his anti-churchly views about 1125. By the middle of the twelfth century, Arnold of Brescia was driven from Rome, condemned as a heretic, and finally hanged because of his religious austerity and because he advanced the opinion that the clergy should abandon all property and worldly power. Arnold bitterly attacked the whole system of ecclesiastical property rights and advocated the return to apostolic poverty. He taught that clerics who owned property, bishops who held tenures by royal grant, and monks who had possessions of land and wealth could not possibly be saved. Later, in the thirteenth century other individuals who were not preachers took up this idea. Frederick II, the Hohenstaufen emperor, advocated that the clergy be humbled from their worldly position and pride to which their wealth had exalted them, and that the church as a whole should practice apostolic ideals of living.[5] Dante also attributed the ills of the church to its excessive wealth.[6]

In the course of the twelfth century a number of anti-churchly sects emerged and spread over parts of Western Europe advocating apostolic poverty as one of the highest religious ideals. Of these groups the Waldenses and the Cathari were the most important, though there were other minor ones such as the Humilatati and the Fratricelli. The Cathari, or Albigenses, hark back to the Manichaeans of the later Roman Empire, and were particularly strong in southern France and northern Italy, also in northern Spain. By the opening of the thirteenth century they proved a grave peril to the Roman church. In this movement the ascetic spirit of the age found full expression in their ideal of the purified which their name implied. They criticized the wealth and power of the church and completely repudiated its clergy and claims. Those among this group who had received the "consolation," the perfect, renounced the right and privilege to hold property. These "perfecti" were the clergy of the sect which seemed to be organized into a sort of hierarchy. One third of the population of southern France, it is thought, belonged to this important sect with its emphasis on apostolic poverty of the clergy.

The Waldenses was a sect founded by a rich merchant of Lyons named Waldo, in the last quarter of the twelfth century. They were sometimes alluded to as the poor men of Lyons. Waldo in seeking the best way to God was told: "If thou wouldst be perfect, go, sell that thou hast, and give to the poor, and thou shalt have treasure in heaven." This he aimed to literally carry out as the true ideal of apostolic poverty. Waldo was opposed by the church because he was misunderstood. He was excommunicated and driven from the church, but he and his followers continued to preach with a stress on simple living. They traveled about by twos, clad in a simple woolen robe, either barefooted or wearing sandals, living wholly on gifts from their hearers, fasting regularly, and rejecting masses and prayers for the dead, the doctrine of purgatory, and other devices used by the clergy to procure money. They were well organized into a hierarchy of bishops, deacons, priests, with a rector at the head of the society. They spread from southern France into northern Spain, Germany, and Austria. Before their repression they wielded a powerful influence in Western Europe.

Besides these anti-churchly sects and individual preachers, of other worldly vision, there sprang up within the church itself new religious orders partly as a direct protest against the worldliness of the clergy and partly as an antidote for the anti-sacerdotal bodies. The chief movements of this kind were the Cistercian monastic revival and the two orders of preaching mendicant friars, the Dominican and the Franciscan. The Cistercians dominated the twelfth century just as the Cluniacs dominated the eleventh and like the Cluniacs they originated in France and spread throughout Western Europe. Founded at Citeaux in 1098, shortly after the beginning of the first crusade, the Cistercian monasteries numbered six hundred and seventy-one a century later, all under the authority of the abbot of Citeaux. The ideals of the Cistercians were withdrawal from the world, religious contemplation, strenuous self-denial, and the practice of apostolic poverty. The chief exponent of the movement was St. Bernard who mixed an unusual degree of monastic self-immolation with a far-reaching evangelism. Strange to say, Bernard attempted to convert the anti-worldly heretics of southern France, and his bitterest enemy was Arnold of Brescia, but he differed in methods rather than in ideals from these other movements. Bernard and the Cistercians were as radical in their ideals of apostolic poverty as was Arnold of Brescia who suffered martyrdom for his stand.

The Dominican order grew out of an attempt to offset with equal zeal, asceticism, and devotion to the ideal of apostolic poverty, the work of the Cathari and the Waldenses. It was an attempt to convert these heretics by meeting kind with kind, a great social service project that abandoned the common practice of contemplation apart from the world and sought access to men in their need. St. Francis, the founder of the Franciscan mendicant order espoused poverty as a bride and determined to preach repentance and the kingdom of God in plainest of garments, without money, living only on what was given him. His ideal was the imitation of Christ in absolute poverty. This was a most radical attitude toward worldly possessions, but it was apparently timely. Without St. Francis of Assisi, said Sabatier, the church would have foundered on the rocks of worldly wealth and corruption: "The little poor man, driven away, cast out of doors by the creatures of Innocent III, saved Christianity." [7] Unhappily all these antiworldly movements either died out, degenerated, or reverted to type. The Dominican and Franciscan orders ultimately became unusually wealthy. Yet in their time all these movements described here represented a strenuous protest against the wealth of the clergy that later reëmerged and brought forth effective results in regard to the disendowment of the church.

II. Precursors of Disendowment in England before Wyclif

With John Wyclif and the Lollards, disendowment took an organized and consciously directed course by the opening of the fifteenth century both in the way of propaganda against and practical application of the idea. But Wyclif did not build up this movement from the ground floor, for already in his time the alienation of church property on account of its abuse, mismanagement, or danger to the secular power had become a matter of open threat and established precedent. This was manifest in one of his own statements, for in answer to the friars who asserted that it was an error that the king and the secular lords had the right to confiscate the goods of churchmen, Wyclif pointedly contended that:[8]

> Since our king hath done so and other kings his predecessors have done so many times by lawful cause as pertaining to their power, and of the common law, by council of the peers of the realm; it followeth that not only our king now hath erred, but also his predecessors have erred, and generally all his counsellors, lords and prelates and all men of parliament counselling thereto (have erred).

Many other authorities also show that before the end of the fourteenth century the practice of seizing the goods of the church on various pretexts had become more or less common.[9]

One of the earliest hints as to the possibility, under moral obligation, of the secular authorities appropriating ecclesiastical property when misused came in the turbulent days of the middle thirteenth century. At that time the abbots writing the pope warned him of dangers threatening the church on account of a reckless papal financial policy. The abbots pointed out that open schism was imminent unless immediate remedy was applied; they showed that Italian priests occupying English livings was a misapplication of funds, and the lay lords were regarding this misuse of benefices as a reason for confiscation by the state: They said:[10]

> For the nobles and men of rank declare that if the churches bestowed on monasteries by them are con-

ferred on Italian clerks, they will have a just right to recall those churches and other benefices into their own possession; because the revenues proceeding from them ought by right be applied to the benefit of the poor and of pilgrims, since this was the intent of the giver and the cause of their being given.

A number of the provisions of a document promulgated by the Synod of Merton held in 1258 reveal a spirit of discontent and a manifest complaint on the part of the English clergy over lay encroachment on their property rights. Some of the articles of this instrument show that the secular authorities were ready to take advantage of the minutest flaw in legal technicalities regarding grants and charters of churches to deprive religious men of their holdings.[11] Grosseteste, Bishop of Lincoln, complained of lay and regal irregularities touching the seizure of church property.[12] Thus a number of things go to show that the idea of sacredness and immunity attached to church property was crumbling.

The provisions of Westminster in 1259 made it illegal for men of religion to enter into any man's fee, without the license of the chief lord by whom the fee was immediately held.[13] This step was a precursor of the Statute de Religiosis, or Mortmain, of 1279 which aimed to do away with abuses that were a matter of complaint as far back as the time of Bede.[14] While the Statute of Mortmain cannot be looked upon as an act of direct disendowment, it was indirectly a step in that direction. The motive of King Edward and the barons was partly to prevent an increase of the wealth and power of the church, and partly to prevent more lands falling into the hands of clerical owners, who were not so able to fight the king's battles as lay lords. Being a matter of military defense, the very necessity of the law implied that the abuses it aimed to correct were a danger to the survival of the secular power. From this negative step of checking the growth of clerical wealth for reasons of defense of the realm was only a short step in taking over the wealth of the church for purposes of positive defense in time of war.

In the reign of Henry III an ecclesiastical struggle took place that united all classes in England against the papacy; but in the time of Edward I a new alignment of forces emerged that placed the king and the national party in opposition to the pope and the English clergy. This struggle between church and state was due to the policy of Edward I to bring order and regularity in the political administration of the realm. His policy was one of centralization and concentration of power into the hands of the king. The first half of Edward's reign was marked by a series of legislative enactments to this end that gave him the name of the English Justinian.[15] In carrying out this policy the new commercial classes began to play their rôle. The influence of the merchants was much in evidence. Englishmen themselves were now engaging in trade instead of leaving it to foreigners, there was much legislation in regard to trade, and the forces that gave rise to mercantilism were already at work.[16] Not only had the burgher class been called to take part in the parliaments, but Edward made use of special merchant assemblies in consultation on his policies.[17] The interests and ideals of the merchants favored the centralization of authority.

Against the tendency toward concentration of power into the hands of the king, the wealth and influence of the church proved a dangerous barrier. Edward was determined to remove, or at least to curtail, the evil. The church was daily increasing in wealth through the Dead Hand, a practice that decreased feudal dues by which the royal exchequer was still partially supported and indirectly

menaced the defense of the realm. The church claimed
exemption from secular taxation on property that the king
felt was needed to help bear the expenses of government.
The situation gave rise to two grave crises, one ending
in the promulgation of the Statute of Mortmain, and the
other bringing forth the papal bull Clericis Laicos. In both
cases the clergy was whipped into submission, for church
property was subjected to secular taxation, and a law was
enacted to put a check on its increase.

But Edward did not stop with mere attempts to limit
the growth of ecclesiastical wealth and to subject church
property to taxation in support of the state. During the
course of his reign he seized and confiscated the goods of
the clergy on several occasions. In 1283 the king, pressed for
lack of funds in carrying out his Welsh campaigns, laid
hold of the crusading tithes that were being collected
throughout England. On this occasion when Archbishop
Peckham, encouraged by the papacy, attempted to thwart
the design of the king, the latter forced the doors of the
treasury of Lincoln cathedral, and other places were violently entered and the money taken. But the protests
against such action became so strong that Edward was compelled to make restitution.[18] Again, in 1293 the king seized
the funds and treasures of the cathedral churches, religious
houses, and mendicant orders to assist in carrying out
his military project in Gascony.[19] These he did not re-
store. At the same time he confiscated the wool of the
Cistercian monasteries.[20] In his trouble with the clergy concerning taxation in 1297, the king took over for a time
the monasteries as well as some of the property of the
secular clergy.[21] On the whole the reign of Edward I
marked a definite phase for the decline of the property
prestige of the English clergy. This was true of the period

as a whole that followed the crisis over papal finance just after the middle of the thirteenth century.

III. The Confiscation of the Alien Priories in England

The secularization of the foreign religious houses in England, consummated in 1414, may be regarded as a definite step toward the disendownment of the English church, serving as a precedent to the wholesale confiscation of monastic property.[22] The attitude toward the alien priories in the two centuries antedating their ultimate extinction may be looked upon as the first symptoms of the growing discontent over the entire monastic system.[23] Their requisition began in the time of King John and continued during the reign of Edward I until their final sequestration in the early years of Henry V. Several motives were involved in these institutions being taken over by the secular power, the most important of which were their alleged danger to the defense of the realm, their rundown economic status, and the devotion of their revenues to philanthropic ends.[24] That they were a menace to the state in times of war was obvious because of the fact that they seemed to harbor spies, and the money sent abroad by them could be easily used to give aid and comfort to the enemies of the kingdom.[25] Their mother houses were in France and their inmates were Frenchmen of anti-English sympathies.[26] This in itself proved a plausible justification for their sequestration especially during the time of the Hundred Years War. But the primary motive was, after all, mercenary rather than patriotic.[27] The confiscation of the alien priories was another indication that as early as the thirteenth century ecclesiastical property in England was no longer looked upon as inviolable, but its use was tolerated for secular purposes.

The alien priories originated with the Norman Conquest although there are instances of a limited number being planted before that as early as the time of Edward the Confessor and even of Alfred the Great. The time of the Norman Conquest was coterminous with a great medieval monastic revival and that alone accounts for the founding of many new religious houses especially of the Cluniac imperialistic type. But the new Norman barons installed by the conquest had a particular devotion to the abbeys of their native Normandy, and thus gave strong encouragement and support to the establishment of branch cells from beyond the Channel. In this manner colonies of French monks found lodgment in England. In this movement lay the roots of the alien priory problem in England. The secular invaders of England in time became thoroughly Anglicized with their interests and patriotism wrapped up on the insular side of the Channel, but the ecclesiastical immigrants gave themselves over to no such transformation, the priories remaining French and alien in personnel and in attitude. From the time of the Conquest until the end of the reign of Henry II, that is, in a century and a quarter, 102 of these foreign houses were founded in England.[28]

As long as the kings of England had common interests and great feudal appendages on both sides of the Channel, these foreign houses presented no problem, but with the loss of the Norman and Angevin possessions due to the victories of Philip Augustus in the late twelfth and early thirteenth centuries they at once became a menace to the realm for the reason that they now became alien in the true sense of the term. This accounted for the first seizure in 1204 by King John. The Normans in England were at that time classed as traitors and their property confiscated by the crown. The alien monasteries were included in this policy. That economic motives played a part in this sudden seizure was manifest in the fact that no revenues of the alien priories were to be sent from the realm, and that their restoration was accompanied only by the payment of heavy fines. This money came into the exchequer of the king. Some of the priories paid as high as 100 pounds sterling for their release, while others of the richer class were forced to pay out of their annual revenues 100 pounds sterling to the king a term of years after their release.[29]

The next epoch that marked a step in the fall of the foreign religious houses in England came in the reign of Edward I, though there was a single instance of seizure in the time of Henry III.[30] But the last named monarch was too ecclesiastically minded to take drastic steps adverse to the interests of the monasteries. In 1295 Edward I, pressed for money to carry on his wars and made nervous over the danger of espionage on the part of the foreign monks, seized the alien priories in England and appropriated their revenues to his immediate uses. The position of Edward in this year was a difficult and a serious one. Scotland was in revolt and trouble was brewing in France over Gascony, so that a war was imminent in which Scotland and France were allying themselves against England. Edward stood in need of money and the undivided loyalty of his people. Instead of this the French monks on English soil were supplying money to France in the revenues of the alien priories which were thought also to be harboring spies, betraying military secrets, and giving useful information to the French.

The king therefore sent the sheriffs of the various counties bordering the sea, or watercourses leading to the sea, to arrest all the alien men of religion and remove them farther into the interior. In their places he substituted

English monks who were pledged to pay over to the royal exchequer all revenues accruing from the seized houses.[31] This sequestration included about sixty houses.[32] Each alien monk was given an allowance of eighteen pence a week for food and ten shillings a year for clothing from the houses suppressed. The remainder was to be turned over to the exchequer. A guardian was appointed to inventory all the goods. Later all the alien priories throughout England were similarly taken over by the secular power. A few of these sequestered houses were restored several months later on condition that a fixed annual sum be paid into the king's treasury by the priors. This yearly farm was to be kept up for the duration of the war, and it was not relinquished until 1306.

The alien priories were again seized in 1324 when war with France once more threatened, but they were restored on the accession of Edward III, in 1327, when peace was once more assured. But they remained free for only a decade, since in 1337 at the outbreak of the Hundred Years War all the lands, tenements, benefices, possessions, etc., were again taken over by the state. This time they were farmed out by the king to their priors, and an incomplete list of these farms showed that the royal exchequer was enriched by 5559 pounds sterling through this arrangement.[33] Besides the payment of the farms, fines were imposed for release so that the king realized an additional sum of 876 pounds sterling to carry on his wars. In the course of the Hunderd Years War the alien priories seesawed back and forth under sequestration by the state and under periods of freedom according to the interims in the fighting. Finally in 1414, their confiscation was consummated by Henry V as a necessary war measure.

An interesting and significant development in the process of secularization of the alien priories was the atti-

tude and action of the people toward them, expressed in
the petitions and activity of the Commons. During the
Hundred Years War, as early as 1346, a petition of the
Commons appeared asking that all alien monks be ban-
ished from the kingdom and supplanted by English men
of religion. The Commons also asked that a check be
placed on letters sent across the sea by foreigners. The seizure of 1369 was preceded by a petition of the Commons
deploring the fact that the alien monks betrayed the secrets of the realm. The protest was renewed in 1373 in
spite of the sequestration that had taken place, and to the
charge of treason was added that of sending money out
of the kingdom. After this petitions became frequent put-
ting forth various reasons why the French churchmen
should be expelled from the realm. The most common
complaint was that the secrets of the kingdom were carried abroad and money was being taken into France. This
money, the Commons pointed out, could be well used by
the English against the French instead of the opposite
course. So great was the agitation of the Commons that
actual expulsion of many of the alien monks was effected
by 1377.[34] It continued until the final confiscation of 1414
which immediately followed such a petition. The propaganda of Wyclif and his followers going on in the later
phase of the movement against the priories must have had
much to do with the ever growing discontent of the
Commons in this respect.

The various motives leading to the ultimate confiscation of the alien priories have already been pointed out,
but among them the economic one could not help being
very prominent. Need of money by the kings from time
to time was most easily satisfied by imposing on the help-
less monks of the alien houses, and doubtless the idea of
danger to the defense of the realm was used only as a

major pretext. The fact that the forced priories were handed back to the former priors after payment of a heavy fine and on condition of paying an annual farm is indicative of the possibility that money for the exchequer rather than danger of the realm was the real issue. Why take them away merely to return them if they were believed to be disloyal? The considerable sum amounting in all to some 7000 pounds sterling per annum realized by Edward III in the confiscation of 1337—an enormous figure reckoned in values of that time—was an all powerful inducement to change the status of the alien priories. The fact that the process of denization, or naturalization, progressed so slowly and the exorbitant fines imposed for such denization was another indication that merely Anglicizing the French houses was not alone the object of sequestration.

IV. UPHEAVAL AND UPRISING IN THE LATE FOURTEENTH CENTURY

By the last quarter of the fourteenth century the movement tending toward the final disendowment of the church in England had acquired considerable momentum. Besides the attacks on the alien priories legislative checks on ecclesiastical privileges manifested themselves in such measures as the Statute of Carlisle in 1307 and the Statutes of Provisors and Praemunire in the middle of the century. It has been asserted that had the sentiment that brought about the enactment of the two last named laws been carried to the point where the forces of the times were leading it, the Reformation would have been precipitated in England a century and a half before it actually did take place.[35] This may be an overstatement of the fact, but nevertheless in the last quarter of the fourteenth century movements were on foot that shook the power and prestige of the church to the very foundation and left the whole edifice in a precarious condition. During that time, social, economic, and political factors were at work and a leadership was present that was rapidly molding public opinion to effect an ecclesiastical revolution. The situation was allowed to dissipate in the reign of Richard II and the church recuperated again under the patronage and championship of the early Lancastrian dynasty.

But the matter of confiscation of church property by the end of the fourteenth century was no longer a mere attitude as in the reign of Henry III. A new phase of disendowment had come to the front marked by a violent propaganda aiming to undermine all justification for an endowed priesthood and translating itself into drastic steps toward confiscation of the goods of the church. Two leaders emerged in this period who did much to precipitate a crisis, one of them was John Wyclif and the other John Ball. The propaganda and agitation of both these men were of the utmost significance in regard to shaping anti-clerical attitude of the times, and to this end they unconsciously coöperated. To say the least their work cannot be segregated into separate fields of activity, namely, secular and ecclesiastical. The attitude toward the wealth of the clergy held by the Oxford radical was only a phase of the larger movement that brought on the so-called Peasants Revolt of 1381, due to the preaching of the mad priest of Kent and the social, political, and industrial discontent of the time.

There was a lapse of over two centuries between the incendiary teaching of Arnold of Brescia and the propagandist doctrines of Wyclif regarding the disposal of church property. The two were similar in the main point

of view, but there was little, if any, historical connection
between them. There is no reason to believe that the English
reformer borrowed his ideas from the Italian radical. The
primary fact that accounts for the immediate failure of
the earlier innovator and the ultimate success of the later
one was a tremendous change in the social, economic, and
political order in Western Europe. In the span of years
from 1155 to 1384 Europe had taken a long stride out
of the Middle Ages. The same era that marked the Crusading Movement and the enrichment of the church witnessed also the development of commerce with the emergence of forces destined in the end to strip the church of
its wealth. In the wake of a growing commerce came the
rise of national monarchies, the growth of towns, the
emergence of a middle class, and various agrarian read-
justments. In England a commercial, industrial, and agrarian revolution was going on setting loose new forces
which were rapidly disintegrating the old régime after
which the wealth of the church was organized. The Black
Death in England had so accentuated these forces that a
social upheaval and a political revolt resulted by 1381.

It is only under the light of these circumstances that
the work of Ball and Wyclif may be understood. The attack of Wyclif was on the church directed against the misuse of its wealth in particular. The attack of Ball was on the
social, economic, and political order as a whole; and it
was in this way that he assailed the churchmen as well as
the whole aristocracy of wealth and power. He had much
to do with giving shape and strength to the sentiment for
disendowment of the clergy. The emphasis of Ball was on
social and economic equality, preaching that villeinage and
servitude were contrivances of the wealthy to keep ordinary men in subjection and teaching that all goods should
be held in common.[36] Men were from the beginning cre-

ated equal and that equality ought to be restored and maintained by force if necessary. "Whan Adam dalfe and Eve span, who was thanne a gentleman?" was a famous text of this preaching priest. Tithes were not necessarily due to the church, and the authority of the clergy was to be set at nought.[37] Ball was essentially a communist and a leveler, attacking the hierarchy of wealth embodied in the church as a part of a nefarious system of the aristocracy of wealth as a whole.[38]

For twenty years John Ball continued to preach these social and economic ideas which were distinctly revolutionary in character. He greatly annoyed the authorities who sought to restrain him with frequent prison sentences without success. His teachings and agitation had much to do with the outbreak of the Peasants Revolt in 1381 which was immediately precipitated by a new poll tax, and which was the result of a long season of economic discontent. The Great Revolt started in Kent, but disturbances broke out all over England so that it was a widespread and apparently concerted movement. The plan was to kill all lords, gentlemen, and great churchmen. The chief object was the emancipation of the villein, so that archives were rifled to get possession of deeds, court rolls, and all legal bonds of serfdom and destroy them by fire. Lords and churchmen were forced to surrender in written statements their feudal rights.[39] The numerous serfs on the great abbeys of St. Edmundsbury and of St. Albans rose against their monastic landlords and demanded enfranchisement. Similar instances occurred in many other places in England. It was in this uprising of 1381 that Sudbury, Archbishop of Canterbury met his death through the violence of one of these mobs. To the insurrectionist, Sudbury was the impersonation of the economic oppression of the people.

Authorities differ as to the exact time Wyclif launched

into ecclesiastical politics, but whether early or late his career was marked by an extensive literary and propagandist activity regarding the disendowment of the church.[40] His activity was manifested long before the Great Revolt of 1381, and his influence no doubt had much to do in bringing on the insurrection. His teachings affected primarily academic and political circles, but he also adopted means of disseminating and popularizing them. He sent his preaching priests throughout England, and his influence reached into Bohemia. His followers, known as the Lollards, were a well-organized sect with decided socialistic and communistic tendencies. Whether Wyclif was influenced by Ball, or whether the latter was a disciple of Wyclif as some contend is quite aside from the point.[41] Both men were products of the times and at the same time molded the currents of thinking, each making his peculiar contribution. The influence of Ball was temporary. He was primarily a sentimentalist and an agitator—a soap-box orator of his day without an organization to perpetuate his work. Wyclif was a thinker, a philosopher, and a preacher. But he was also an organizer and writer and his work was thus given permanency.[42]

The outstanding contribution of Wyclif was his attack on the wealth of the English clergy. In this respect he may certainly be regarded as the "Morning Star of the Reformation" because this teaching found its way into early sixteenth century thinking. He not only believed in the disendowment of the church, but his writings are so freighted with the idea that one is led to believe it was with him an obsession. In the study of his theory of disendowment, now to be perused, a number of major historical facts should be kept in mind. One of them was the social, economic, and political upheaval that has just been alluded to in the preceding paragraphs. Economic forces were at work tending to change the existing order of things. The church belonged to the old feudal régime and with the passing of feudalism it either had to change its economic organization radically or be subjected to criticism in regard to the use of its wealth. A second fact was the course of the Hundred Years War. Wyclif not only became the champion of a growing nationalism which this war and the commercial revival were stimulating but an enemy of the church. The papacy located at Avignon and subservient to French influence made it look as though the revenue derived from English lands sent abroad by churchmen to support the papacy was being used to aid and comfort the enemy. A third fact was the Great Schism of 1378 when the prestige of the papacy was shattered by the existence of two heads of the church neither of which could be logically regarded as legitimate.

It was under these conditions that Wyclif promulgated his teachings against the wealth of the clergy. His theory for the disendowment of the English church involved four major points: endowment was contrary to the divine order of things; it tended to the moral and spiritual decay of the clergy; it militated against the best secular interests of the realm; it was the duty of the lay lords to forcibly deprive the clergy of their goods.

V. Wyclif's Theory of Disendowment—Endowment Is Contrary to the Divine Order

Wyclif laid the ax at the root of the tree of ecclesiastical endowment by asserting that dominion was founded on spiritual grace and not on a basis of material wealth and power.[43] Again, in a treatise called "Concerning Civil Lordship" he put forth the opinion that God was chief lord of all things, who forbade in his revealed word the endowment of the clergy.[44] The fundamental right of the church to hold property was thus undermined by direct revelation. But indirect logic also eliminated an immoral and unfaithful priesthood from God's tenantry, for Wyclif's ideal of tenure was feudal as well as theocratical. God was the supreme suzerain of all earthly domain who apportioned lands, possessions and wealth by subinfeudation on condition of service to be rendered. The clergy failed to render the services required. Instead of using the wealth left in their charge to advance the best interests of God's kingdom, they proved evil, disloyal, and unworthy tenants. Wyclif showed that the more churchmen increased in wealth the more corrupt they became until the papacy itself was looked upon as the Antichrist.[45] Because of this corruption and unfaithfulness to God, the supreme suzerain, most of the wealthy ecclesiastics should be disendowed.

The law forbidding endowment found in the Scriptures had never been abrogated.[46] Therefore the Donation of Constantine was wrong in principle and Pope Sylvester was beguiled of the devil when he persuaded the first Christian emperor to subsidize the church.[47] Christ, the ideal minister, lived in poverty and the clergy ought to deem it a privilege to follow him in this, for "Christ who gave poverty was greater than Caesar who gave property."[48] The greatest boon that the church could request would be divestiture of its temporal possessions, for was not poverty the divine plan for the clergy?[49]

In the tract "Concerning Civil Lordship," Wyclif went on to show that God had delegated all secular authority and all worldly possessions to the temporal lords and not to the great churchmen.[50] The clergy was in possession of great property because the secular lords, contrary to the law of God and to the divine plan, had alienated their holdings to the spiritual lords. Both the lay lords and the clergy were to be blamed for this situation, and they were now under the curse of God because of it.[51] For even if Magna Carta itself upheld churchmen in their rights of property, the law of God was above Magna Carta and could not be ignored or explained away. The clergy according to divine plan was to live on the income of no land or possessed wealth, but on tithes and free will offerings of the people. The law of tithes the clergy tacitly confessed to be still in force and operation by accepting them, why did they not in like manner regard the law that forbade the possession of property. Christ who came to reveal and exemplify the divine plan for the church preached poverty and lived without property, but the clergy now reversed the order of Christ and hence that of God. The clergy had become worldly wise instead of heavenly minded; they surpassed lay lords in riches, pomp, and worldly show; they engaged in secular business and neglected the service of God; they were contrary to the law of Christ and of God. Because of the reversal of the divine order all suffered: the clergy in moral decay; the lords and commons in material and spiritual impoverishment; the kingdom as a whole with discontent, disturbance of the peace, and religious unrest. Because the law of God expressly forbade endowment, Wyclif concluded in this tract, the clergy ought to give up their property and they ought to surrender it joyfully.

In another English treatise, "The Clergy may not Hold Property," Wyclif put forth the same idea.[52] He asserted that Sylvester, Bishop of Rome, committed simony in accepting from Constantine the first endowment of the church. Because ecclesiastical property was on the increase and because it was illegally acquired, the secular lords should not hesitate in alienating it. It was false to class

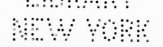
LIBRARY
NEW YORK

church property as alms like the clergy tried to make out, rather, as contrary to the divine order of things, church property was "alle-a-mysse." Endowment was a wasting of goods, a misappropriating of funds, and a breach in God's plan detrimental to clergy, lords, and commons alike.

In a Latin tract entitled: "Dialogus, sive Speculum Ecclesia Militantis," Wyclif drew up at considerable length just what the divine order of things was meant to be and just how it had been broken into by the churchmen. The church militant was composed of three orders; namely, the clergy, the secular lords, and the commons. These three classes of society were knit together, ideally at least, in mutual love and common interests. The three orders were to coöperate in promoting the general welfare of the realm, each having a peculiar mission and aim in life and each living up to certain well defined ideals. The God given ideal of the clergy was poverty, contemplation, prayer, and heavenly mindedness; following in the footsteps of Christ and living on alms and tithes. The temporal lords, holding their possessions as a sort of divine trust, were to acquire wealth and power so as to defend the realm from its enemies and so as to make effective the royal administration. The commons working at manual labor and following commercial pursuits were to give support to the other two groups in every endeavor to promote the welfare of the kingdom. These three estates by a divine arrangement of things were rigidly fixed and mutually exclusive in status, duties, and privileges; and it was only in the event that this divine order of things was ignored that confusion and adversity resulted.[53]

Such confusion of affairs was at the time apparent, for contrary to the heavenly arranged order of society, in defiance to the revealed word of God the clergy was usurping the position of the secular lords and supplanting them

in their offices. The clergy holding temporal possessions were forced to aid in war and to assume secular responsibilities. Here again Wyclif called attention to the fact that the Scriptural law forbidding the priesthood to hold property was still in full force, and the clergy were committing simony and heresy in breaking that law. Here again he also repeated that Christ both in practice and precept showed that the true life of his ministers was one of poverty.[54] Ecclesiastical endowment came in only through a law of the Antichrist. Was it meant that the law of Christ was to be kept in force only during the course of the first two Christain centuries while the law of the Antichrist was to continue forever? [55] The clergy ought not to be deceived by misleading terms, for alluding to church property by such pious expressions as "alms" and "patrimony of the crucified" did not help matters. Neither by shifting the responsibility of endowment on the generosity of pious laymen could the clergy be exonerated. The only remedy for the sin of endowment was restitution of the goods wrongly acquired. In case this was neglected by the ecclesiastical lords, confiscation by the state was both right and urgent.[56]

Such was the position of Wyclif in this dialogue between Truth and Falsehood whom the author pictured debating the issue. When Falsehood objected that the authority of the saints was on the side of a subsidized clergy, Truth replied that the saints were not sinless, and granting that the ones holding the view were guileless their dictum could not stand against that of Christ and Moses. If property holding saints were in Heaven it was not due to the fact that they owned worldly goods, neither were they to be imitated in the practice. All true saints that ever took worldly gifts abjectly repented of it.[57] When Falsehood objected that disendowment would lessen the number of the clergy to the detriment of religious activities, Truth replied that spiritual perfection did not necessarily come because of numbers. If Christ decreed that the clergy live without worldly goods and secular dominion, his will ought to be carried out regardless of all consequences. Poverty and obedience were much better than wealth and infidelity, and the church would be benefited even if many of its wealth loving priests and prelates were weeded out.[58]

In this colloquy Wyclif also pointed out that the friars were supreme hypocrites because they chose a life of poverty yet approved and accepted gifts. The prayer they offered for the dead was a mere delusion to fatten their purses, for to such prayer God was deaf and the affluence of the intercessors did not help to quicken the divine ears. The temporal dignity upon which the prelates as a whole rested merely qualified them for hell. This was the reason why the church should revert to its primitive status of apostolic poverty by reducing its secular dominion and doing away with clerical functions kept up merely for gain.[59] Idleness was the bane of the priesthood, making them unfitted for clerical duties. The abundance of wealth in the church not only fostered loafing, but it attracted idlers to the clerical class.[60] The existence of a leisure class of non-producers wasting their time and wealth was not an economic asset to the kingdom.[61] Let the clergy do honest work instead of selling useless prayers or exacting usury; let them work for a fixed salary, or write books, or teach grammar, or even give themselves to manual labor, or let them be checked by some other condition that will make them responsible for remuneration paid them.

Thus it was that Wyclif showed that an endowed church was contrary to the divine order of things. Poverty was the ideal and original condition of the clergy. That was a law of God given to Moses, approved by Christ, and honored by the Apostles. From this law the church was seduced by the devil, accepting the law of Antichrist which was endowment. The church militant should make amends for this situation; that is, the three orders ordained of God as the church militant should coöperate in reëstablishing the divine order. All three classes would benefit by such an arrangement; the clergy would be brought under the rule of Christ; the lords would be able to defend the realm and not be forced to oppress their tenants; and the commons of the land would enjoy prosperity.[62]

VI. Wyclif's Theory of Disendowment—Endowment Degraded the Moral and Spiritual Standards of the Clergy

Wyclif throughout his voluminous writings contended that disendowment would confer a blessing upon the clergy because their vast wealth corrupted their morals and rendered them unfitted for spiritual duties.[63] The business of priests, monks, and friars was to promote the religious interests of the people and from these pursuits wealth was drawing them to other employments and worldly diversions.[64] Greed for money, also, led the clergy to indulge in practices that degraded the offices of the church and the lives of the churchmen.[65] On the part of the people, open sin was often permitted for the payment of money, and indulgences for wrongs committed were freely granted in case the stipulated price was paid.[66] For this reason the church ought to be deprived of its temporal holdings and checked in its mercenary methods since these things defeated the ends for which the clergy existed and made a mockery of the church.[67]

That the opulence of the church debased the priesthood, perverted the offices of the ministry, and obstructed the spiritual edification of the laity, Wyclif clearly and repeatedly pointed out. In all of the seven sacraments money was not only accepted but it was often extorted for administering the sacred offices.[68] He showed that unfit men paid their way into ecclesiastical positions while the more proper candidates were turned down because they lacked money.[69] The outcome of such a policy was that incumbents of high posts and dignities in the church were morally unqualified to occupy those places.[70] He mercilessly exposed and denounced the petty graft practiced on candidates for holy orders.[71] He did the same for various clerical fees that seemed unfitting:[72]

> For they take for writing and sealing of a little scroll with six or seven lines, from twelve pence to two shillings; and certainly this is foul extortion. For they need no seal or letter according to God's law, but only the witness of their fellows and other true men that they were ordained at such a time. And they needeth not many times to be shaven and if they did they might be shaven of the common barber, and clipped the entire year for the money their barber takes at one time.

What was true in regard to appointment, ordination, consecration, and the various steps toward holy orders, was the case also in regard to penance and indulgences.[73] In this connection a blanket indulgence called a "sin-rent" was given to the ones who were able and willing to pay for it.[74] Thus for the payment of twenty shillings per annum some men were privileged to go on unchallenged in a life of open sin from year to year, or they might by paying a sufficient lump sum make the contract extend over a term of years.[75] Certain bishops procured by such arrangements additional incomes ranging from 2000 to 3000 marks a year.[76] One prelate in particular was known to have collected in this manner the sum of 60,000 marks within a period of twenty years: "Thus he robbed of the people and sent souls to hell at the same time." [77]

The injustice of this system was pointed out in that the rich were able to pay for absolutions covering a thousand years and the extremely poor could get no relief at all.[78] The worst phase of this tendency to extort money was that the practice extended to all the offices of the church and to all the duties of the clergy. Besides the ones mentioned above fees were collected for marriages, christenings, prayers of all kinds, extreme unction, and burial of the dead.[79] And in the majority of cases if the money failed to materialize the office was not performed.[80] This situation, according to Wyclif, not only demoralized the clergy but, as he caustically pointed out, the king and the realm were little helped by the prayers and services of such simoniacs, who by their rapacity and extortion got possession of the goods of rich and poor alike, wasting their substance in pompous show, gluttony, drunkenness, and worldly living.[81]

In another Latin work called "De Simonia" the great Oxford doctor insisted that the besetting sin of the clergy was simony, and the main bulwork of simony was the endowment of the church.[82] And the term simony was expanded into a broad definition which meant "an inordinate will to exchange spiritual for temporal things." [83] It was simony for a churchman to take more than he absolutely needed.[84] It was also simony for a layman to give needlessly and profusely to the clergy.[85] His ideal of the clerical life was one of poverty, and his ideal for clerical support was one of alms. All spiritual promotions were procured by simony which was universal among the clergy though the higher prelates were the worst offenders. The latter forsook the poverty of Christ to procure the property of the pious rich by means of flattery and for worldly power.[86] Most dangerous of all was the simony of the Roman court, for it robbed the realm of vast treasure needed to build it up. Englishmen traveled to Rome for benefices, pardons, first fruits, and special favors, spending one-fifth of the wealth of the realm and bringing back only "a little lead and much mischief." [87] The net results of simony for the clergy were extreme worldly-mindedness and general immorality to the utter neglect of spiritual things.[88]

Wyclif accused the churchmen of misappropriating the revenues of various ecclesiastical foundations, so that abbeys and monasteries were ruined and hospitals reduced to half their capacity that priests might live sumptuously on costly wines and meats.[89] In this manner the original purpose of the founders of religious houses was not only defeated but immorality on the part of the clergy was fostered. The picture was one of the spiritual as well as economic decay of some of the monasteries. Worldly-minded prelates made "sotel marchandise with pore mennus lifelode and holy Chirche goodis," and many abbeys were turned into "pig-stys, stables, and barkhouses." [90]

With respect to a decline in ecclesiastical standards, moral and spiritual, the friars also were charged as being responsible.[91] They connived at sin in the confessional because they feared frankness and honesty would react on the remunerative fees they received for this office as well as for other ecclesiastical services they were accustomed to perform. Thus they brought moral and spiritual confusion on the land.[92] In order to secure easy penance, vicious wrongdoers were accustomed to forsake the settled parish priests for the auricular chamber of the itinerant friars who would gladly absolve them for money. This was looked upon as a dangerous social menace, so that Wyclif advocated banishment for the mendicants.[93] Notice the following quotation from "The Grete Sentence of Curs Expouned".[94]

And for esy penaunce of money that they enjoyen men for trentalis and masse pens and makyng of gaie wyndowis and grete housis, that the world mau see and preise, the most viciouse men as avouteris, extorsioneris, usureris, and open theves gon to these hypocritis and forsaken there owne curatis that wolden sumwhat telle hem the perilis. And herefor of false purchas, of wikid extorsion and robberis, cometh never restitucion for siche privey schriftis and penaunce of masse pens; and where thei regnen most in household, prechyng and stryvyng, there regneth most synne. And sithen discencions withinforth and open werris withoutinforth comen most from synne and norischyng of synful men in here myslyvyngs, these weiward and coveitous confessouris disturblen most the pees of the kyng and his rewme.

VII. Wyclif's Theory of Disendowment—Endowment Jeopardized the Social and Economic Welfare and Endangered the Military Defense and Political Stability of the Realm

In a large Latin treatise, Wyclif taught that depriving the priesthood of their temporal possessions would be a national boon in at least three ways; it would benefit the clergy as an ecclesiastical group, the church as a national institution, and people as a social, economic, and political entity.[95] How happy and prosperous England would be, he exclaimed, if every parish church had its own resident rector with his family and every estate in the land had its just lord with his wife, servants, and a moderate family. For then there would not be so much plowable land lying barren; there would be no scarcity of corn and cattle; and there would be an abundance of servants, farm laborers, and artisans. Thus the kingdom would possess an abund-

ance of all kinds of goods. He then went on to say that
under the existing régime hirelings of the ecclesiastics,
who indignantly held civil dominion, brought about all
sorts of abominable evils. The land was occupied by tenants bearing the rule of the clergy reluctantly who cared
little about tilling the fields because they did not own them.
These tenants lived by theft because they lacked proper
oversight. Their wantonness disturbed the kingdom. The
clergy laden down with temporal possessions sought to
equal and even to surpass the splendor of the lay lords.
Things would be different if the temporalities were given
over to poor laymen; marriages, families, and freemen
would increase; the state would be greatly benefited; and
priests could devote their time to pious contemplation and
spiritual edification.[96]

In other words, the great wealth of the church was not
merely injurious to the clergy as a class but it indirectly
affected the welfare of the nation as a whole. This idea he
again enlarged upon in his tract "The Grete Sentence of
Curs Expouned." [97] In this treatise it was claimed that the
church aimed at nothing less than overthrowing the secular power and setting up its own. The church was in fact a
state within the state, posing as a rival, claiming in theory
its first obedience to Rome, and denying the jurisdiction
of the king over the persons and goods of its rulers. The
church controlled a third of the taxable property of the
realm and claimed exemption from taxation for secular
ends without papal approval. The assertion of a separate
obedience encouraged men to rebel against the king, taxes
sent abroad weakened the means of military defense at the
same time aiding the enemies of the kingdom, and the
vast wealth of the church was a menace to the social and
political integrity of the nation.

This position of Wyclif may in part be understood in the following quotation:[98]

> How stronge theves and traitours ben thei now to kingis and lordis in denying this obedience and in geving ensaumple to alle men in the lond for to rebel agenst the kynge and other lordis. For in thys thei techen lewid men and comyns of the lond, both in wordis and lawis and opyn dede, to be fals and rebel agens the kyng and lordis. And thys seemeth wel by here newe laws of decretalis where the proude clerkis have ordeyned thys—that oure clergie schal paie no subsidis, ne taxe, ne helping of oure kyng and oure rewme withouten leve and assent of the worldly prest of Rome; and sith many tymes thys proude worldly prest is enemye of oure londe, and prively meyteneth our enemyes, and to weren agenst us with oure ownen gold. And thus thei makyn this alien proudest prest of all othere to be cheef lorde of alle goodis that clerkis han in the rewme, and that is most part thereof. Where ben more traitours bothe to God and holy Chirche, and namely to here lege lord and his rewme, to make an alien worldly prest enemye to us, cheef lord of most part of oure rewme?

The dominant economic position of the church as a menace to the general welfare of the kingdom appeared again in an English tract entitled "Clerkis Possessioneris." [99] In this short treatise Wyclif taught that a highly subsidized clergy was detrimental to the realm because it destroyed the real usefulness of the priesthood, the knighthood, and the commons. The priesthood was turned from spiritual duty to vain worldly business or else gave itself over to idleness, gluttony, and drunkenness. The knighthood was weakened by the amortizement of its lands to pay for the empty prayers of the churchmen. The commons were injured because the church made good government impossible, failed to give good teaching, and robbed and oppressed by fines and rents. Because the clergy were guilty of these things, and because they paid tribute to a foreign lord, the pope, they were traitors.

In another short tract called "Concerning Church Temporalities," [100] the matter of the misuse and confiscation of church livings was again discussed. Prelates were not only worldly-minded, neglectful of religious duties, and even wanton in their lives; but they wasted the substance derived from their possessions which was meant to take care of the sick, the poor, and the needy. In this manner a great social service was being neglected, and the means for carrying it on were being wasted and misapplied. The prelates spent so much money coming from their benefices in feasting and entertaining great lords and wealthy magnates that little was left for distribution to the poor and needy in the vicinity of cathedrals and large convents. Incidentally it was mentioned that the prelates entertained and fêted these magnates because they feared confiscation. They tried to keep on the good side of the secular powers. Thus they avoided reproof of lords, and great men failed to censure their covetousness, and connived at their false dealings out of self-interest. This proved another social and moral bane to the kingdom laid at the door of endowment.

The gross misuse of ecclesiastical property was thus a just cause for its secularization, and this step was urged even to the point of using force to bring it about. Three reasons were given all of which tended to promote the general welfare of the realm. Secularization would improve the morals of both clergy and laity; the temporalities of the church would improve the military defense of the kingdom; and coercion on the part of the secular lords would be commendable because the law of the Scriptures against endowment would be enforced:[101]

> And secular lordschipis that clerkis han ful falsly agenst Goddis lawe and spent hem so wickedly schulden be goven wisly by the kyng and witti lordis to pore gentlemen that wolden justli governe the peple, and meytene the lond agenst enemeyes. And than myghte oure lond be strengere by many thousand men of armes than now is, withouten ony cost of lordis or talliage of pore comyns, be dischargid of grete rente and wickid customes brought up bi coveitouse clerkis and of many talliagis and extorsions, bi whiche thei ben now cruely pillid and robbid. And thus bi restorynge of lordschipis to secular men, as thei duwe bi holi writt and bi bryingyng of clerkis to mekenesse and wilful povert and bisy gostly traveile as lyvenen Christ and his apostlis, schoulden synne be distried in ech degree of the Chirch, and holi lif brought in, and secular lordis moch strengthid, and pore comyns relevyd, and good governale both gostly and worldly com agen, and rightwisenesse and treuthe and reste and pees and charite; and hereto schulde ech Christene man helpe bi al his wille, herte, kunnynge, and powere.

In his appeal for social and economic amelioration by a secularization of church property, Wyclif looked both toward the past and toward the future, bringing forth ideals new and old. He cited not only the Scriptures but Roman and English law, ecclesiastical canons, and historical precedent to justify his ideal for a confiscation of the wealth of the clergy.[102] But he also advanced along a new line of thought; namely, community of goods. He looked upon a sort of communism as an ideal condition of social and economic organization, but he did not advocate a communistic reorganization under existing conditions.[103] In this outlook he perhaps had his mind on the New Testament communism of the early church with its failure to successfully develop.

VIII. WYCLIF'S THEORY OF DISENDOWMENT—IT WAS THE DUTY OF THE LAY LORDS TO DIVEST THE CHURCH OF ITS WEALTH

On account of the abuse of ecclesiastical wealth, its menace to the social, economic, political, religious, and military interests of the kingdom; Wyclif came forward with the teaching that the temporal lords had a legal right and a religious sanction for seizing the goods of the clergy.[104] "*Per idem tempus,*" wrote Walsingham, "*surrexit Oxoniis quidam, dictus Johannes Wyclef, Doctor in Theologia, tenens opiniones a toto damnatas Ecclesia videlicet.* . . . *Item, si Deus est, domini temporales possunt legitime ac meritorie auferre bona fortunae ab ecclesia delinquente.*"[105] Unless the clergy radically reformed there was no alternative to actual dispossession. Any sort of superintendence by the lay lords or control of the revenues from church lands would prove inadequate to meet the existing situation.[106] The king was the natural leader in any policy of disendowment, and he should be held responsible under the law of God to confiscate the goods of the clergy. The king was the true vicar of Christ, but he also had power to act in this capacity as the chief of the secular arm. The king was now to undo the evil work of the English Constantine.[107] Disendowment was the only recourse to do away with the abuses of the clergy and the dangers of the nation, and the king now had a great opportunity to effect it. The lordship of even the secular princes was a questionable matter when it was abused, but in regard to the clergy it was absolutely forbidden.[108]

There was a time in the career of Wyclif when he seemed satisfied merely with reform. The demoralization of the clergy, their spiritual neglect of the laity, the use of their wealth for ulterior purposes could possibly be changed by less drastic means than by complete secularization of ecclesiastical property. At least he came forth with a long program of reform in his tract entitled: "Concerning Poor Priests."[109] The treatise contains twenty-one points covering all the abuses of the clergy, but thirteen of these relate to evils arising out of money matters. In these he advocated that simony be destroyed, sin-rents be stopped, and curates hold no secular offices. He likewise would do away with illicit fees, annates, usury of clerks, and amortizements. He also would have the treasure collected at the shrines of saints used in the defense of the realm, and some sort of taxation imposed on church property.

But this was a passing expedient rather than a fixed ideal, for endowment was looked upon as the cause of all the abuses in the church and no remedy outside of disendowment could bring adequate relief. The subsidizing of the church with expansive worldly possessions had transformed it from a Christian to a Caesarean body from the start and the ever grasping policy of the clergy had tended to perpetuate such a status. Papal provisors, Peter's pence, annates, tithes, and various sorts of taxation added in a later day all went to aggravate the situation. The money extorted in connection with the sacraments and the confessional came in their turn. All this involved simony and no one could tell where the thing would end. So long as endowment was allowed to continue it would be impossible to extirpate simony since all simony was due to it.[110] Ruin threatened the realm under the existing situation, and the only alternative was a complete disendowment of the clergy. Only depriving the church of its wide worldly in-

terests would eliminate the misappropriation of funds.[111]
It would also force the religious men to live on tithes and
offerings according to the original intention of the founder
of the church.[112]

Such a seizure of the goods of the clergy would not be
an act of robbery, but it was on the other hand a duty
which the king and the secular lords owed to the nation.
Wyclif for that reason called upon the king to bestir himself in order to save the kingdom which was daily being
robbed of men and money and which was rapidly falling
from his hands into the power of Rome.[113] Looking to the
advantage of the civil and military welfare of the people
was a distinctive contribution made by Wyclif to the movement of disendowment. Arnold of Brescia, the anti-churchly
sects, and the early mendicants advocated apostolic poverty
because wealth was a hindrance to spiritual growth.
Wyclif did this and more. He was the pioneer and the
exponent of a new point of view by proclaiming a highly
endowed clergy a danger to the whole civil order.[114] Time
and again he called upon the civil authorities to remedy
this situation by confiscating the wealth of the church and
his admonition soon bore fruit.

IX. The Aftermath of Wyclif's Theory of Disendow-ment—Attempts at Confiscation

The answer to the attitude and propaganda of Wyclif
was the Lollard movement, springing up in the wake of his
career and freighted with significance both as to immediate effects and ultimate bearing on the reformation of
the sixteenth century. The course of the Lollard movement was marked by three well defined phases, the first
of which ended with the execution of Sir John Oldcastle
and a group of Lollard insurrectionist leaders in 1417. The

crushing of this rebellion meant the end of Lollardry as an aggressive social and political revolutionary force. The second phase of the movement was characterized by little open activity of the adherents of Lollardry due to the relentless suppression by the authorities and the absorbing issues of foreign and civil wars. It ended about 1485. The third phase of their activity came with a revival of Lollard propaganda in the time of Henry VII and continued until it merged into the greater Reformation movement of the sixteenth century.

The first phase of this movement was one of the utmost significance for the history of disendowment, showing that the doctrines of Wyclif persisted, that they were widely propagated, and that they became a vital revolutionary force for a quarter of a century after the death of the founder.[115] His teachings were popular throughout the south of England and particularly in London itself.[116] An incident told in the Chronicle of Caxton, repeated by Tyrell, illustrated the vengeful feeling of the hierarchy as well as the influence of the Lollards about this time. A servant of the Bishop of London took from a baker a loaf of bread in the open street. The baker demanded pay but was met with a blow that struck him down, and the Bishop's man took refuge in his master's house near by. A mob gathered insisting that the culprit be delivered up, threatening to burn down the episcopal residence, and resorting to various acts of violence. The riot was quelled by the soldiers, but the Bishop of London insisted on arresting and prosecuting the offenders "because of an old grudge he held against the citizens as favoring the doctrines of Wyclif." [117]

The Lollards were not limited to London nor to the south of England, but they were scattered more or less throughout the realm, thanks to Wyclif's propagandist movement in the shape of poor preachers.[118] One of their chief complaints was against the wealth and power of the clergy.[119] If the contemporary historians are to be believed, the increase in the numbers of the Lollards after the death of Wyclif was extraordinary. Some of the statements of these chroniclers were either gross exaggerations, or they indicate a grave menace to the church. Knighton pointed out that one half of the population of England at the time was Lollard, and others corroborate the statement.[120] One writer said that by the time of the accession of Henry V, in 1413, 23,000 of the Lollard sect had suffered death.[121] These may be overstatements, but nevertheless Sir John Oldcastle was able to rally 100,000 of the sect to his standard of revolt. The fact that after his defeat, Oldcastle was enabled to hide from the authorities so long in spite of the price on his head was indicative of wide Lollard sympathy and following.[122] For a long time it was hard for the sheriffs to enforce the statutes against the Lollards because of their strength.[123] In the reign of Richard II sixty preachers were spreading the doctrines of Wyclif in Leicester alone.[124] The king was forced to suppress conventicles of Lollards in London, check their literary activity, and even to arrest their leaders.[125] The Lollards were not recruited from the poorer classes alone but many knights and nobles, sometimes men of great wealth and influence, joined the sect. Among them were found such names as the Cliffords, the Nevilles, and the Montagues.[126]

The inevitable result of the spread of the Lollard movement was a series of efforts to confiscate the property of the church. At least six attempts were made to despoil the clergy of their property in the period between the death of Wyclif and the end of the reign of Henry V. But as early as the year 1371 the idea had been advanced of the advisability of taking over the temporalities of the church as a necessary war measure. Wyclif at that time showed how a certain lord "more skilful than the rest" in an address before the Parliament pictured the church as an owl that had stolen the feathers of the other birds and was allowed to use them under ordinary conditions. On the approach of the hawk, however, the birds formerly robbed suddenly snatched back their feathers as a means of protection.[127] The parable was obvious and its import was immediately grasped by the prelates. The speaker then openly asserted that in time of war the wealth of the church could legitimately be used for the common defense.

But the first attempt actually made to seize the goods of the clergy by violence and appropriate them for state purposes did not materialize until 1385. In that year at a parliament held in London, the king asked the usual pecuniary support of both laity and clergy. But the clergy refused to contribute asserting that the church ought to be free and in no manner taxed by the secular authorities. Archbishop Courtney even went so far as to swear that he would rather lose his head than to submit to the bondage of a tax. This attitude angered many of the knights and a number of the peers; and they began to answer that the church held too many temporalities, and that it would be a real act of piety on the part of the laymen to take over its vast possessions. This would humble the proud churchmen. The disgruntled laymen then drew up a tentative plan for the partition of the ecclesiastical property that was to fall under condemnation. However, when the scheme was presented to the king he refused to accept it, saying that so long as he was sovereign the clergy would not be molested in their right of property.[128] Yet this show of aggression by the laymen brought the prelates suddenly to terms, so that they volunteered to give a tithe to the king. Notwithstanding his attitude on this occasion the king had earlier seized the goods of the bishop of Norwich as well as the temporalities of the archbishop of Canterbury.[129]

Nine years following this episode, at another parliament held in London, the threat of confiscation again faced the clergy. On this occasion the Lollards were directly implicated in bringing about the issue. While Richard II was carrying on a campaign in Ireland, followers of Wyclif posted on St. Paul's Church a catalogue of accusations against the churchmen charging them with various crimes.[130] The bishops tried to silence by force the agitation that followed as a result, but with no success. In the list of propositions catalogued on the posted document, one advocated that the property of the clergy be taken from it. The trouble became so serious that the king was forced to return from Ireland to take the situation in hand, and the conference in London was the result. Apparently many of the nobles were back of the agitation, for the king threatened one of them with death in case such an episode was repeated under his leadership. But it took more than mere threats to put a stop to the Lollard agitation, for two years later the pope was forced to write the king asking for the condemnation of certain Lollard heretics as a menace to church and state alike.[131] And only a few years after this came the famous act of Parliament *"De Hæretico Comburendo"* by which Lollardry became a crime punishable by burning.[132]

Two more attempts to confiscate the property of the church closely followed one another in 1403-4.[133] Henry IV, after the victory of Shrewsbury, was hard pressed for funds to carry on a campaign against the Welsh. In the emergency the principal supporters of the king suggested that he seize the money and equipage of the bishops. But the strenuous opposition of the Archbishop of Canterbury caused the king in the end to desist from such an undertaking. An effort at confiscation much more sweeping and serious came in the parliament at Coventry soon after.[134] When the king made known his usual need of money, he was reminded by certain of the knights that his necessities might be provided without too great burden to the laity by taking over the wealth of the church and applying it to public uses. The knights argued that the riches of the clergy made them careless in regard to religious duties, and that diminishing their exorbitant revenues would prove beneficial to both church and state. In the sharp altercation following the proposal, Arundel, Archbishop of Canterbury, took up the challenge of the laymen. He claimed that the property of the church could not thus be violated without impunity, censuring the knights for their cupidity and successfully appealing to the king. That the time was not ripe for so startling an innovation was manifest in the decision of the monarch, the division among the peers, and the final apology that the knights offered for their conduct.

But a little later, in 1410, a parliament strongly Lollard in composition made proposals for a complete disendowment of the church.[135] In a petition presented to the king, commons and peers alike seemed joined in pointing out the immense pecuniary resources of the clergy and the reasons for their confiscation. If the lord the king saw fit to take possession of the temporal goods of the bishops, abbots, and priors which was spent in useless show and grandeur, the crown and the realm would receive much advantage from such a measure; for it would support fifteen earls, fifteen hundred knights, six thousand squires, and a hundred new hospitals. Another manuscript added that by such a move the king would place in his coffers

the sum of 20,000 pounds sterling per annum; that each
earl would have an income of 3,000 marks; that each
knight would likewise have an income of 100 marks; and
that all the poor of the land would be amply provided
with sustenance. The church, according to this document,
had an income of 332,000 marks per annum which ought
to be spent on the poor. It also had property sufficient
to subsidize 40,000 priests and clerks with an annual stipend of 7 marks apiece.[136] The scheme of the parliament
was thwarted by the attitude of the king who said he had
vowed to leave the church in a better state than he had
found it.[137]

A similar project was brought forward four years later
in a parliament held in Leicester under Henry V.[138] Here it
was represented that the church possessed 18,400 ploughs
of land and that its revenues were 485,000 marks per annum, an amount equaling to one third of the entire wealth
of the realm. When a measure for confiscation was presented to the parliament, the Chronicler Edward Hall said
that it made the fat abbots swear, the proud priests frown,
the poor friars curse, the silly nuns weep, and indeed all
her merchants were made to fear that Babel would down.[139]
At first the parliament favored the measure, but the
newly elected Archbishop of Canterbury, Chicheley, championed the cause of the churchmen effectively by divert-
ing the interests of the young king to more tempting projects in France.[140] This was the last recorded attempt at
open violent seizure of church property until the final confiscation of the sixteenth century.

X. THE AFTERMATH OF WYCLIF'S THEORY OF DISENDOW-
MENT—ITS UNDERCURRENT AND REVIVAL

There were a number of reasons for the period of lull
in the propaganda against endowment during the three-

quarters of a century following the year 1410. A very important though indirect cause was the reopening of the Hundred Years War and the dynastic conflict following its close known as the Wars of the Roses. But the immediate cause of the cessation of attack on church property doubtless was the blow given to Lollardry in the defeat of the insurrection of Sir John Oldcastle, and the relentless way in which the sect was suppressed by Henry V. Oldcastle claimed a following of 100,000 open adherents besides some 50,000 servants and apprentices in London that gave him open sympathy.[141] In 1414, acting under the false impression that the king had embarked for France, he congregated a number of his followers in St. Giles Field, planning to attack and destroy certain abbeys and churches in and about London. One of his objectives was the famous abbey of St. Albans. But he was frustrated in his design by the quick action of one of the king's officers who dispersed the insurrectionists and forced their leader into hiding. Thirty of the conspirators were executed immediately, and after three years spent in hiding Oldcastle met the same fate. This debacle seems to have wholly disconcerted the Lollard movement as an organized force of direct-actionists.

But there was some evidence to show that their activity as propagandists persisted in an undercurrent at least during this period of lull in spite of foreign and domestic war and relentless suppression. In a document known as the "Festival" compiled in the time of Henry VII but antedating this period, the denunciatory sentences evidently were meant for the Lollards. The "Festival" was a catalogue of curses that solemnly condemned to dark perdition the following offenders: [142]

Al those that deprive holy chyrch of ony right to make of holy chyrch ony lay fee that is halowed or

sanctified. And also al those that with holde the rightes
of holy chyrche; that is to say offeryngs, tithes, rents,
or freedome of holy chyrche. . . . And al those that
ony maner of moveable goodes, or unmoveable, away
bear wyth strength or wrongfully bear away or waste:
of the wych cursing they may not be assoyled til they
have made satisfaccion unto whom the wrong is done.
And al those that ony maner of goodes with vyolence
or malice beare out of holy chyrche stede or abbaye or
hous of relygyon which that there in is layd or done
for warandyse of socoure or for to be kepte: and al
those which that there to procure or assent. And al
those that them mayntayne or sustayne. . . . And al
those that with holde tythes or with drawe their tythes
wytyngly or malycyously to the harm of holy chyrche;
or tythes let to be gyven of al goodes which they are
commanded and ordered to be gyven by the law of
holy chyrche.

The whole document savors of an attempt to offset the
doctrines of the Lollards regarding the payment of money
to the clergy. Its anti-Lollard tendency was also seen in
the curse it pronounced against all that did not believe
in the sacrament of the altar as it was commonly looked
upon.

A probable cause for the reticence regarding the Lollards during the period was the gradual disappearance of
their persecution as the prestige of the Lancastrian dynasty
began to wane. This was true specially after 1431.[143] With
persecution at an ebb there was little to attract attention
toward the Lollards. Again, their methods of propaganda
changed and their influence consequently became more
subtle: the itinerant preacher speaking in the open gave
place to the traveling preacher reading the tracts of Wyclif to select and trusted groups hiding in barns, stables,
and lonely parts of the woods.[144] Then again during the

Wars of the Roses any notice of them would naturally have ceased; for, as Fuller said: "The very shadow of the storm sheltered them."[145] Finally, silence was due to the sterility of the period in learning and literature. Of poetry there were only the smallest fragments of the rudest sort and prose was little more prevalent.[146] The work of Walsingham ended in 1418, and no eminent annalist succeeded him, for the chronicles of the following years were fragmentary and confined to the local interests of uninteresting monks.[147]

An exception to the lack of literary activity was the labors of Reginald Peacock, Bishop of Chichester; and strange to say, it is in his works that one has the strongest of indirect proof that the opinions of the Lollards were quite influential in the middle of the fifteenth century. This forerunner of the English Renaissance was a strange combination of radicalism and reactionism, attacking the Donation of Constantine as a fable and upholding at the same time such crying abuses as absenteeism, pluralities, annates, papal provisors, and even simony itself.[148] He strongly defended at great length the endowment of the clergy.[149] As a reactionary he was hated by many of the laity and as a heretic he was opposed by the clergy. Supported for a time by the powerful Duke of Suffolk he was finally crushed; he abjectly recanted and spent his last days in prison.

Of the eleven literary works of Peacock, the majority were directed against the teachings of the Lollards.[150] "They were addressed to the common people to reclaim them from Lollard errors (as he deemed them) which were widely prevalent."[151] He himself said his works were written "for to conuicte and ourcome the erring persoones of the lay peple which ben clepid Lollardis."[152] Of these writings the "Repressor of Overmuch Blaming of the Clergy" was likely typical of his anti-Lollard sentiment. It was written in English and fills two moderately sized printed volumes given over entirely to the refutation of Lollard opinions in spite of the fact that the name Lollard appears only once.[153] He upheld the use of images, pilgrimages, ecclesiastical property, and other ideals and institutions assailed by the Lollards.[154] The fact that a large proportion of the Repressor was devoted to a defense of endowment indicated that the Lollards had not ceased to attack the right of ecclesiastical property.[155] In his arguments, Peacock refuted step by step the position of Wyclif, proving by both the New and the Old Testament that endowment was not forbidden. He concluded that whatever the Scriptures, reason, and human enactments did not disapprove was lawful; and since none of these prohibited the clergy to possess lands and goods, endowment was not illegal.[156]

A revival of Wyclifism appeared at the beginning of the reign of Henry VII and continued with ever increasing vigor in the first quarter of the sixteenth century.[157] John Foxe, on consulting the bishop's registers, discovered the names of forty persons of the Lollard heresy who suffered death between the years 1509 and 1527.[158] A Lollard by the name of Thomas Man traveled throughout the south of England preaching to numerous groups of these believers. At his trial in 1518, he boasted having turned seven hundred people to his way of thinking.[159] The sect grew so rapidly that the Bishop of Lincoln despaired of checking them by the usual machinery of the church and called on the aid of the secular arm. The king responded by a writ ordering mayors, sheriffs, bailiffs, constables, and all good subjects to coöperate in exterminating the heresy.[160] Strype showed by a similar and further consultation of the bishops' registers that Lollardry was specially active in and about London.[161] An entry of the State Papers showed that Henry VIII, in 1512, issued a commission to the Bishop of Coventry and Litchfield, and others "to inquire into insurrections, rebellions, Lollards, etc.," in South Wales, in the counties of Salop (sic), Hereford, Gloucester, Worcester, and Flint.[162]

The name Lollard was not forgotten, and it continued to be associated with heretical teachings in the period of the Reformation. But the names of Lollard and Lutheran were at times badly confused.[163] When Hugh Latimer, court preacher of Henry VIII, preached at Bristol to ever increasing crowds against pilgrimages as time wasting and economically non-productive labor, a poetically inclined priest played on his name thus:[164]

L   for Lollard standes in thys place.
A   for error of great iniquities.
T   for traytour to God, lackyng grace.
I   for ignorance of true Trinitie.
M   for maynteyner of those that are nought.
E   for eretick as lerned men seyth.
R   for rebeller agaynst Chrysts feyth.

CHAPTER IV

REVOLT OF THE REFORMATION PARLIAMENT AGAINST
ECCLESIASTICAL EXACTIONS IN ENGLAND
1529-1536

FINANCIAL abuses of the Roman ecclesiastical system on the eve of the English Reformation fall into four typical groups centering around (1) vacancies, (2) administering the sacraments, (3) the church courts, and (4) papal taxation. The matter of vacancies involved papal provisions, the payment of annates, installations, the spoilia, the servitia, pluralities, absenteeism, bestowal of the pallium, and the collection of innumerable petty fees.[1] Administering the sacramental offices multiplied absolutions, indulgences, masses, dispensations, and fees for all the seven sacraments.[2] The dispensing of justice was made oppressive by the excessive fees and fines of the church courts, probating of wills, and expensive appeals to Rome.[3] The regular taxation included tithes, Peter's pence, mortuaries, visitation fees, and various kinds of customary dues.[4] Other economic abuses were manifest but not so outspoken, such as a tacit obligation to pay the delinquent tribute money promised by King John. There was an alleged maladministration of ecclesiastical wealth, and complaints as to losses of time and money in the observation of needless holy days, in pilgrimages, and in mendicancy.

Most of these financial irregularities were long standing ones, and some of them had been the cause of acute crises, even calling forth threats of schism from the papacy, in the course of the three centuries preceding the Reformation. The medieval church had developed intricate financial machinery by means of which it collected large sums derived from fees, lands, fines, and regular taxation.[5] Its economic interests covered all Western Europe and the papal exchequer was organized accordingly. The church had long enriched its coffers by impoverishing the people and its methods had long been resented. Men in constant touch with the papal court were at times amazed at the ready show of money. The Spanish confessor of John XXII said.[6]

> I have frequently entered into the office of my lord the pope, where I have seen bankers, tables loaded with money, ecclesiastics occupied with counting piles of crowns. May Christ, who was poor, cast out now and forever this business from the church.

Some of the popes spent the money as fast as it came in while others hoarded it until they became immensely wealthy.[7] Clement V was said to have amassed a fortune of about fourteen million dollars.[8] Innocent IV exclaimed to the relatives gathered about his deathbed: "Why do you weep, wretched beings, have I not left you all rich?"[9] A fourteenth century writer spoke as follows:[10]

> Money does everything at the court of Rome. If you do not know this turn to its customs and ways. It loves causes, suits, and quarrels because they cannot be carried on without money, and a cause that once enters the court proves almost unending. . . . High persons receive dispensations so long as they have sufficient money. This marvellous vanity and cupidity of the court has aroused scandal against it throughout the whole world.

This is the eighth year that pope Clement V has ruled the whole church, but whatever he did to benefit mankind has escaped the memory. At Vienna he gathered a council, conceded indulgences for the Holy Land and collected an immense amount of money, but in no way benefited the Holy Land. Far better were it for the rectors if there were no pope, than to be daily subject to such exactions. But whether or no it is possible for me to discuss this, because it is equivalent to sacrilege to question the power of that prince. Among all other provinces of the world, England feels most the oppressions of the lord the pope. . . . Lord Jesus, either take away the pope from our midst, or lessen the power he assumes among the people.

Thus it was that papal exactions fattened the coffers of Rome by draining wealth from all Europe and affecting all classes of people. According to Lagarde, nothing did so much as the pontifical financial system to detach the nations from the Apostolic See.[11] Statements to this effect may be found at many places both in the sources and in the later authorities.[12]

I. Minor and Surviving Forms of Financial Abuses on the Eve of the Reformation in England

Neither the geographical isolation of England nor the growing spirit of nationality saved that land from the financial and economic abuses of the church. England long had been a principal source of papal exploitation and remained such until the final break with Rome in the sixteenth century. A pope of the twelfth century alluded to England as his inexhaustible fountain of riches,[13] and the writer just quoted above mentioned England as feeling most keenly the oppressions of the pope. From the

Anglo-Saxon period onward William of Malmsbury, Oder-
icus Vitalis, Gerald of Cambridge, Matthew of Paris, Wyclif, Langland, and Chaucer make mention of the abuses
of the church.[14] England abounded in great natural wealth,
and the English clergy were richly endowed in lands
and revenues. It was for this reason that it had been a
fertile field of papal exactions in the past and remained such
until the final ecclesiastical revolt of the sixteenth century.
It was this also that was one of the most exasperating
causes of the final break with the papacy in 1533. A description of the nature, origin, and popular reaction toward certain outstanding forms of ecclesiastical taxation
and financial abuses is quite necessary in determining the
part they played in consummating this ultimate breach
with the Roman See. The four typical groups of financial
abuses given at the opening of this chapter contain both
major and minor forms of financial irregularities that
brought discontent and disapproval on the part of the
English people and that formed a basis for which the Reformation Parliament saw fit to voice its protests, and pro-
mulgate its legislation. Only the minor and the more faintly
surviving forms of abuses will be discussed at this point.
The description and discussion of the others will be reserved for the place where the acts passed by the Reformation Parliament abolishing them are taken up.

The immense mass of exactions imposed by the Roman
court may be seen in the catalogue of them set forth in
some of the acts passed by the Reformation Parliament.[15]
In one of the petitions, the Commons despair in the enu-
meration of them all. For many years past, and still at the
present time, they complain, the subjects of the king have
been plundered and the land impoverished and decayed
by the intolerable exactions of great sums of money on
the part of the bishop of Rome in the form of censuses,

Peter's pence, procurations, fruits, suits for provisions, bulls, delegacies, rescripts, appeals, legatine jurisdictions, dispensations, faculties, grants, relaxations, writs of prinde valere, rehabilitations, abolitions, "and other sorts of bulls, briefs, and instruments of sundry natures, names and kinds . . . the specialites whereof be overlong, large in number, and tedious here to be inserted."[16] A similar list of petty and numerous exactions may be found in the act for the conditional restraint of the papal annates passed in 1532.[17]

In regard to that group of abuses centering about vacancies, the matter of papal provisions was still the cause of grave misgivings in England on the eve of the Reformation. This practice which meant the filling of English ecclesiastical livings with incumbents of foreign birth and interests had resulted in a number of grave crises in the past, and has already been spoken of above.[18] Neither the statute of 1351 nor that of 1390 succeeded in entirely checking this evil. Papal patronage of this sort was looked upon as a national menace in two ways: it jeopardized the defense of the realm by filling England with men of foreign extraction, and it impoverished the kingdom by the export of vast wealth to the papal court.[19]

The spoilia also survived on the eve of the break with the papacy. This was a papal claim on the personal property of a bishop in case of his demise. The demand grew out of a popular local custom of an earlier day by which the episcopal residence was violently sacked when made vacant by death. The kings had put a stop to mob assault of this kind, but they appropriated the property themselves. When church councils objected to this sort of secularization of ecclesiastical wealth, Innocent IV finally had such intestate property revert to the Apostolic See. The claim had never been relinquished.[20]

The servitia were fees paid by bishops, abbots, and high prelates in general for nomination, consecration and confirmation to office. The tax did not appear until the thirteenth century, but it continued until the Reformation.[21] The monks of St. Edmundsbury were forced to pay to the papacy 800 marks for the confirmation of their abbot in 1248.[22] In 1218 the Bishop of Lincoln paid 1000 marks to be installed into the episcopal office by the pope, and he paid an additional 100 marks to the papal legate.[23] "Clement V lived cheerlie by the monie which he got from bishops that came to him for confirmation." [24] A regular tariff was eventually fixed for the various papal promotions, but the fee usually amounted to a third of one year's revenues of the office involved.[25]

The conferring of the pallium also comes under this group of exactions connected with ecclesiastical vacancies. It entailed the payment of large sums of money by archbishops when the insignia of their office was imposed by the pope. King Canute was said to have complained that vast sums of money were extracted from the archbishops by this means. The practice had begun, in fact, with Pope Gregory the Great and continued still to be a papal demand in the early sixteenth century.[26]

The second class of financial abuses, namely, the exaction of fees for administering the ordinary offices of the church was also much in evidence in the early sixteenth century, and it contributed towards the break with the papacy in 1533. In 1529, the Commons petitioned the king that the sacraments and sacramentals be freely administered by the clergy.[27] All the seven sacraments together with indulgences, dispensations, chanting of mass, prayers, and kindred spiritual services were made the means of procuring money much resented by the people. It had long been so, for Piers the Plowman in the "field full of folk" portrayed the greed of priest and prelate in the fourteenth century. One sees priests acting as confessors for the salary involved, pardoners running about as hucksters of papal bulls, and parsons "singing for simony."[28] The "Complaint of the Plowman" portrayed the clergy as becoming so rich that their power exceeded that of the king:[29]

> These have more might in England here,
> Than hath the king and al his lawe,
> They han purchased hem such powere,
> To taken hem whom list not knawe;
> And say that heresie is her sawe,
> And so to prison will hem send,
> It was not so by elder dawe;
> God for his mercy it amend.

Wyclif painted a similar picture. The priest bribed the bishop to be ordained, and after ordination refused to say mass except for money either in the form of an annual stipend or immediate fees. Long time permits to indulge in immorality, called "sin-rents" were often procured from priests by men of wealth and influence.[30] Ordination, penance, marriage, baptism, confirmation, extreme unction, and burial of the dead involved talliages of money.[31] If a parish priest refused to connive at sin, all the parishioner had to do was to go to the nearest friar in order to get easy absolution.[32] Priests encouraged the rich to found chapels and endow chantries in which the clergy led lives of uselessness and ease.[33] Payment for shanting masses became a matter of royal bounty and subsidy. Henry III paid the clerks of the royal chapel for special singing.[34] Henry VII bought 10,000 masses "en bloc" at a penny a mass for the souls of dead Knights of the Garter.[35] In his will he provided for 10,000 more at six pence a mass.[36] The divorced queen, Catherine of

Aragon, made provision in her will for 500 masses for the dead.[37]

Absolutions, dispensations, and indulgences were also a source of serious grievance. The trade in them sprung up in the twelfth century as a means of financing the Crusades. They soon proved useful in other ways, and by 1300 began to supply the daily needs of the popes. The custom was developed by Innocent III, who for the payment of money granted freedom to excommunicated persons.[38] In the reign of Henry III, absolution became a scandal tending toward schism.[39] These privileges soon were sold at the papal exchequer for a fixed price, usually a shilling each; and though they were abolished at the council of Basle they persisted until the Reformation.[40] Dispensation to marry within the fourth degree was sold for eight florins.[41] Dispensation to marry on prohibited days could be had for an additional fee.[42] The dispensation became a remunerative source of revenue for the papal chancery.[43] By the middle of the fourteenth century they were extended to the eating of meats, milk, and eggs during prohibited periods.[44] The jubilee years of the popes became a remunerative means of gain, and as a consequence the interim between jubilee years was shortened to 50 and ultimately to 33 years. Ultimately the payment of indulgences was substituted for pilgrimages, the actual journey being made unnecessary provided the cost of the contemplated pilgrimage was forwarded to Rome.[45]

Other offices of the church were likewise made remunerative. In some parts of England two pence per poll were charged by priests for the sacrament of the altar. The matter was a grievance at the outbreak of the Reformation. The petition of 1532 complained that prelates and ordinaries daily permitted parsons, vicars, curates, parish priests, and other spiritual persons having cure of souls ministering

within the realm took and exacted "of your obedient subjects divers sums of money for the sacraments and sacramentals of Holy Church, sometimes denying the same without they first be paid the said sums of money." [46]

A third class of ecclesiastical abuses involving minor and
surviving forms of exactions was the tithe. Tithes seem to
have been collected by the clergy from very early times, but
a special system of this sort of taxation emerged in the
financing of the Crusades. The Saladin tithe imposed for
this purpose first appeared in France in 1146, and it was
introduced into England by Richard I. In the course of
time the papacy came to apply it universally and by 1300
the tithing power was maintained wholly in its hands and
it was until the Protestant revolt. In 1296 the taxation lists of
Nicholas IV were compiled as a basis for reckoning the
tithe in Britain.

Theoretically tithes were of two kinds, one collected on
incomes and the other on the products of the land. A ten
per cent income tax would to-day be thought unbearable
by the small taxpayer, yet that is what the church imposed on the laity. Not only farmers and cottagers were
bound to deliver a strict tithe of all produce, but merchants,
shopmen, and poor artisans were expected to give two
shillings out of every pound sterling they earned. The
tithe on wages and profits was never successfully collected,
but it was nevertheless demanded and the efforts to collect
it were unceasing. At times its payment was made a matter of appeal to the conscience by assuming the tithe to
be an oblation. [47] Tithes on the produce of the land were
definitely fixed and strictly exacted. Schemes were de-
vised to reduce the imposition to a nicety so as to make
sure the payment of the utmost farthing. [48] Between church
and people, tithes, offerings, and oblations were the
source of constant friction continuing to the Reformation.

II. Revival of Discontent and Agitation—Archbishop Bourchier and the Humanists

The discontent over papal financial abuses manifest immediately before the outbreak of the reformation in England was a renewal of popular opposition after a long period of comparative lull. As has been pointed out, John Wyclif had sorely denounced the financial irregularities of the clergy and his followers went to the extreme of attempting to put into practice his theory for the disendowment of the church. From the defeat of Sir John Oldcastle, in 1415, over a century elapsed before the next acute crisis came in 1533; but in the meantime anti-ecclesiastical agitation had again set in soon after the middle of the fifteenth century and in particular upon the accession of Henry VII in 1485. The era of quiet may be attributed to foreign detraction due to a renewal of the Hundred Years War, and to domestic preoccupations incidental to the War of the Roses. The Lancastrian loyalty to the church in suppressing heresy also had much to do with the situation. When peace was again finally assured after the battle of Bosworth, and when the constructive foreign and domestic policies of Henry VII brought on a new prosperity, the discontent over ecclesiastical abuses was suddenly revived.

In the meantime two situations had developed that tended to further intensify the opposition toward the clergy. In spite of the secularization of the alien priories consummated by Henry V, the wealth of the church had actually increased in the fifteenth century by the endowment of free chantries. Again, the moral decline of the clergy went on apace or, to say the least, saw no improvement. What Wyclif, Hus, and the Conciliar Movement had aimed to accomplish by active, organized, well directed, and conscious efforts was by no means realized when things were allowed to drift. The church instead of taking warnings by such movements, and instead of seeking to adjust itself to the rising spirit of nationality and individualism continued to satisfy its avarice by antiquated financial demands. By the end of the first quarter of the sixteenth century such demands had overreached the bounds of endurance both in England and on the Continent.

The answer on the Continent had already been the outbreak of the Protestant Revolt led by Luther and Zwingli, and centering about the abuses of indulgences and other financial irregularities. At the Council of Nuremberg, in 1520, the German princes drew up a list of a hundred causes for complaint many of which concerned financial matters. The Germans protested that forbidden meats, marriage during Lent, and remission of sins were being allowed for payment of money; excommunication was imposed for pecuniary advantage; holy days were an economic loss; useless ceremonies were performed for gain; and spiritual courts out of avarice trumped up charges against the innocent.[49] The following proverbs were rife: "When bulls from Rome come, bind well the purse." "Rome regardeth not the sheep without the wool."[50] In England where popular protest had twice in the past reached an acute stage, a renewal of the struggle was inevitable. A crisis was the more imminent in that papal prestige had declined, the moral status of the clergy had deteriorated, and the spirit of nationality and individualism had advanced.

To such an extent had the extortion and oppression of the church extended on the eve of the reformation in England that some men began to despair of relief. This was the confession of no less a churchman than Edward Fox, Bishop of Winchester, a leading light of his time. When Cardinal Wolsey undertook a visitation of his ec-

clesiastical province, Fox wrote him a word of encouragement but expressed a doubt of the feasibility of the project. His letter showed that a similar reformation had
failed to materalize in a like effort within his own diocese in spite of three years of continual "study, labour, and
vigilancy, and pains:" [51]

> Wherein I came to understand (which I could not
> so much as thought of before), that all that belonged
> to the ancient integrity of the clergy, and especially the
> monks, were so depraved by license and corruption . . .
> that it increased both pains and labor in me, now spent
> with age, and took away all hope ever of seeing a per-
> fect and absolute reformation in this my privy diocese.

That gross irregularities existed in the church and were
the cause of much scandal may be seen in the commission
issued by Archbishop Bourchier in the middle of the fifteenth century to correct and reform defects, crimes, and
excesses in his province.[52] The commission was given because of the "constant and noisy clamor of many" in regard to the condition. Absenteeism on the part of rectors
and vicars caused churches to be neglected and ecclesiastical wealth to be misappropriated, and the incumbents
"like vagabonds and profligates run about through the
kingdom and apply themselves to worldly gain, to revel-
ings, to drunken bouts, to wicked adulteries and forni-
cations. They spend their time on all manner of vices,
and waste the property and goods, fruits and revenues
of their benefices." The result was that church buildings
went to ruin, and the wealth of the churches was wasted
and misapplied.

The following specified irregularities are mentioned in
the document, all leading to moral mischief or economic
waste. There was the evil of secular appropriation of benefices in which laymen, posing as monks, got possession

of churches and vicarages; non-residence of ecclesiastical
incumbents who used the goods of their charges for personal and selfish ends rather than for public and charitable
purposes; careless and unlicensed priests holding cure
of souls who refused to pay the usual tithe to the diocese;
for the procurement of money, marriages legally contracted
were annulled; and in the making of wills, witnesses were
not procured so as to make it easy to annul, set aside, or
make void the instrument. All these things taken together
led to many crimes daily committed by the people, contempt for religion, neglect of the poor, decay and ruin
of church edifices, spoiling and wasting of ecclesiastical
goods, and intercepting of property by tampering with
wills and testaments.[53]

The revival of Lollardry in the reign of Henry VII
and its increasing importance has already been alluded to
in another connection, but others besides these so-called
heretics were assailing the misuse of the wealth of the
clergy in the early Tudor period. The most outstanding
of these were the humanists Colet and Erasmus. Extreme
discontent over the financial abuses of the English clergy
and criticism of their worldly living was in particular expressed by John Colet. Nothing, he said, had so disfigured
the face of the church as the secular and worldly living
of the clergy. In a sermon delivered before Convocation
at St. Paul's, in 1512, this outspoken critic of the ecclesiastical system roundly denounced the nepotism, simony, absenteeism, pluralism, secularity, and avarice of priests and
prelates alike.[54] He pointed out to the assembled hierarchs
that the vast wealth of the church permitted the clergy
to live in lazy ease, lust, and gluttony. He deplored the fact
that clerks were merchants and usurers, that monks cringed
to secular lords for worldly preferment, and that the higher
clergy used the wealth of the church to enrich their kinsfolk.

The besetting sin of the clergy, according to this Oxford reformer, was their extreme covetousness, the root of all ecclesiastical corruption: [55]

This abominable pestilence hath so entered the mind of all prelates and hath so blinded the eyes of the mind, that we are blind to all things but only those which seem to bring us gain. For what other thing seek we in the church now a days than fat benefices and fat promotions? That we care not how many, how chargeful, or how great benefices we take, so that they are of great value. Yea, and in the same promotions what other thing do we pass upon than our tithes and rents? O Covetousness, the root of all evil! Of thee cometh this heaping of benefice upon benefice; of thee so great pensions assigned, and so many benefices resigned; of thee all the pursuing of tithes, of offerings, or mortuaries, of delapidations, by the right and title of the church; for which things we strive no less than for our lives. O Covetousness! Of thee cometh the corruption of courts, and these daily new inventions wherewith the silly people are so sore vexed—of thee cometh these chargeful visitations of bishops. Of thee cometh this fervent study of ordinaries to dilate their jurisdictions; of thee cometh this raging contention in ordinaries of the insinuation of testaments; of thee cometh the undue sequestration of fruits; of thee cometh the superstitious observing of all these laws that sound to any lucre, setting aside and despising those that concern the amending of manners. Why should I rehearse the rest? To be short and to conclude in a word; all the corruption, all the decay of the church, all the offences in the world come of the covetousness of the priests.

This lament of Colet was no mere temporary outburst of his reforming zeal, for at the very beginning of his career at St. Paul's he took occasion to point out the evils of ecclesiastical wealth as it was abused.[56] The Lollards heard him gladly, attending his sermons with a keen interest.[57]

Colet pleaded for a reformation in regard to these things. This was to be brought about not so much by the enactment of new ecclesiastical canons as by the enforcement of canons already promulgated. There was not a single evil against which former churchmen did not provide excellent remedies. To adjust matters, he advocated that the canon be enforced against promoting to benefices children and unworthy persons for the sake of gain. "Let the laws be recited against the guilt of simony; which plague, which contagion, which dire pestilence, now creeps like a cancer through the minds of the priests." Absenteeism should be remedied by enforcing the laws requiring the personal residence of curates and bishops. Clerical secularity should be avoided by prohibiting churchmen from becoming merchants, usurers, hunters, and soldiers already provided against by canon. Old laws should also be enforced that prohibited the misspending of ecclesiastical wealth in sumptuous buildings, magnificence and pomp, feasts and banquets, luxury and lust, and enriching kinsfolk and keeping hounds. And above all, he admonished, let those laws be revived that were meant to check the scandals and vice of church courts, thus taking away "those daily newly invented arts for getting money, which were designed to extirpate and eradicate that horrible covetousness which is the root and cause of all evil, which is the fountain of all iniquity." [58]

In a similar manner, Erasmus depicted the corruption of the church, the passionate fondness of the clergy for money, and the corresponding indifference of the prelates to spiritual matters. The popes sought riches, honors, lands, offices, indulgences, and worldly show; but all the drudgery and toil of their office they were willing to turn over to Peter and Paul who had plenty of time to mind such things.[59] The higher clergy contented themselves fingering money through a pair of thick gloves, and fighting with fire and sword all who challenged right and title to their fields, treasures, and vast dominion.[60] The lower clergy were busy fighting for their tithes, using their syllogisms as fiercely as they might use swords.[61] The high craft of the clergy was the procuring of money, and like all craftsmen they attained skill and technique until they were expert in their vocation of gathering tithes, offerings, perquisites, etc.[62] Every order of clergymen was content with reaping profits, while the burden of office was shifted to others. Thus along the whole line of the hierarchy the tendency prevailed to evade spiritual responsibilities. The secular priests turned the burden of godly living over to the monks who passed it on until, he said, it reached the Carthusians; "this order alone keeps honesty and piety among them, but really keep them so close that nobody ever yet could see them": [63]

> Thus the popes, thrusting in the sickle into the harvest of profit, leave all the other toil of spiritual husbandry to the bishops, the bishops bestow it upon the pastors, the pastors on the curates, and the curates commit it to the mendicants, who return it again to such as well know how to make good advantage of the flock by securing the benefit of their fleece.

III. Revival of Discontent and Agitation—"The Very Beggars' Supplication against Popery"

On the very eve of the break between Henry VIII and the papacy there appeared in England an important pamphlet that reflected popular attitude toward the financial abuses of the ecclesiastical system. It was commonly known as the Petition of the Beggars. The document bears all the marks of propaganda as to bias, overstatement, incendiarism, and even willful misrepresentation; yet comparing it to a number of contemporary writings, it seems to reveal with some degree of accuracy the sentiment of many among the ruling classes in England toward the clergy. The tract attacked the existing religious régime as a social, political, and economic menace to the commonwealth. It catalogued the whole list of the current papal financial abuses, criticized and denounced the system of ecclesiastical graft, and sounded a note of warning to the secular authorities as to the dangers of the situation. It also suggested a remedy for the evils of the times by depriving the clergy of their position, confiscating the wealth of the church, and setting the churchmen to work at productive secular labor.

The author of this anti-clerical booklet was Simon Fish, a lawyer of Gray's Inn, who having taken a hand at lampooning Cardinal Wolsey in a London play was forced to flee to the Continent. While a refugee abroad Fish seems to have written the tract, which came into the hands of the king through Ann Boleyn. The king was very much pleased with the tract, reading it with avidity, and giving protection to its author. The attitude of the monarch may be seen in the following statement from Foxe: [64]

> The king after he had received the book demanded of her who made it: whereupon she answered and said, a certain subject of his, one Fish, who was fled out of the Realme for feare of the Cardinall. After the kyng had kept the booke in his bosome iij or iiij. dayes, as is credible reported, such knowledge was giuen by

the kynges seruantes to the wife of ye sayd Symon Fishe, yat she might boldly send for her husband, without perill or daunger. Whereupon she thereby beyng incouraged, came first and made her sute to the kyng for the safe returne of her husband. Who vnderstandyng whose wife she was, shewed a maruelous gentle and chearefull countenance towardes her, askying where her husband was. She answered "If it like your grace, not farre of." Then sayth he "fetch him, and he shall come and go safe without perill, and no man shall do him harme."

When Fish came into the presence of the king, the latter embraced him, engaged him in a long conversation, took him out riding and hunting, and finally gave him his own signet ring as a token of safety against those who were seeking his arrest. The book had a considerable circulation, coming out in a German and Latin translation on the Continent in 1529 and 1530.[65] Attempts were made to broadcast it in the streets of London, but the efforts were thwarted by Wolsey. The book was important enough to bring forth an answer by Sir Thomas More in a counter tract called "Supplicacyon of Soulys."

The first part of the pamphlet was a complaint against the yearly exactions of the clergy and the disproportionate amount of wealth under the control of the church. The churchmen received a tenth part of all produce, profits, and incomes; and they had managed during the four centuries past to get within their grasp a third part of the wealth of the realm. "The goodliest lordshippes, maners, londes, and territories are theyrs. Besides this they haue the tenth part of all the corne, medows, pasture, grasse, wolle, coltes, calues, lambs, pigges, gese, and chikens." An enormous amount of money was exacted yearly by probating of testaments, offerings toward pilgrimages, masses and dirges, mortuaries, hearing of confessions, absolutions, and alms given to all the five orders of begging friars. The quarterage alone, collected by these mendicant orders, totaled the sum of £43,333, 6s., 8d. in a year. That was an exorbitant sum of money for the times, amounting to nearly a million pounds sterling in present day values. Yet four hundred years before this time, according to the booklet, the clergy had not a penny.[66]

The clergy, according to the tract, consisted of a very small minority that owned or controlled an undue proportion of the wealth of the country. Only one out of every four hundred of the population of England was a churchman, yet combining these yearly exactions extorted from the people and the fact that they owned a third of the land, the clergy were in possession of one half the substance of the realm. "Ley then these sommes to the forseid therd part of the possessions of the realme that ye may se whether it drawe nighe vnto the half of the hole substaunce of the realme or not, So shall ye finde that it draweth ferre aboue." Such an unequal distribution of wealth was a serious economic menace to the commonwealth. "Whate subiectes shall be abill to helpe theire prince that be after this facion yerely polled?" "Is it any merueille that youre people so complaine of pouertie?" "Is it any merueille that the taxes fifteenes and subsidies that your grace hath taken emong your people to defend theim from the threatened ruine of theire comen wealth haue ben so sloughtfully, yea painfully leuied?" It was the policy of the church to ever acquire property and never alienate any, so that eventually all the wealth of the land would fall within its grasp. "Whate kingdome can endure that euer gyuith thus from him and receyueth nothing agein?" "O howe all the substaunce of your Realme

forthwith . . . rynneth hedlong ynto the insaciabill whyrle-
pole of these gredi goulafres to be swalowed and devoured." [67]

The economic ascendancy of the church was also a grave
political danger to the state, for the clergy were using
their wealth to alienate the obedience of the people from
the secular power to themselves. What does this greedy
sort of sturdy, idle, holy thieves do with the yearly exactions taken from the people, it was asked. The reply was:
"Truely nothing but exempt theim silues from the obedience of your grace. Nothing but translate all the rule power
lordishippe auctorite obedience and dignity from your
grace to theim. Nothing but that all your subiectes shulde
fall ynto disobedience and rebellion against your grace
and be vnder theim." It was the power of the church that
had reduced King John to submission and that brought
England to a state of vassalage, hence let the present king
take warning. "Where was the obedience of all his subiects
become that for maintenance of the comen welth shulde
haue holpen him manfully to haue resisted these bloudsup-
pers to the shedinge of theyre bloude? was not all to
gither by theyre polycy translated from this good king
to theim?" [68]

The wealth of the clergy was also represented in the
Supplication of the Beggars as the source and occasion of
grave social and moral irregularities. Vagrancy was increased, the cause of the poor was neglected, loose family
life was encouraged, homes were broken up, venereal diseases were spread, and race suicide and social degener-
ation were pronounced: [69]

> These are they that by theire absteyning from mar-
> iage do let the generation of the people wher by all
> the realme at length if it shulde be continued shall be
> made desert and inhabitible.

These are they that haue made a hundred thousand ydell hores yn your realme whiche wolde haue gotten theyre lyuing honestly yn the swete of theyre faces had not theyre superfluous rychesse illected theyme to vnclene lust and ydlenesse. (Here follows several lines on the spread of venereal diseases.) These are they that when they haue ones drawen mennes wiues to such incontinency spende awey theire husbondes goodes make the wimen to runne awey from theire husbondes, yea, rynne awey them silves both with wif and goodes, bring both man wife and children to ydlenesse theft and beggeri.

Yea who is abill to nombre the greate and brode bottomles occean see full of euilles that this mischeuous and sinful generacion may laufully bring vppon vs vnponisshed. Where is youre swerde, power, crowne, dignitie, become that shulde punisshe the felonies, rapes, murdres, and treasons committed by this sinful generacion? Where is theire obedience become that shulde be vnder your hyghe power yn this matter? ys not all to gither translated and exempt from your grace vnto theim? Yes truely. Whate an infinite nombre of people mightee haue ben encreased to haue peopled the realme if these sort of folke had ben maried like other men.

So strong and influential was the clergy that they not only were in a position to thwart legislation being enacted against these evils but they made ineffective important statutes promulgated in the past. What is the remedy? Fish asked. Make laws against them. The writer doubted whether it could be done. The clergy were stronger in Parliament than the king himself because of the great number of bishops, abbots, and priors that sat therein. All the king's counselors and learned men, with few exceptions, were in the fee of the church to speak against the best in-

terests of the king in the parliament house. The statutes
of praemunire and mortmain had been largely ignored,
and it was hard to indict a priest under the former law.
If any man was bold enough to indict a churchman he
would be sorry for it in the end. The celebrated case of
Richard Hunne was cited as an example, who had he not
"commenced accyon of praemunire ageinst a prest he had
ben yet a lyue and none heretik at all but an honest
man." [70] The statute of mortmain was meant to put a
check upon the growing wealth of the clergy. "But whate
avayled it? haue they not gotten ynto theyre hondes more
londes sins than eny duke in ynglond, the statute notwithstanding?"

Laws and statutes will not bring relief so long as the
clergy dominate Parliament and so long as the chief counselor of the king is chosen from among the churchmen.
What then was the remedy? "If ye will eschew the ruyne
of your crowne and dignitie let their ypocrisye be vttered
and that shalbe more speedfull in this matter than all the
lawes that may be made." The remedy was to disclose
their hypocrisy, confiscate their possessions, put them to
productive labor; and if they refuse to conform use cor-
poral means of persuasion: [71]

> Take from theim all these thynges. Set these sturdy
> lobies a brode in the world to get theim wiues of theire
> owne, to get thier liuing with their laboure in the swete
> of theire faces according to the commandment of God
> (Gene. iii) to gyue other idell people by theyre ex-
> ample occasion to go to laboure. Tye these holy idell
> theues to the cartes to be whipped naked about euery
> market towne til they will fall to laboure that they by
> their importunate begging take not awey the almesse
> of the good christen wold giue vnto us . . . bedemen.
> Then shall aswell the nombre of oure foresaid mon-

struous sort as of baudes, hores, theuss, and idell people
decrease. Then shall these great yerely exaccions cease.
Then shall not your swerde, power, crowne, dignite,
and obedience of your people be translated from you.
Then shall you have full obedience of your people.
Then shall the idell people be set at worke. Then shall
matrimony be moche better kepte. Then shall the gen-
eration of your people be encreased. Then shall your
comons be encreased in richnesse. Then shall none
begge oure alms from us. Then shall we haue ynough
and more than shall suffice vs.

The "Supplicacyon for the Beggers" was a very important document of the period but it must not be taken
too seriously as representing the ecclesiastical situation.
"What a picture of the cruel, unclean and hypocritical
monkery that was eating at the heart's core of English
society is given to us in this terse and brave little book,"
wrote one commentator; [72] "we cannot but shudder as
we try to realize the then social condition of our country."
This is perhaps taking the little tract too seriously. The
Beggars' Petition has all the ear marks of propaganda.
The few statistics it contains cannot in any way be relied
on. There is throughout the pamphlet gross exaggeration
and overstatement. Almost every point made in it must
be taken with a grain of salt. But these very points mark its
importance. Like the cartoon and the lampoon of the
present day, the tract must have stimulated a great deal
of sentiment adverse to the church. Especially was this
the case owing to the fact that a definite thread of truth
ran through the entire booklet. The importance of the
petition lay not in the fact of its picturing a true situation,
but in arousing popular opinion against the clergy.

IV. ATTITUDE AND ACTION OF THE REFORMATION PARLIAMENT
—FIRST PETITION OF THE COMMONS

The Petition of the Beggars had appeared about the year 1527, and it marked the climax of unofficial opposition and protest against the abuses of papal finance. Its attacks upon the clergy were very bold and very bitter, yet its author lived unmolested in England under the aegis of the king's signet. For nearly half a century since the accession of Henry VII discontent and opposition had been given expression and had been gathering force until a rupture in the church was inevitable. It is only against this background of a period of preparation that the attitude and action of the Reformation Parliament can be understood. That body met in 1529 and extended its sessions for seven years. It was to some extent subservient to the Court, which it is likely was responsible to a large degree both for the point of view and action of the Parliament. But the point of interest is that this body passed a series of measures that tended to sever England from the papal jurisdiction and that the bulk of these measures had to do with financial and economic relations between the church and people, particularly in the matter of monetary exactions. Such were the first and the second Petition of the Commons, the Act for Annulling the Annates, the Restraint of Appeals to Rome, the Act forbidding Papal Dispensations and the Payment of Peter's Pence, and such also was the Act for the Dissolution of the Smaller Monasteries.

Immediately after assembling and organizing, the nether house of the Reformation Parliament "began to common their grefes wherewith the spiritualitie had before tyme grevously oppressed them, both contrarie to the

lawe of the realme, and contrarie to all righte." [73] The result was the First Petition of the Commons presented to
the king in 1529. In this instrument the Commons complained of six major abuses of the clergy from which they
prayed for relief. The six included excessive fees collected
in the probating of wills, mortuaries, exorbitant rents on
church lands, prelates engaged in secular occupations,
pluralities, and absenteeism. The step once taken by the
Commons marked a crisis in opposition to the church and
may be regarded as the opening move in the reformation of the English church. Edward Hall, the contemporary biographer of Henry VIII, wrote that "these
thynges before this tyme might in nowise be towched
nor yet talked of by no man except he would be made a
heretike. . . . But now when God had illumed the eies
of the kynge, and that there subtell doynges were once
espied then men began charitably to desyre a reformation, and so in this parliament menne began to shew
there grudges." [74]

The immediate result of this agitation against these
grievances was a series of legislative acts aiming to eliminate the evils against which complaint was directed. Most of
these earliest parliamentary measures seem to have been
ineffective in this first official onslaught against the excesses of the clergy. The probating of testaments, for instance, came up again in the second petition of the Commons in 1532. England had suffered long in regard to the
questionable practices of churchmen relating to wills.
In the "Complaint of the Plowman," it had been written: [75]

> For who so woll prove a testament,
> That is not worth all tenne pound,
> He shall payment make for the parchement,
> The third of the money all round.

Wyclif made mention of the fact that in the probating of testaments the clergy robbed the Commons of the land of many thousands of pounds "against Holy Writ, the pope's law, the statutes of the king, and a good conscience."[76] Archbishop Stratford tried to remedy the evil by drawing up a tariff of fixed fees for each legal process a will had to undergo, but he apparently failed.[77] Edward III had a statute passed against "grievous and outrageous fines for the probate of wills."[78] This had to be renewed in the time of Henry V, because of the continuance of the evil, and because fees had increased ten times in amount.[79]

The exactions connected with probation of wills had not been mitigated on the eve of the breach between England and Rome. On the contrary, oppressions and exactions had "greatly augmented and increased against all right and justice, and to the great impoverishing of the kings subjects."[80] The settlement of the estate of Sir William Crompton was one of the scandals of the times. Henry Guilford asserted that he was forced to pay the Cardinal (Wolsey) and Archbishop Warham, in 1529, the sum of 1000 marks to probate this will.[81] "What money pull they not in the probating of testaments" was the exclamation of the Beggars' Petition alluding to the clergy. Nor did this statute of 1529 seem to remedy the abuse, for a few years later, in the second petition of the Commons complaint was again registered concerning the delays and fees connected with procedure regarding wills, thus:[82]

> And also where, in the spiritual courts of the prelates and ordinaries, be limited and appointed so many judges, scribes, apparitors, summoners, appraisers, and other ministers for the approbation of testaments, which coveting so much their own private lucres, and satisfaction of the appetites of the said prelates and ordinaries, that when any of your said loving subjects

do repair to any of the said courts for the probate of any testaments, they do in such wise make so long delays, and excessively take of them so large fees and rewards for the same, as is impotable for them to bear, directly against all justice, law, equity, and good conscience.

A second act that grew out of the protest of the Commons in 1529 affected the imposition of the mortuary, seeking to assuage if not to eliminate the practice. This was also a survival of a medieval custom originating in the attempt of the churchmen to imitate the lay lords. The lord of the manor came in to claim the heriot on the death of a tenant, the prelate came to take away the mortuary. The heriot took the best animal, the mortuary the second best.[83] In case there were no livestock, personal property could be seized.[84] By this injustice not only was the bread winner removed from many a family, but a main source of livelihood was taken away. In many cases, however, the cow, horse, or pig was bought back by the estate for a cash payment, but this form of commutation did not make the burden of the tax any lighter.[85] The mortuary was closely connected with the tithe and oblation; in fact, it was a means of assuring payment of tithes after death, for it was assumed to be a gift left by the deceased to make good for the failure to pay his tithes and offerings during life. Neglect in tithing was looked upon as a mortal sin, and the mortuary was a surety for absolution from such sin.

For a long time the method of exacting the mortuary varied in different parts of England; there was no fixed standard or ruling and the practice was always abusive. At Torksey, for instance, the best animal could be taken and the very last animal could be demanded. Abuse became so manifest that Archbishop Winchelsey ruled, in

1305, that there must be at least three animals in the estate and the priest was entitled only to the second best.[86] This ruling was confirmed by Langham half a century later,[87] but that the evil was not mitigated may be seen from the following quotation from a mid-thirteenth document: [88]

> They ought to give the mortuary fee, which is called the corpse-present, to the parson; namely, the best animal for the husband and for the wife the second best animal if they have another. And if there be only one animal and the husband or wife is dead, the value of that animal shall be divided into two parts so that he or she shall answer for half the price to the parson in the name of mortuary. . . . And if they have no animal, then they must give their upper tunic, or tunic, cape, tabard, or mantle. And no other thing of their chattels should they give to the parson as mortuary. And if the husband dies, the parson should have his best garment as a mortuary. And if the wife dies, the parson shall have the wife's garment as above said.

As the middle class developed, their property was also imposed on. It was over a mortuary involving personal property that Richard Hunne a rich merchant of London was sued in the spiritual courts, imprisoned, and, it was alleged, secretly murdered in prison at the instigation of the churchmen just on the eve of the Reformation. All the parish demanded in this case was the death sheet of the merchant's dead child, which Hunne partly out of principle and partly out of sentimentality refused to give. The case stirred London to its depth.[89]

The statute of 1529 confirmed former enactments against mortuaries, fixed the tax to be imposed, defined the nature of property involved, and provided for the restitution of the tax if the act were violated by the clergy.

But it had little effect and a reënactment was necessary a few years later. In spite of the promise of the clergy to reform and amend their practices regarding mortuaries "they were augmented and greatly increased, against all right and justice, and to the great impoverishing of the king's subjects." [90]

A third measure was aimed against clerical secularity. Prelates monopolized a number of secular occupations. "Abbotes, Priors, and spiritual men kept Tanne houses, and bought and sold woll, clothe, and all manner of merchaundise as other temporal merchauntes dyd." [91] The clergy controlled lands also for which they charged exorbitant rental, or kept up the price of the produce grown upon their holdings: "Priests beyng surveiors, and stuardes and officers to Bishoppes, Abbotes, and spiritual heddes had occupied Ferms, Graunges, and grasing in every countrey, so that the pore husbandman coulde have nothynge but of theym and yet for that they should pay derely." [92] The matter of clerical secularity was closely connected with pluralities and absenteeism. Spiritual men were accused of affecting courtly living. Instead of living upon their charges they drew the revenues therefrom and either gave themselves to pleasure or "followed divers trades and occupations secular: some were surveyors of land, some receivers, some stewards, some clerks of the kitchen, many gardeners and orchardmakers. . . . If they wanted a sermon to be preached now and then in their churches, they got the friars to do it for them." [93]

The matter of pluralities and non-residence was a fourth evil met by legislative enactment growing out of the first petition of the Commons in the Reformation Parliament. Foreign pluralities especially were looked upon as a menace because under them churches decayed and much wealth was exported abroad. "By reason of the present foreign

incumbents dwelling abroad, all the spiritual offices of
the diocese are decayed, and great quantities of gold,
silver, and treasure to the amount of 3000 pounds yearly
have been conveyed out of the realm . . . to the great impoverishing of this realm," one document asserted.[94] Another document not only pointed out the economic loss
involved by pluralists that gathered and conveyed great
sums of money out of the realm, but it showed a grave
strategic menace connected with the practice. For "by sem-
blance of visitation they do undermine, to knoe the secrets
of the king and of the realm; which disclosed doth great
hurt as well to the merchants of this realm, as otherwise." [95]

Pluralities and absenteeism were closely connected with
provisors, dating far into the past and occasioning much
discontent.[96] Certain provisions drawn up by a national
synod in 1268 would have rendered these evils impossible
had they been enforced, which they were not. A single
priest was known to hold as many as twelve benefices.[97]
John Mansel, court chaplain of Henry III, controlled much
wealth coming from plural benefices.[98] One writer asserted
that Mansel possessed as high as seven hundred livings.[99]
In 1369 the Bishop of Ely was shocked to find that certain clerks in his diocese held as many as twenty benefices apiece.[100] In 1283 Archbishop Peckham made a strenuous but abortive effort to remedy the abuse.[101] Pluralities
tended to monopolize clerical livings and concentrate power
and wealth into the hands of the few; absenteeism drained
the local parishes of the means essential to their spiritual
upkeep and caused communities to be neglected. The law
of 1529 aimed to make void automatically the right of
a churchman to a living he was already holding if he accepted another. In case an incumbent of a benefice accepted an outside living to the value of eight pounds
sterling per annum, he forfeited the living he was on.

If any churchman accepted a living from the Roman court, contrary to the act, he was fined two pounds sterling. An absence from a benefice protracted to two years incurred a fine of ten pounds sterling. All livings above four in number, held at the passage of the act had to be relinquished, and all new appointees were required to live upon their benefices.[102]

Much bitterness of feeling was aroused by the legislation growing out of the petition of 1529. The clergy strenuously opposed the measures. The priests referred to the Commons as schismatics and heretics because of their action and attitude toward the churchmen, and to such a degree did the clergy carry the matter that many of them were arrested and punished. The churchmen argued that usage and long custom made the practices being abolished legal. In answer, a certain lawyer among the Commons said: "The usage hath ever been of thieves to rob on shooters hill, ergo, it is lawful." This implied that the commons regarded the clergy as thieves and robbers in the matter of these monetary exactions.[103]

V. Attitude and Action of the Reformation Parliament —Second Petition of the Commons

The second petition of the Commons appeared in 1532. There has existed a question as to its origin, some claiming that it came directly from the Commons and others holding that it originated at the royal court itself. Most of the originals of the document are either entirely written in the hand of Cromwell's secretary, or are annotated by Cromwell himself.[104] But these facts alone do not establish the authorship of Cromwell, much less would they be conclusive evidence that the Commons had nothing to do with the petition.

There are a number of reasons for thinking that the

document was genuine, or at least that it was a true reflection of popular feeling and opinion of the times. Grievances over financial irregularities of the clergy were expressed three years before this in a similar petition. Bishop Fox, writing to Cardinal Wolsey in 1523, stated at that time that only a reformation would pacify the common people, who "were continually crying out against clerical abuses."[105] When Henry VIII was addressing the rebels of Lincolnshire, he said: "We have known also that ye our commons have much complained in tyme past that the most part of oure goodes, landes, and possessions of thys realm were in spiritual mennes hands."[106] He also wrote to Cardinal Ghenucci at Rome admonishing him that: "Whenever the Act (of Annates) is mentioned, you should instil into their ears (Roman Court) how incessant have been our efforts to resist the importunities of our people for passing the statute."[107] Finally, as a proof of the fact that public discontent was deep seated in the popular mind, an anonymous letter appeared asserting that the laity were beginning to cry out against the clergy on account of exactions: "cut them down, why cumber they the ground." This letter as a whole was a severe and outspoken denunciation of the clergy: Bishops connived at the vices of the people instead of correcting them. Many sinned, but the sword of excommunication fell only on such as were delinquent in money matters. Churchmen instead of nourishing and protecting the flock, devoured it by exactions. Visitations, elections of priors and abbots, and promotions were used as a means for getting money. The luxury of the prelates was an outrage, living at court and hunting for benefices. Simony was a universal sin of the clergy.[108] Many things go to show that if the petition of the Commons did not originate in the parliament, it could easily have done so.

Of the twelve charges brought against the clergy by the second petition of the Commons in 1532, the majority had to do with abuses connected with the church courts.[109] Cases concerning mortuaries, wills, tithes, marriages, heresy, moral delinquency, and many secular matters were tried in these ecclesiastical tribunals. They were numerous, efficiently organized, constantly in session; and they possessed adequate machinery for enforcing their decisions.[110] Popular in an earlier day when these courts championed causes neglected by the old feudal courts, success had led to corruption; and at the time of the Reformation the criticism and outcry against them was general.[111] Archbishop Warham had made an effort to reform them but had abjectly failed. Cardinal Wolsey, on the other hand, not only opposed the attempt of the primate of York, but was debauching the functions of these courts in such a way as to stir more deeply the popular unrest now manifest against them.[112]

A particular evil of this system of ecclesiastical courts was the influence of—to use a modern term—the shyster lawyer who was interested in promoting litigation because it paid him good financial returns to do so. He usually came from the poorer sort of priests whose marriage debarred them from aspiring to the higher preferments.[113] "Every offence contrary to piety, justice, and sobriety might be tried in the Courts Christian. Hence there was scarcely a single person in any parish who might not receive a citation to appear before an ecclesiastical judge, if a pettifogging clerical attorney scrutinized his conduct with a malignant eye, or with a view of proffering his silence as a marketable product." [114] The result was innumerable citations to the religious courts and vexatious fees by which the poorer classes especially were oppressed. This may be seen in the petition itself: [115]

And where also many of your said humble and obedient subjects, and especially those that be of the poorer sort, be daily convented and called before the said spiritual ordinaries . . . being very light and indiscreet persons, without any lawful cause of accusation or credible fame proved against them, and without any presentment in the visitation—be disquieted, disturbed, vexed, troubled, and put to impotable charges for them to bear, and many times be suspended and excommunicated for small and light causes upon only certificate of the proctors of the adversaries made under a feigned seal which every proctor has in his keeping; whereas the party suspended and excommunicated many times had no warning; and yet when he shall be absolved, if he be out of court, he shall be compelled to pay his own proctor twenty pence, and twenty pence to the scribe, besides a privy reward to the judge, to the great impoverishing of your said poor subjects.

Closely connected with the system of ecclesiastical courts was the Convocation of prelates which had made in the past, and continued to make, laws, constitutions, and ordinances without royal knowledge and assent, which the courts were wont to observe. The petition objected that the laity had no part in making these laws, which were for that reason "against all equity, right, and good conscience." Laymen were likewise put to "impotable charges, costs, and expense" due to limiting the number of proctors in the courts of Arches and Audience. This caused both delay in litigation and suspicion of a conspiracy of the churchmen to thwart the course of justice. The petitioners thought that additional proctors ought to be appointed by the king to whom accused laymen could resort in order to expedite cases in litigation and insure a square deal to the accused.[116] The fees collected in these courts of Arches and Audience were both excessive and grievous. For every citation two shillings and six pence were charged; for every inhibition six shillings and eight pence; for every proxy sixteen pence; for every certificate sixteen pence; for every libel three shillings and four pence; for every statement requiring record four pence; for each decree of the court three shillings and four pence; for every sentence or judgment twenty-six shillings and eight pence; for every testimonial upon the sentence an additional twenty-six shillings and eight pence; for every *significavit* twelve shillings; for every commission to examine witnesses twelve shillings. After reciting this catalogue of fees imposed, the petitioners stated that they are "impotable to be borne by your said subjects, and very necessary to be reformed.[117]

Ecclesiastical courts powerfully helped to precipitate a religious revolution in England. The nuisance was of long standing and effort after effort was made, especially after the time of Wyclif, to amend the evils of these church tribunals. "Not only Reynolds," said Stubbs, "but Meneham and Stratford, and almost every primate to the time of the Reformation strove earnestly against the abuses of the spiritual courts which were really alienating the nation from the church and from religion." [118] The Courts Christian were the principle cause of friction between laity and the clergy in the early sixteenth century; [119] or, as one authority put it, the corruptions of the ecclesiastical tribunals "certainly gave the final impulse to the Reformation under Henry VIII." [120]

Other evils of a financial nature denounced by the Commons in this petition were the exactions by the parish clergy in connection with the sacraments; simony in regard to accepting fees and first fruits in the transfer of office; nepotism, or the practice of prelates conferring offices on their very young kinfolk in order to secure the revenues; and the excessive number of holy days observed by the church as an economic loss of time and money especially in the harvests. The Commons pointed out that all these things were the cause of a "marvelous disorder" within the realm, and that a remedy ought to be applied immediately by the king.[121]

VI. Attitude and Action of the Reformation Parliament—Annulling the Annates

The payment of the papal annates was another form of abuse with which the Reformation Parliament was forced to deal. Two measures appeared that forbade these exactions being sent to Rome, one of them was the conditional restraint of the annates passed in 1532 and the other was their absolute annulment in 1534.[122] To whatever origin these taxes date back, they were of long standing in England. Clement V seems to have been the first pope to make use of them as revenues for the papal exchequer. At first the collection of the annates was purely local and temporary sometimes taken by the Archbishop of Canterbury and sometimes by the king. In this form they appeared first in 1246 and 1256, but by the time of Pope John XXII the annates were made permanent and general.[123] The annates were a tax upon clerical livings, usually including the revenues of the first year of the benefice conferred. In an earlier period they were collected from the monasteries, but later they were restricted to archbishoprics and bishoprics. This limitation was probably due to the bitterness of the protest that they incurred.[124]

The origin of the annates, then, can be traced back at

least two centuries before the Reformation as far as the
pontifical annates are concerned, and their exaction was
strenuously resisted from the very beginning. Already in
1307 this papal claim proved a grievance in a council held
at Carlisle.[125] Again in 1376, the Parliament complained
that by the first fruits the papacy laid violent hands on the
bishoprics in England to the extent of draining from the
realm a sum of 20,000 marks per annum; this was an
intolerable burden, and the practice needed to be reformed.[126] The Parliament further objected that at times
the annates were increased five times the actual amount
due.[127] Wyclif objected to payment of the annates because the popes managed to get more than the revenues
of one year and because they translated bishops from see
to see just to collect and multiply the annates.[128] A statute
directed against the payment of first fruits passed in 1304
speaks of them as "horrible mischiefes and damnable cus-
tomes." This act spoke of bishops having to treble the annates before their election could be confirmed by Rome;
and it limited the sum to the revenues of one year because
too much wealth was taken from the realm by this sort
of inflation.[129] Complaint was made against the annates
at the Council of Constance, and they were officially abolished at the Council of Basle, but the practice persisted
until the Reformation.

Clergy as well as laity were adverse to the payment of
the annates. In fact, when it came to the matter of their
suppression at the time of the reformation in England,
the clergy seemed to take the initiative. For in 1529 there
appeared a startling document called the Petition of the
Clergy in which the churchmen urge the king not only
to abolish the payment of annates but to separate from
the papal jurisdiction in case the papacy insisted on collecting these exactions.[130] The reasons advanced by the

Convocation in the petition for abolishing the annates are illuminating. They may be summarized as follows: the payment of first fruits conveys too much wealth from the realm; it involves the prelates in heavy debt; it ofttimes ruins men who serve as bondmen for the bishops; it robs the dioceses of their necessary support; it is a misappropriation of ecclesiastical funds; it is simony according to the spirit of papal law; finally, annates are forbidden at the council of Basle.[131] After enumerating these objections, the Convocation suggested to the monarch that in case the papacy "should insist on requiring the payment of these taxes the obedience of England should be withdrawn from the See of Rome."[132] The clergy also pointed out that the annates exhausted the treasure of the realm, brought the English people to penury, and caused no small decay to the whole land.

But the protest against the payment of annates was not limited to the clergy. The tax was an object of general discontent, and the vast sums of money they drained from the kingdom made the annates play an important rôle in consummating the break with the papacy. The act providing for the conditional restraint of these papal dues speaks of the "great and inestimable sums of money daily conveyed out of this realm to the impoverishment of the same." Since the second year of the reign of Henry VII, the document records, 160,000 pounds sterling were paid over to Rome from the various dioceses of England.[133] In a paper drawn up by Cromwell it was shown that the king by taking over the annates would be enriched by 40,000 pounds sterling. Besides this the paper asserted, the king could devote to the repair and erection of hospitals the sum of 10,000 marks annually. His Grace might also furnish himself with two hundred serving gentlemen at a cost of 20,000 marks annually; devote 20,000 marks to the additional defense of the realm; and spend 5000 marks for repair of highways and other public works.[134] According to one authority, the annates collected from Canterbury and York amounted to 2000 pounds sterling a piece. The diocese of Winchester paid 2400 pounds, Durham 1800, Ely 1400, Salisbury and Exeter 1200 each, Lincoln and Norwich 1000 each, etc.[135] Besides this the archbishoprics of Canterbury and of York paid an additional 1000 pounds sterling for the pall.

In fact besides the pall, the filling of a diocesan vacancy involved many other payments paralleling the annates. Confirmations, elections, admissions, postulations, provisions, collations, dispositions, institutions, installations, investitures, orders, holy benedictions, palls, and other things requisite to attaining promotion are all spoken of in the document. All these seemed to have entailed extra fees, so that the filling of a vacancy was a great expense "by occasion whereof the treasure of this realm has been greatly conveyed out of the same." [136]

The annates not only drained the nation at large of vast sums of money, but they were oppressive upon the bishops and worked a hardship upon the local diocese. If a bishop elect were a poor man, or financially straitened he was forced to borrow the money to pay the inevitable first fruits. In case he had no property, his friends had to be surety for him. The king himself complained that his bishops were thus driven to the bankers. "The question of the annates is an old one, and the amount has become so great that the bishops have complained of it, and very lately the bishops of Winchester and York had to borrow money for the payment of their bulls." [137] The Convocation of 1529 put forward the same objection.[138] The matter of loans worked well enough in case the incumbent lived long enough to make repayment, otherwise his bondsmen had to make good the balance, a contingency that sometimes threw them into bankruptcy.[139] The fact that the men chosen to fill diocesan vacancies were advanced in years aggravated this situation, but worse than that it tended to multiply the years for the payment of annates. The matter of aged prelates and often repeating annates had been taken up with the papacy only five years before the act for annulling the first fruits.[140] The average incumbency of a bishopric in England was six years, but there were cases when three vacancies occurred in a single year.[141]

This matter of aged prelates was now advanced as an argument for annulling the annates by the Reformation Parliament. By frequent and unexpected death of episcopal incumbents, bondsmen that advanced money to the prelates in payment of the annates were caught in a financial trap and ruined, and the realm was also drained of immense treasure: [142]

> By occasion of the same (payment of annates) not only the treasure of this realm has been greatly conveyed out of the same, but also it has happened many times, by occasion of death, to such bishops and archbishops, so newly promoted, within two or three years after his or their consecration, that his friends, by whom he had been holpen to advance and make payment of the said annates, or firstfruits, have been thereby wholly undone and impoverished:
>
> . . . the said exactions of annates, or firstfruits, be so intolerable and impotable to this realm, that it is considered and declared, by the whole body of this realm now represented by all the estates of the same assembled in the present Parliament, that the king's highness before Almighty God is bound, as by the duty of a good Christian prince, for the conservation

and preservation of the good estate of the common-wealth of this realm, to do all that in him is to obviate, repress, and redress the said abuses and exactions of annates, or firstfruits: and because that divers prelates of this realm be now in extreme age, and in other de-bilities of their bodies, so that of liklihood bodily death in short time shall or may succeed unto them: by reason thereof vast sums of money shall shortly after their deaths be conveyed unto the Court of Rome for the unreasonable and uncharitable causes abovesaid, to the damage, prejudice, and impoverishment of this realm, if speedy remedy be not in due time provided.

In the repeal of the annates no question of principle in the payment of the tax was involved. No pro-test arose against annates as annates, but dissent was cen-tered against the payment of the tax to Rome. The same parliament that suspended payment of the annates to Rome granted that they be paid into the royal exchequer. Even the reactionary malcontents of the North in the Lincolnshire insurrection agreed that the tenths and an-nates belonged to the king.[143] Suppression of protests likely had much to do with the silent submission by which the annates were voted into the royal treasury. When it came to paying the moneys into the papal curia they were alluded to as "great exactions and intolerable charges"; but when it came to turning them over to the crown they became "good revenues for the defence of the realm."[144]

VII. Attitude and Action of the Reformation Parlia-ment—Abolition of Appeals, Dispensations, Peter's Pence, Census, etc.

In two separate acts passed in 1533 and 1534 the Reformation Parliament put an end to the matter of ex-

pensive appeals made to the court of Rome.[145] Two reasons were given in these measures for taking such a step,
one was that the royal jurisdiction was encroached on, and
the other was that appeals were the occasion of needless
expense to the realm.[146] The courts of the king, spiritual
and temporal, were now made the sole channels for procuring justice and heavy penalties were attached to ig-
noring the newly enacted law. A number of times in the
past England had made the attempt to free itself from
this sort of papal jurisdiction, Edward I, Edward III, Richard II, Henry IV, and other kings had "made sundry laws,
ordinances, statutes, and provisions for the entire and sure
conservation of the prerogatives, liberties, and preëmi-
nences of the said imperial crown of this realm, and of the
jurisdiction spiritual and temporal of the same to keep
it from the annoyance of the See of Rome"; but without
success.[147] The acts of 1533 and 1534 are England's declara-
tion of independence from papal legal jurisdiction.

Because of the indifference toward these former statutes, and also because of new dangers arising out of appeals in the matter of testaments, causes of matrimony and
divorce, rights of tithes, oblations and obventions, the new
acts were promulgated. These things especially led to "great
inquietation, vexation, trouble, cost and charges of the
king's highness, and many of his subjects and residents
of this his realm." They also led to delays, involving extra
costs, and the blocking of speedy justice.

The final act of the series of statutes promulgated by the
Reformation Parliament to put a check on financial exactions imposed by the Roman court had to do with the
abolition of dispensations, Peter's pence, census, and a
host of other petty charges that went along with them.[148]
These exactions were a bitter grievance to the English
people. Wyclif outspokenly resented these evils in his

day. Priests, he said, ran out of the land over great seas, through enemy countries, in peril of their lives, in cold, hunger, storms, and tempests. It was a wonder that they ever returned alive. They bore vast sums of gold out of England, which they exchanged for worthless sealed paper. "For good gold they bring back dead lead, heresy, and simony."[149]

In procuring dispensations there was often great losses in time by delays willfully manipulated by the Roman court. There was loss of money in exchanges, in hiring couriers, in the necessity of a military escort. Trained solicitors were needed to make the appeal to the Roman court, tavern expenses ran high, and bribes had to be given to expedite cases:[150]

> Forasmuch as the charges of obtaining licenses, dispensations, faculties, and other rescripts at the court of Rome, by losses and exchanges and in conducting of couriers and waging solicitors for them have been grievous and excessive to your people, and many times greater sums have been demanded for the speedy expedition in the court of Rome, than be expressed in the old tax limited to be paid for such expeditions . . . and by reason thereof (the people) have been constrained to pay more than they were wont to do, to the great impoverishing of this realm: and sometimes the speeding of such dispensations . . . has been so long delayed that the parties laboring for the same have suffered great incommodities and loss for lack of quick speed.

An old manuscript points out that Peter's pence was first paid to the papacy by King Ina of the West Saxons as early as A.D. 882.[151] It was suspended only once from that time on until the Reformation, though it may not have been paid regularly.[152] Its origin seems to have been in alms sent in support of the Schola Saxonum, a harbor for English pilgrims early established in Rome. When this hospital was no longer used, the money was transferred over to the papal treasury.[153] It was perhaps one of the oldest forms of money sent by Englishmen to Rome, and whatever was its origin it goes far back into the past.[154] In 1883, there was found on the site of an old papal palace a hoard of over eight hundred English coins none of which were issued later than the year 974. All of these coins were Anglo-Saxon pennies, and they are thought to be an installment of the denarius of St. Peter as it had been collected in England some time shortly after that date.[155] Canute, the Danish king, made mention of the payment of the Romfeoh in a letter written in 1027, and made provision for its collection by law.[156]

The denarius of St. Peter was a hearth tax, and when fully collected it affected every family within the kingdom.[157] And the gathering of it was pretty well assured, for there was an efficient organization to that end made up of fifteen prelates. These were the two archbishops, nine bishops, and four archdeacons. Later the number was increased to eighteen. The total amount of the tax was always small, not exceeding 300 marks when only the sum actually due was paid. But even this was a large amount of money in a time of sparse population and of limited coinage; besides, very often much more than this stipulated sum was gathered. In 1214, Innocent IV wrote that the English prelates sent the 300 marks to Rome, but kept at least 1000 marks for themselves.[158] In 1306, one of the Avignon popes was accused of trebling the hearth tax.[159] As early as 1170, Pope Alexander warned the archbishops of England against covetousness in regard to the Romescot. Attempts were also made to increase the quota of this tax by collecting a penny for every 30-pence value of property.[160]

At first the Peter's pence was regarded as alms, but with the surrender of King John in 1213 it was regarded as a tribute. From either standpoint it was unwelcome, and Englishmen sought release from it. In fact it was regarded as an odious tax both because of its universality and its annual regularity. Bishop Stubbs said that nothing aroused the national feeling in England against Roman taxation more than did the notorious Peters' pence. He likened its effect to the poll tax that occasioned the revolt of the masses in 1381.[161] It was looked upon as a symbol of subjection to the Roman court, and as a tribute paid to a foreign power. It was a financial burden from which the English people were determined to be freed, but which in spite of this act of Henry VIII continued to be paid until the time of Elizabeth.[162]

The census (censes) was another charge that was dispensed with in this act of 1534. It was a tax of medieval origin, and it was feudal in its nature.[163] It was paid by monasteries and also by princes, so that the tribute money of King John may be classed within this apostolic tax. In feudal days of rapacity and loot, the founder of a monastery "recommended" the new unit to St. Peter whom he asked to protect from the plunder of brigands and barons, of bishops and kings. For this patronage the founder promised to pay annually a stipend to the papacy. Monasteries thus "recommended" to St. Peter were pledged to pay this annual tax. Kings too weak against a powerful neighbor sometimes made a similar promise to pay annually a fixed sum for the protection of the Apostolic See. All this was well enough so long as protection was needed, but with the passing of the feudal régime, and the rise of powerful monarchies the need of papal protection disappeared. By the time of the Reformation it was looked upon as an oppressive tribute, and it was abolished by the act of 1534.

A vast swarm of papal abuses of a financial nature was done away with by this statute of 1534. Besides the ones described above there were abolished pensions, procurations, fruits, "suits for provisions, and expeditions of bulls for archbishoprics and for bishoprics . . . and other infinite sorts of bulls, briefs, and instruments of sundry natures, names and kinds." [164] In this and the other acts passed during the period, the action and attitude of the Reformation Parliament was one of revolt against and repudiation of these ecclesiastical financial abuses: [165]

> And because that it is now in these days present seen that the state, dignity, superiority, reputation, and authority of the said imperial crown of this realm, by the long suffering of the said unreasonable and uncharitable usurpations and exactions practiced in the time of your most noble progenitors, is much and sore decayed and diminished, and the people of this realm thereby impoverished, and so or worse be like to continue if remedy be not therefor shortly provided: It may therefore please your most noble majesty . . . that all such pensions, censes, portions, and Peterspence (etc.) shall from henceforth clearly surcease, and never more be levied, taken, or perceived, nor paid to any person or persons in any manner of wise; any constitution, use, prescription, or custom to the contrary thereof notwithstanding.

In all these acts of the Reformation Parliament: the Petitions of the Commons, the Conditional Restraint of Annates, the Restraint of Appeals, the Act Forbidding Papal Dispensations and the Payment of Peter's Pence, one cannot help being impressed with the fact that the major grievance of the Commons was the financial and economic losses sustained by the English people through the impositions of the papacy. Economic reasons were a powerful factor in separating England from the papal jurisdiction. Discontent and unrest that had been centuries long in duration came finally to a head in the legislation undertaken between 1529 and 1536. But on top of this action came also two other measures economic in their motive. These were the two acts for the suppression of the monasteries that brought great changes in the use and distribution of ecclesiastical wealth.

CHAPTER V

THE forces that played a part in the sudden confiscation of ecclesiastical wealth in England after the break with the papacy in 1533 were at least four in number. There was (1) a fear of national disintegration; (2) the interests of the public weal and of the national defense; (3) the cupidity of the ruling classes; and (4) the passing of an old, outworn economic order of things. Each of these factors as it reacted toward the secularization of church property had its basis in motives and conditions essentially economic. A rift in the state was threatening by an apparent defection of the clergy who were thought to be using their wealth to aid and comfort the enemies of the realm. Laymen coveted the wealth of the church as a means of strengthening the defenses of the kingdom and of mitigating the burden of taxation. The king, the nobles, and the new middle classes wanted the monastic lands to enrich themselves personally and to enhance their power politically. The new economic organization rapidly developing, based on commerce and industry rather than on agriculture, left little hope for the old feudal régime of the church to remain immune from attack.

Whatever else may be said as to the motives back of precipitating the ecclesiastical revolution of 1533, it is quite evident that a desire for doctrinal reform played little part.

Henry VIII and the group interested in the movement were either openly opposed or tacitly indifferent to radical changes in doctrine and dogma.[1] The king was preëminently an opportunist in the matter, guiding his policy to suit the shifting political developments of the period. At first he posed as "Defender of the Faith" upholding the church against the Lutheran heresy, but later one sees him fostering a rapprochement with the German Protestants by promulgating the Ten Articles. But that this indicated no sincere or permanent change of attitude may be seen in the reversion to the orthodox Six Articles when a German alliance proved no longer advantageous. In ecclesiastical administration, organization, and polity changes were similarly slight. The outstanding fact of the Henrican phase of the English Reformation was a set of economic and financial changes affecting the church. According to Hugh Latimer, the opulence of the church was so reduced that its power to function properly was curtailed at times for lack of funds.[2]

I. Fear of National Disintegration—Foreign Interests of the English Clergy

The study of contemporary documents plainly reveals that a danger regarding the unity of the realm was secretly feared, openly expressed, and carefully guarded against. The cause of the fear was a possible defection of the clergy whose material wealth made such a contingency a grave danger. Evidences of disloyalty were plainly visible both in the regular and secular churchmen.[3] The Act of Supremacy aimed to counteract it; for it gave to the king full power and authority in the church to repress all offenses "for the conservation of the peace, unity, and tranquility of the realm." [4] It is true that the Convocations of both Canterbury and York abjured the papal supremacy by the middle of 1534; but if this was not a mere feint it was, to say the least, official rather than representative.[5] The existence of a secret allegiance between the secular clergy and the papacy showed itself in a number of ways despite the protest of Convocation voiced against the annates and its demand for a separation from Rome as early as 1529.[6] This attachment of the secular clergy to Rome went far beyond a mere sympathetic attitude, and approached disloyalty to England. Prelates and priests alike joined in a concerted movement to spread propaganda favorable to the Roman jurisdiction in England.[7] The Government thought it unsafe for the bishops to collect the tithes after its break with the papacy because it feared the misappropriation of such moneys for the reinstatement of papal authority.[8] The clergy were suspected not only of weakening the national defense by transferring money abroad, but of revealing military secrets of the realm.[9]

The patriotism and loyalty of Cardinal Wolsey certainly was beyond question, yet the subsidies he received from the Continent awakened apprehension at home. Although none of Wolsey's grants came directly from the papacy, he took revenues from Francis I and Charles V that exceeded the income of the king.[10] This was a sort of foreign entanglement that looked dangerous, and in the midst of a growing spirit of nationality such alien relations of the clergy contributed to the desire for an ecclesiastical reorganization. The case of Fisher, Bishop of Rochester, was on the other hand one of outspoken disloyalty. He boldly asserted that the correcting arm of the papacy was far too lenient toward the revolt of Henry VIII.[11] Fisher urged the emperor, Charles V, to take matters in hand and by military duress force the English king to again submit to the papacy. Such an act, he urged, would be as meritorious in the eyes of God as a crusade against the Turks. Bishop Fisher even went so far as to suggest Reginald Pole as the regal prospect about whom the reactionaries should rally to depose Henry VIII.[12] He was leader in a conspiracy to form a confederation of Christian princes against the English king.[13] Cromwell in attempting to justify the execution of Fisher to the French king, said: "The Bishop of Rochester with suche others as were executed here, their treasons conspiracies and practices secretly practised as well within the realme as without to move and styrre discension and to sowe sedycyon within the realme, intending thereby not onely the destruction of the kynge but also the hole subuersion of his highness realm." [14]

One of the most serious implications comprising the loyalty of the secular clergy, and involving at the same time an excuse to confiscate their goods was unearthed in connection with an oath which they made jointly with the abbots to the papacy.[15] In a solemn attestation, now revealed to the secular authorities, the prelates swore never to divulge the secret counsels of the papacy, to communicate to Rome any danger threatening the papal curia, to receive papal legates, and to alienate no property without consent of the papacy. It is highly improbable that the king had been ignorant either of the existence or the nature of this oath. If he knew of it he had failed to take action against the clergy out of fear of their power. But now that papal prestige was crumbling in England he took drastic action. He pointed out to a select group of the members of Parliament called before him for council that the oath was not a symbol but an actual evidence of divided allegiance. Taking the position that the clergy had turned against him, he said: [16]

> Well beloved subjects, we had thought the clergy
> of our realm to be our subjects wholly, but now we

have well perceived that they be but half our subjects; yea, and scarce our subjects. For all the prelates at their consecration make an oath to the pope clean contrary to the oath they make unto us, so that they seem to be his subjects.

Technically the clergy were now traitors in the eyes of the royal court, and consequently their goods were subject to confiscation by the state. Such a step Cromwell evidently had in mind. His motive even according to his supreme eulogist, John Foxe, was extremely mercenary, but he had the complete accord of the king.[17] Cromwell suggested to the monarch that this predicament of the clergy be made a pretext for filling the royal exchequer and crippling forever the power of the prelates. "His majesty might accumulate to himself great riches, as much as all the clergy of the realm was worth, if it pleased him to take the occasion now offered. The king gave good ear to this, liking right well his advice."[18] In fact the king received the proposition with so much favor that he gave Cromwell practically unlimited power to act in the case. Cromwell appeared before the Convocation and pointed out to the assembled clergymen that both by act and attitude they had made their property subject to seizure by the crown. Because they had assented to the legatine court of Wolsey, he said; and because of the oath they had sworn to the pope, they had forfeited to the state "their goods, lands, chattels, possessions, and whatsoever they had."[19] But apparently the time was not ripe for such a drastic step of complete confiscation that Cromwell had in mind, for both the king and his minister seemed now to shrink from such an undertaking. When the Convocation humbled itself confiscation was compounded by the payment of an exorbitant fine.[20] The oath was now outlawed and abolished and a new one imposed by the king claiming undivided loyalty to himself.[21]

The divulging of this oath which the clergy made to the papacy was one reason for abolishing the papal jurisdiction in England.[22]

An incident connected with the collection of the fine imposed on the clergy goes to show how far disaffection had spread in the ranks of the lower clergy. When the Bishop of London tried to gather the money he was violently opposed by the parish priests. The local clergy refused to pay toward the levy, and when the Bishop of London tried coercion a demonstration verging on riot forced him to desist. The doors of a chapter house were forced to prevent a packed assembly of clergymen to impose the levy locally. Despite the fact that a number of priests and laymen were arrested and imprisoned, the money was not raised as planned so that the burden of the fine fell on the upper clergy.[23]

The unity of the realm seemed also to be threatened by the suspected disaffection of the regular clergy. It was this that led to the attack upon the monasteries and the ultimate secularization of their wealth. Traditionally, the tie between the monks and the papacy was a close one and it was feared that this situation bred an undue influence of Rome in the monasteries. The latter were, indeed, the protégés of the papacy in theory and thus suspicion was aroused. Archbishop Cramner looked upon the monks as the pillars of the papacy. "Under colour or pretense of obedience to their father in religion (which obedience they themselves made), they were made free by their rules and canons from the obedience of their natural father and mother, and of all temporal power, from obedience of emperor and king, whom of very duty by God's law they were bound to obey." [24]

A privy counselor of king Henry VIII wrought up over suspicion as to the patriotism of the monks and their attachment to Rome became somewhat of an alarmist. The account was given by Lord Herbert of Cherbury in his History of Henry VIII:[25]

> But Sir, when I consider again how the pope, the bishop of Rome, hath threatened to join all Christian princes against your highness, and that in these monasteries . . . he nourishes a seminary of factious persons that oppose your supremacy; and what instruments they may be in stirring up sedition in your highness' kingdom at the same time that some foreign power may invade it, I cannot but wish that some good order were given. . . . As for the suppression of any, not I, but some violent and inexcusable necessity must be your counsellor. I should think it fit that they instantly be visited. If your highness have any other way to defend yourself against the threatened invasion, I shall never advise you to this, and yet that no further than to bring your estate to a just temper.

By "some good orders" of course confiscation was meant. The historian Speed gave two reasons for the suppression of the monasteries, one was patriotic and the other economic. He accused the monks of making false gains out of their religious duties and alluded to the religious houses as "the Nests and very Receptacle of all traitorous attempters against the peace of the Lande and the Supremacy of the Crowne."[26] "The monks notwithstanding their subscription to the casting off of the pope's supremacy were generally thought to be against it in their hearts, and ready to join any foreign power which should invade the nation."[27] The State Papers abound in seditious statements emanating from the monasteries.[28] Since the monasteries controlled vast wealth, the best way to remedy the situation would be to destroy the economic power of the monks which gave a material basis to the danger.

II. Fear of National Disintegration—the Rebellion of the North

The apprehension regarding the fidelity of the abbots and monks was to some extent justified when rebellion broke out in the North of England in 1536. The secular power had already gotten a taste of the obstinacy of the Observant and the Carthusian friars in forcing their subscription to the Act of Supremacy; but the insurrections at the North threatened much direr consequences.[29] The immediate cause of the Rebellion of the North was the suppression of the smaller monasteries.[30] It is a mistake to think that the secularization of the religious houses in England was popular at the time.[31] The movement was at best the work of a small minority of the upper classes that seemed to see in them a danger to the state and that hungered lustily after the spoils. Though the opposition against confiscation was general, it was particularly virulent in the North. In the more progressive South which had caught the spirit of the new age of growing commerce and industry there was a great deal of indifference to the confiscation of the monasteries. There the king and his party had little trouble in rooting out opposition.

But a different situation prevailed in the North of England in that it was isolated. Far removed and out of touch with the greater trading ports of the South, the North of England had advanced little in commercial and industrial enterprise. For that reason it had begun to break with the past in no noticeable degree; it remained agrarian in economic organization; it was conservative in its thinking; and its ideals were primarily linked up with the old régime.[32] The North was also remote from the political influence of the central government, so that sudden military interference with any movement was difficult and opposition had a chance to be sown and to take root. In the South, More, Fisher, and others were speedily put to death in opposing the Act of Supremacy; but men were boldly traveling throughout the North Country preaching against the policies of the king and the Parliament.[33] Thus conditions in the North of England were favorable to re-action; opposition and discontent had a chance to ferment; irregular military organization was possible; and ultimate open rebellion was inevitable.

There were two main areas of insurrection, one in Lincolnshire and the other in Yorkshire. The Lincolnshire rebellion broke out in October, 1536, but it was soon quelled. It was led by a friar who posed as a local cobbler.[34] Lacking good leadership and proper organization the movement soon collapsed, but not before its adherents presented a complaint to the king criticizing him for surrounding himself with upstart counselors, deploring the suppression of the monasteries, and denouncing the sequestration of the annates.[35] Much more serious and threatening was the Yorkshire Rising a few weeks later led by Robert Aske and terminating in the Pilgrimage of Grace; it was well equipped, carefully organized, and adequately led. Forty thousand men were ultimately gathered under its banner as the movement pushed southward under the guise of a pilgrimage. Only the excuse of a swollen stream prevented the king giving battle to this determined group of malcontents, and to the end they showed a spirited resistance to the royal authority.[36]

A significant feature of these revolts was the number of clergymen involved in them. The centers of the disturbances seem to have been the religious houses, though the secular clergy and even some of the nobility were instigators in the affairs.[37] Many abbots and monks were executed in spite of the promise of leniency. Among those put to death

were John Paslowe, Abbot of Whaley, and two monks of
the same house; Robert Hobs, Abbot of Worborne, and
two monks of the abbey; The Abbot of Sawley, and the
prior of that house; William Wold, Prior of Burlington;
a parson of Puddington; and the cobbler-captain of Lincolnshire with six priests of the same district.[38] Some of
the bishops were implicated in the movement; and Edward
Lee, Archbishop of York, was looked upon as a partisan
in the revolt because of the ease with which the castle of
Pomfract capitulated under his hand.[39] Ten or twelve
prominent noblemen of the North of England also partici-
pated in the revolt.[40] The demands of the rebels made to
the king and Parliament were wholly reactionary in tone.
They insisted that the upstart minister, Cromwell, be dis-
missed from the service of the king, that the Reformation
doctrines be eradicated, that the papal authority be rein-
stated, that the annates be restored to the pope, that the
suppressed monasteries be revived, and that the clergy have
a voice in the disposal of the tithes.[41]

The discontent out of which these uprisings grew was
by no means confined to the North of England, but the
spirit of dissatisfaction was more or less general. A contemporary letter written by one clerk to another stated that:
"Until the king and the rulers of this realm be plucked by
the pates and brought to the pot, as we say, shall we never
live merrily in England; which I pray God may chance
and now shortly be brought to pass." It then goes to show
the wide extent of the discontent: [42]

> Ireland is set against him, which will never shrink
> in their quarrel, to die in it. And what think ye of
> Wales . . . ? They will join and take part with the
> Irish, and invade our realm. If they do so, doubt ye not
> but they shall have strength and aid enough in Eng-
> land; for this is truth, they go about to bring this realm

into such miserable condition as is France, which the Commons well perceive as sufficient cause of rebellion and insurrection in the realm. And truly we of the church will never live merrily til that day come. This is truth, three parts of England is against the king, as he shall find if he need.

Discontent evidently was wide spread and deep seated, and it penetrated to an alarming extent the army of the king sent to crush the Yorkshire "pilgrimage." [43] This alone explains the reason why the king avoided the risk of a battle at a very critical time in the march of the forty thousand.

A rumor was current that the king refused to join battle with the insurgents because he feared disloyalty on the part of his own troops made up mostly of volunteer Commons. In a letter of Cromwell to Gardiner and Wallop, English envoys in France, he maintained that paternal and humanitarian impulses moved the king in avoiding a clash with the insurrectionists.[44] This he did to correct the rumor, which stated in Cromwell's own words was that "the commens assembled for the kings partie were so faynte and unwilling, that they wold not haue doon their dieuties if it had comen to extremytie." [45] Cromwell tried to explain matters by asserting that the king had given orders to his captains beforehand that they should in no case risk a battle. The king, he intimated, had compassion on his subjects and recoiled from the thought of shedding their blood.[46] But this was contrary both to fact and also to the character of Henry VIII. Just a few weeks before this, Cromwell showed how drastic and unrelenting would be the punishment of the insurrectionists the king was preparing: "His highness haith putt every thyng now in suche parfitt order that if thes rebelles doo contynue eny lenger in their rebellyon, dout you not but ye shall see theym so subdued as their example shalbe fearfull to all subgiettes whilles the world dooith endure." [47] After all, the only satisfactory explanation is that the spirit of insurrection was quite general.

But the danger once passed, the king suppressed the greater monasteries without mercy. He also renewed his attack on the wealth of the secular clergy. Many among the influential ruling classes now supported the monarch because they saw the danger that lay in vast wealth controlled by disloyal churchmen, and because they were personally enriched by the spoils. The break-up of the monastic system in England and the distribution of ecclesiastical property among men faithful to the crown was a masterstroke of statecraft on the part of Henry VIII. It not only unified the kingdom but it rendered permanent the results of the schism of 1533. [48] National solidity was particularly solicited at this time because of the menacing continental developments which threatened to embroil England in a foreign war. Could the pope and the emperor compromise their differences, they were bent on bringing Henry VIII to terms over his breach with the papacy. The danger of the situation was aggravated by the machinations of Reginald Pole, the regal rival of Henry, who was doing his utmost to widen the breach between Henry and his enemies on the Continent. From his retreat in Italy, Pole published his book against Henry, entitled *Liber de Unitate Ecclesiae*, and strove to unite the Catholic powers against the English monarch.

Patriotic subjects now favored the suppression of the monasteries because the monks seemed completely out of sympathy with nationalistic ideals, and because it was believed that their wealth was being used against the best interests of the commonwealth. For this policy of the king in suppressing the religious houses, Cromwell must be given the credit. He frankly told the king that the

wealth of the church would be a facile means of replenish-
ing the royal exchequer.[49] It was Cromwell who advocated
the policy of distributing the monastic lands among secular
owners as a means of permanency for the revolution, for:
"the more that had interest in them the less they would be
revocable."[50] The aim and ideal of Cromwell was to con-
solidate the realm by eliminating the conflicting elements
therein. Under his régime there was a carefully directed
policy toward political absolutism.[51] Through a well organized system of espionage, Cromwell was conscious of
the attitude of the clergy. Nothing, he reasoned, could
operate more injuriously against national unity than the
disaffection of the clergy, and nothing could make disloyalty more dangerous than the wealth of the church.

The scattering of the monks and giving their property
to men faithful to the crown did render permanent the
results of the reformation. It effectively hindered future attempts to return to the papal allegiance. The dispersed
monks stripped of their wealth could give reaction no organized direction or financial support. In the Marian settlement of 1554, the disposition of ecclesiastical property made
in the earlier reign was the one great exception to the
process of repeal. The grantees of monastic property confiscated under Henry VIII and Edward VI were confirmed
in their estates.[52] This economic triumph of the favored
classes, who were as a whole anti-papal in attitude, made a
return to the old Roman ecclesiastical régime practically
impossible. John Foxe was right:[53]

> In such realms and kingdoms as this, where laws and
> parliaments be not always one, but are subject to the
> disposition of the prince, neither is it certain always
> what princes may come; Therefore the surest way to
> send monkery and popery packing out of this realm is to
> do with their houses as King Henry here did, through

the motion and counsel of Cromwell. For else, who seeth not in queen Mary's time, if either the houses of monks had stood, or their lands had been otherwise disposed of such as they were, how many of them had been restored or replenished again with monks and friars in as ample a wise as they ever were. And if dukes, barons, and the nobility scarce were able to retain the lands and possessions of abbeys distributed to them by Henry, from the devotion of queen Mary seeking again to rebuild the walls of Jerusalem, what then could the meaner sort have done.

III. Common Interests of the Realm—Provision for the National Defense

One of the major motives for depriving the English clergy of their vast possessions, exploited continuously in the contemporary documents, was the seizure of church property as a means of building up the defenses of the realm and of lessening the burden of taxation. The idea was a hold over from the Wycliffian theory of disendowment; for Wyclif taught that it would be lawful to pull down churches as a means of building towers, and to melt chalices as a means for paying soldiers.[54] Furthermore, the Oxford reformer taught that the possessions of the church should be distributed among knights and others capable of defending the land against enemies. Such a policy would strengthen the military defense, mitigate the burden of taxation, solidly unify the kingdom, and advance the general welfare of the people.[55] It was owing to the influence of Wyclif's point of view that the Good Parliament began to suspect the papal collectors of betraying the military secrets of the realm; and to doubt the wisdom of the fact that five times as much taxes was raised in England for the pope as was raised for the king.[56]

The Supplication of the Beggars likewise pointed out the danger to the national defense due to the endowment and financial policy of the church. The tract showed that many times in the past the subsidies for the defense of the realm had been curtailed either by a refusal of the clergy to contribute or because the country had already been drained of funds by papal exactions. The king was reminded that the wealth of the church could be the means of military defeat in case of a crisis; that political ruin and national survival were threatened by the control of this wealth from abroad. "What kingdom can endure that ever giveth thus and receiveth not again?" King Henry VIII was facing a situation which, under similar conditions, would have ruined other monarchs in the past. King Arthur could never have resisted the Danes encumbered to the same extent by such an ecclesiastical financial hindrance. The Greeks could never have taken Troy nor the Romans expanded to a world power encumbered in such a manner. Likewise the king of England could not expect to win victories on the Continent, gain glory for the nation, or even hold his own in case of war with such a drain on his resources. Part of this pamphlet by Simon Fish was a powerful appeal for national self-preservation threatened by the wealth of the clergy.[57]

The spirit of the times now played into the hands of agitation of this sort; for the reign of Henry VIII was a way mark in the policy of military and naval defense. This plan of action had in fact been initiated by the king's father, though Henry VIII has been regarded as the real founder of the English navy.[58] But the king gave no less attention to the land defenses of the nation than to the naval. A portion of the spoils reaped from the confiscation of the monasteries was devoted to this purpose. Defense of the realm was also given as a motive in the legislation that turned

over the annates to the royal exchequer. One of the documents connected with their annulment stated that owing
to the excessive charges for maintaining the defense of
the realm during the past twenty years some mitigation
of this burden ought to be provided. For this reason it was
granted that the king receive the first fruits of all livings
from an archbishopric to a free chapel.[59] The people were
groaning under the weight of taxation almost unendur-
able, and they were only too willing to listen to any voice
promising them immediate relief. Giving utterance to such
a motive as defense of the realm in seizing church property
had two advantages; it served as a pretext to lay claim on
such property, and it promised relief from taxation.[60]

The political situation on the Continent was also at this
particular time making military and naval precautions
necessary. An acute crisis emerged in 1539 which drove the
English king to a program of both conciliation and defense.
Despite the Ten Articles of 1536, Henry had little real
sympathy with the German Protestants, and he refrained
from joining the League of Schmalkald in the end.[61] The
king distrusted the German Reformers because they were
making concessions to Charles V.[62] Mutual fear of the ever-
advancing Turks at the southeast was drawing Charles V,
Francis I, and the German princes together, and the English king was fearful that such a coalition might be used
against himself. In fact, a fleet had been concentrating at
Antwerp; the French and Spanish envoys had left London;
and a general coolness and uncertainty prevailed.[63] The
crisis was the more threatening in that Reginald Pole was
consolidating these forces in his own interests as claimant
to the English crown.[64] There was even talk of the Catholic
groups uniting in alliance with the Turks to crush the
reformation: "The bishop of Rome and his adherentes do

studye, nothing more than to haue the princes of thair
alliances to be at peace and trues not only bitwen them-
selfes but also with the turkes and other to theutent that
they may extinguishe the veray sincere sorte of the Evan-
gelicall princes, and their assisters." [65] Again: "In Spayne
all thynges be waxen from colder to coldest. Pole is lately
arryved there. In conclusion Themperour sayeth. . . . If he
were his own traytour commyng from that holy father of
Rome he can not refuse him audience. . . . As for any
treatie of streighter allyaunce they saye in dede that they
shal not fayle to obserue the hole tenour of their treaties." [66]

As a result of these movements, Henry VIII took two
important steps in defense of his position one of which was
diplomatic and the other military. After failing to arrange
a marriage contract with either royal house, of France or
Spain, to offset the combination against him, he finally
married Anne of Cleves to gain the good will of the German Protestants. He also had passed by Parliament the
Six Articles to assure the Catholics of his doctrinal conservatism. His next step was to take careful and definite
precautions to put in proper condition the military and
naval defenses of the kingdom. He sent his military experts
to inspect the strategic points along the exposed seacoasts,
and he made a personal tour of inspection for a similar
purpose to various places within the realm: [67]

> Wherefore his Majestie in his awne persone, with-
> out eny deley toke very laborious and painful journies
> towardes the sea coastes. Also he sent divers of his
> nobles and counsellors to viwe and searche all the
> portes and daungers on the coastes where eny mete
> or convenient landing place might be supposed, as
> well on the borders of England as also of Wales. And
> in all soche doubtful places his highness caused divers

and many bulwarkes and fortificacions to be made. And further his highnesse caused the lorde Admiral erle of Southampton to prepare in redenesse shippes for the sea, to his grete cost and charges.

Moreover the king ordered both the land and naval forces to be in readiness as if expecting an invasion of the realm.[68] It was these preparations that were a factor in bringing about the confiscation of the greater monasteries. Herbert of Cherbury wrote thus:[69]

All which preparatives being made against a danger which was thought to be imminent, seemed to excuse the king's suppressing the abbeys; as the people willing to spare their own purses, began to suffer it easily; especially when they saw orders taken for building divers forts and bulwarks upon the seacoast; many of these if not most, we have this day, being thought not so exact as the modern, yet of his raising.

The same writer stated that this motive of building up the defenses of the kingdom was in mind when Parliament suppressed the smaller monasteries in 1536, but the object was defeated by the cupidity of the king.[70] The failure to apply these funds according to the original intention was likely due to the fact that danger was not so imminent. Later authorities agreed with Lord Herbert.[71] Strype, a collector of contemporary memorials of the Reformation, also bears this out in a document.[72] Lord Herbert said that the king protesting he would suppress none without parliamentary sanction, but seeing that some of his subjects for conscience sake and others to avoid the charges of war wanted the goods of the monasteries confiscated, agreed to their secularization.[73] He said that:[74]

They were the seminary of those who opposed the regal authority in secular matters; to which some have thought the reason formerly touched might be added, that the parliament was willing to lay the burden of furnishing the king's necessities from themselves. And thus were the lesser monasteries dissolved. But whatever the reasons were, it was certain that use was not made of them as might have been, while the revenue of the crown was so little improved thereby. If the profits of those dissolved had been employed for a settled entertaining and payment of a royal army by land, and a great fleet at sea, our king might have given (besides securing the realm) the law in great part to his neighbors.

IV. COMMON INTERESTS OF THE REALM—PROVISION FOR THE GENERAL WELFARE

The defense of the realm, the alleviation of taxation, and provision for the general welfare of the kingdom became favorite arguments justifying the confiscation of the wealth of churchmen both regular and secular. "Not only the monasteries were to feel their punishment," said Strype, "but the archbishops and bishops, and all other dignified churchmen were to bear their share." [75] Detailed and graphic schemes for lessening the weight of taxation were sometimes presented, though it is doubtful whether the attempt was ever made to carry any of them out. One plan suggested in order that the royal exchequer be forever enriched, the kingdom and the nobility strengthened and increased, and the common subjects be acquitted and freed from all former taxation and services, the following program should be put into effect: suppress the wealth of the abbots, friars, monks, and nuns; and out of the revenues thus assured, raise up in their stead forty earls, sixty barons, three thousand knights, and forty thousand soldiers and trained captains. By so doing, the king and his successors would never lack treasure, while the common people would never have to be charged with loans, subsidies, and fifteenths in the future.[76]

Cromwell himself seems to have worked out some such scheme of amelioration. In a document found among his papers there appeared a plan promising relief from taxation and increased revenues for the king by means of the confiscated revenues of the clergy in case the plan was carried into effect. The church was to be relegated to the place of a mere department of state and the clergy to be paid fixed sums per annum according to their position and importance. The paper made ample provision for the defense of the realm and for the royal exchequer, but the needs of the deprived prelates, priests, and religious men were also kept in mind. It also promised relief from the galling taxation of the time. It was to be provided by parliamentary act that the Archbishop of Canterbury receive 2000 marks per annum and not above; and that all the rest of the revenues of the archiepiscopal see be paid over to the king and his heirs for the defense of the realm and the maintenance of his royal estate. In like manner the Archbishop of York, the various prelates, etc., were to get incomes in proportion to position. The monks, canons, and abbots were to be provided for but their revenues turned over to the king's treasury.[77]

Some of the plans for confiscation and secular appropriation were based on a broad social and economic outlook rather than on immediate relief from a state burden. One paper in particular revealed a scheme with unusual vision and sense of altruism.[78] It advocated that only a portion of the wealth of the church be appropriated by the state so that the clergy retain enough to live comfortably. It urged that the part taken over by the crown be devoted to the advancement of the general public welfare. For one thing it should .be used to counteract the evils of the enclosure movement. The confiscated resources of the church were to be used for the better administration of justice, giving employment to sturdy vagabonds, aiding the poor and unfortunate, building up new towns, restoring decayed manors, reclaiming unprofitable parks, and constructing new roads throughout the kingdom. Such use of church property would both benefit the masses and also exalt religion. The wealth of the church was to be used toward socially useful ends.

A very good summary of the economic motives back of Henry VIII's policy of suppressing the monasteries is given in Thomas Wright's collection of documents.[79] It is a memoir of a contemporary writer showing several ways by which the general welfare of the nation was enhanced. Cromwell was given the credit as being the instrument in the hand of God for carrying out the policy of amelioration. He first found the means of persuading the monarch that confiscation could be lawfully done, "and that for his crowne and state in saftie it was necessary to be done":

> Four that he made appeare to the kinge how by their meanes the pope and clergie had so grete aucthoritie, revenue, alliaunce, and principallye captivity of sowles and obedience of subjectes, that they were able to put the kinge in hazard at their will; that for the revenue and maintenance of his estate, warres, and affaires both in peace and warre, at home and abrode, with others, it was most profitable to dissolve them for the augmentation of his treasure. He allyed the kinge so stronglie with mightie forces in Germany and that league of religion, so that their forces and his treasure and the consideration of the common perill by their common enemy the pope he was able to withstande and encounter any foren princes. . . . He knew that

his clargie was attempting the like (deposition) with
the marquis of Exetar (Reginald Pole). He perswaded
the king by maintaining of *equum jus,* and by holding downe of the over-eminent power of soche grete
ones as in time paste, like bellwethers, had led the
sheppeshe flockes of England against their prince, to
knett fast to him the love of his commons and especially the cittie of London. He caused the king to re-
strayne all payment at Rome, and all resorte of his subjectes thither, either for suits, appeals, faculties, or other
causes, whereby he both kept treasure, and held it from
his enemies, and restrayned his enemies from fliinge to
foren partes for conference with them. . . . He caused
the kinge to make such dispersion of the abbies pos-
sessiones as it behooved infinite multitudes for their
owne interest to joine with the kinge in holding them
downe . . . by selling them for reasonable prises to
many men, exchanging many of them with the nobilitie and other for their anchient possessions to the greate
gaine to whome he exchanged, preferring many sufficient persons to the kinges servis, who were soone
rised to the nobilitie and to worship and to goode
calling, and all endewed with maintenaunce out of
the revenue of the abbies.

So far as is known none of these schemes for amelioration
ever materialized, and the conclusions drawn in the last
quoted extract were either theoretical or exaggerated rather
than true to fact. The suppression of the monasteries was
not the financial, social, and political success it was represented to be. At best, perhaps, these documents show but
the exploited motives used to gain popular favor and consent for the confiscation of the wealth of the monasteries.
But if only used as a means of agitation and propaganda,
they show at least a decided economic emphasis determining secularization and suppression. Burnet said that the

king had the greatest opportunity that a king of England ever had to make noble and royal foundations, but whether out of policy to get the good will of the gentry, or in rewarding his courtiers, or out of lavish waste and extravagance he came far short of accomplishing the good he had promised to do with the funds derived from confiscated ecclesiastical property.[80] "He designed to convert 18,000 pounds sterling into a revenue for eighteen bishoprics and cathedrals, but of these he erected only six." [81] Great sums, however, were laid out on building and fortifying many ports in the Channel.

Another thrust at the economic tyranny and waste of the clergy came more indirectly through an attack on the number of holy days and festivals as a time wasting and wealth menacing evil.[82] Wyclif had already made the claim that these were breeding times of vice and corruption. During the less busy time of the year these holidays bred idleness and curtailed production, but in time of harvest they jeopardized the fruits of the fields. Decrease in labor opportunity meant corresponding decrease in the wealth of the nation. The canons of 1362 named forty-two holy days to be observed during the year, and the canons of 1415 show that an average of one day a week was a religious holiday besides the usual Sabbath. On these days work was entirely prohibited. Added to this, the part time cessation from labor demanded on festival days made only four and a half days available for work in every week. Henry VI passed a law in 1427 forbidding laboring men from taking wages on these days, and this was still in force. Thus it was that these holy days led to bitter complaint in the wage earning classes. Latimer, fully awake to the evils of this situation, pointed out its dangers in a sermon before Convocation in 1536: [83]

God seeth the all the whole holidays to be spent in drunkenness, in gluttony, in strife, in dancing, in dicing, idleness, and gluttony. He seeth all this and threteneth punishment. . . . Who is he that is not sorry to see in so many holy days rich and wealthy persons in flow of delicacies and men who live by their travail, poor men, to lack necessary meat and drink for their wives and children; and that they cannot labor on the holiday except they be cited and be brought before the officials. Is it not the duty of good prelates to consult upon these matters and seek a remedy for the same? Ye shall see, my brethren, ye shall see sometime what will become of this our winking.

V. Self-interest of the Ruling Classes—Cupidity of the King

The awarding of confiscated lands and goods of the church to the men of the new middle classes on the one hand, to the country gentry and old established families of the nobility on the other hand was an outstanding feature of the suppression of the monasteries. The immense wealth of the clergy presented a temptation for improving personal fortunes and increasing the political prestige of certain groups that little effort was made to resist it. A recent writer summed up the situation in the statement that most of the landed spoils fell to the nobles and the gentry, and most of the moveable goods soon passed out of the king's coffers after meeting the calls of the moment. Every great lay interest was thus united in the attack upon church property which continued until the death of Edward VI.[84] The king catered to their interests for in this manner, apparently, he aimed to build up a party in England that would uphold the crown in case of a religious reaction.

From the attempts made against the alien priories in the time of Henry IV and Henry V it was evident that the property of these monasteries was coveted by the laity.

The flood of letters and petitions, asking for portions of the suppressed property, that came to Cromwell indicated that such a situation now obtained.[85] The cupidity of the king and the covetousness of the ruling classes may be seen at work on every hand. Direct statement and indirect testimony alike give ample proof that the greed of king and ruling classes was a prominent motive for the economic reform of the church. The result was the creation of a class of the newly rich and highly influential men thoroughly devoted to the dynasty.[86]

Contemporary documents testify to the avarice of the king in regard to taking over the possessions of the church. In spite of the fact that such statements came usually from the enemies of Henry VIII, they evidently contain much truth. One paper stated that the proceeds of confiscated property was occasionally devoted to charitable purposes "lest the accusation of covetousness be brought." A certain clerk under trial stated in the court: "Syth the realm of England was first a realm there was never so great robber and pyller of the commonwealth read or heard of as is our king. He robs not only the spirituality, robbing them of their livings, spoiling them of their goods, and hurling them into prison, but also laymen." [87] Capello, the Venetian envoy held a very low opinion of the financial ethics of Henry VIII.[88] One statement asserted that it would be hard to bring back the king into the Catholic fold because "covetousness is so entered into his sect." [89] There is evidence to show that the king seized the annates largely to satisfy self-gratification.[90] The attachment of Henry VIII to Cromwell was doubtless to a large extent due to the promise of the latter to make the king the richest prince in Christendom out of the spoils of the church.[91]

The assertion has often been made, and it appeared in the Act for the Dissolution of the Lesser Monasteries,[92] that the depraved moral status of the religious houses was the main reason for their suppression. This was no doubt a motive for suppression though it was a minor one. The commission of visitors appointed by the crown made a thorough investigation of the moral and spiritual condition of the houses they inspected, and it was said that when the gross moral enormities they discovered were reported to the Parliament the cry arose: "Cut them down, why cumbereth they the ground." Some of the houses suppressed by the first act, in 1536, were likely very bad, but many were good, and perhaps the great bulk of them indifferent. The strange thing about the matter was that when it came to actual suppression the line was not drawn on a basis of ethical or spiritual conditions but along one of economic rank; that is, houses of a revenue of less than 200 pounds sterling a year were all taken.[93] In regard to ethical status as a motive for an attack on church property, Bishop Fisher was likely right in a speech delivered before Parliament on one occasion. He said: "The church's wealth occasions this first moving. If we were poor our vices would be virtues, and none would be forward to accuse us." [94]

At first the king seemed bent on confiscating all the property of the church to the crown. This would have placed its entire wealth in his own hands and as head of the church he could have doled out salaries to clergymen or granted them scant livings out of the treasury of the state. But he was forced to change his mind for many reasons—especially that such a measure would incur the

undying hatred and opposition of the secular clergy which
he could not dispense with as he could the good will
of the regular clergy. He also feared those persons, or
rather their heirs and successors, who had endowed the
clergy. It would incur the redistribution of a vast amount
of property with which he would be forced to reward and
hence strengthen the ruling classes to a degree he feared
to do. In the end he refrained from his original purpose
of a wholesale secularization of ecclesiastical wealth, but
imposed upon the church a yearly tax of 30,000 pounds
sterling. At the same time he took over the revenues of all
vacant bishoprics and benefices. The avarice of the king
was in this matter gratified by "an inestimable sum of
money." [95] In 1542, King Henry VIII did finally compel
the bishops to deliver up much of their landed property.
As many as seventy manors were taken from the Archbishop of York and many of the dioceses suffered pro-
portionately. The chantries and free chapels were also appropriated by the king.[96]

A mercenary motive on the part of the English king
in attacking the wealth of the church may easily be implied from a study of his doctrinal attitudes. In 1539, after
confiscation of the church property as far as Henry saw fit
to carry it had been accomplished, a rapprochement with
Rome was solicited in the passage of the Six Articles. But
before the suppression of the smaller monasteries in 1536
a similar reconciliation had been sought by the Roman
curia. The latter movement failed. The King of France
took this occasion to express his mind by asserting that it
would be easy to bring the English king back into the
Catholic fold if it were not for his "extreme avarice"
already whetted by profits drawn from the church.[97] The
summer of 1536 seemed a propitious time for healing the
schism between England and Rome as a number of events

indicated: the rival queens were dead; the pope was making overtures; Francis I was lending his good offices to bring an understanding; the king was permitted certain prohibited doctrines to be preached; for the moment he suspended his operations against the monasteries; and the English envoys abroad were rejoicing at the prospect of a reconciliation that would make their king "the most glorious king in the world" and wipe out the stain in his career.[98]

But this era of good feeling suddenly vanished. Instead of reconciliation, Pope Paul III issued his bull of excommunication against King Henry, and the latter replied by giving his consent to the circulation of Tyndal's New Testament. He also resumed his operations against the monasteries. Cardinal Pole looked upon this diplomatic fiasco as due to the king's propensity for plundering the church, and Francis I regarded it as due to the king's cupidity. "Unfortunately," wrote Cardinal Gasquet, "for the accomplishment of this happy return of England to the unity of the faith, other matters besides the divorce of the king were destined to keep the king and the pope apart. . . . A real obstacle was to be found in the fact that the king had already seized a considerable amount of the church's property, and was at that time occupied with schemes of wholesale alienation of the goods of monk, priest, and poor. . . . Reconciliation would have obliterated the vision of untold wealth—dreams which could only be realized by perseverance in the course of destruction embarked upon." [99]

These statements were no doubt true, and the cupidity of the king was a powerful factor in the suppression of the monasteries. But it was by no means all the truth when the rapacity of Henry VIII was put as the real obstacle in the way of reconciliation with Rome. The

monasteries were strongholds of papal influence, the roots
of their loyalty were embedded in Rome, and from thence
they received their nourishment. They threatened the
unity of the realm, and their vast wealth made that threat
a grave menace. Henry was as well aware of this situation
as he was of the fact that great personal gain was to be
derived in the sequestration of ecclesiastical wealth.

VI. SELF-INTEREST OF THE RULING CLASSES—COVETOUSNESS OF THE NOBLES, GENTRY, AND BURGHERS

What was true of the king was the case with the ruling
classes as a whole, whether they were great lords, country
gentlemen, or middle classes of the towns. The entire
realm seemed full of greedy solicitors praying for a share
in the spoils of the church.[100] Letters poured in to Cromwell petitioning the king to reserve for the petitioners slices
of the suppressed lands. The Spanish envoy in England,
Chapuys, writing to Charles V, in 1536, stated: "All the
lords are intent on having farms of the goods of the said
churches. Already the dukes of Norfolk and Suffolk are
largely provided with them." [101] Strype pointed out that:
"When vast and immense treasures were flowing in to the
crown from these endowed houses, there lacked not suitors
to obtain some share in the wealth for themselves. And
Lord Cromwell, to whom they made their addresses for
his favorable recommendation to the king, they made ac-
quainted both their merits and their needs. Divers of
these letters are still extant in our archives." [102]

Prospects for sharing the plunder must have brought
pressure to bear at court, and must have become an inducement to the king in the dissolution of the religious
houses. That such prospects were entertained may be seen
in a letter written by John Huse, one of the commissioners, to Lord Lisle several months before the act of disso-

lution was brought about. Huse said: "When the king proceeds to deal with the abbeys you shall have your share in them." [103] Soon after the act of dissolution came, the Duke of Norfolk wrote to Cromwell saying: "I perceived yesterday that you thought the king would appoint this day such houses of religion as he will appoint me." After asking for certain lands, the letter continued: "If I may have the stewardship of all these lands, so much the better; if not, at least those this side Trent. Where others are speaking, I must speak also." [104]

Others were indeed speaking, and they did not hesitate to offer bribes to get options on the coveted lands. One of the commissioners, Francis Brian, reporting to Cromwell stated that divers persons had been soliciting him for leases of farms belonging to the condemned abbeys, "for which he had been offered much money." [105] The commissioners could accept no money without getting into trouble, but they had no scruples in regard to others getting it; for Brian suggested to Cromwell in the letter: "It is as meet for you to have the money as any man." [106] The commissioners themselves did not hesitate to make entreaty for some of the monastic property they visited, for Brian asked Cromwell to remember him to the king for two houses. His reason for the request being that one monastery joined on the king's hunting forest, and the game might be injured and poached if held by another.

The following letter may be taken as typical of numerous others written by the country gentry soliciting certain properties: [107]

Right worshipfull, yn my most humblyst wise I can commend me to your good mastership, thanckying your mastership ever for the great kyndness and ffavor shewd to me always, and where it may please your

mastership to call to your remembrance that ye prom-
ysed me to be good master unto me when the tyme
came; Sir, your mastership shall understand that whereas yet I am not able to doo suche acceptable service
unto the kynges highnes my master, as my pore and
true hert wold, and if I hadd wherewith to mainteyn
it, so it is, pleasith if your mastership to understond,
that where I desyred Mr. Brian to be so good master
unto me as to mosion unto you to helpe me to the
gifte of the priory of Fynshed, a hous of chanons yn
the countie of Northampton, of the yerely value of
lvj (li), x (s), x (d) yn case it be suppressed. Sir, you
shall understonde that sens that tyme my naturall
ffather willed me to write your mastership, and to
none other, for to be good master unto me for a hous
in Somerset shire called Worspryng where my seyd
ffather is ffounder thereof, and as I doo subpose of
like value thereaboutes. And yf it would plese your
mastership . . . to helpe me to Worspryng priorie, I
were and wylle be wyls I leve your bedeman and
always redy to your mastership with suche service and
pleasure as shal becom me to doo, whillst I do leve,
God wylling, who ever have your mastership yn his
tuysshon. From Bletherweke, this present Palme Son-
day, by your own assured to his little power,

Humffray Stafford, esquyer,

To the right honorable sir
Thomas Cromwell, knyght, secretorie
to the kynges hyghnes d.d. thus.

Letter after letter according to this tenor and fashion could
be given coming from the nobility, the country gentry,
and the tradesmen of the towns. Some offered gifts for
inducing Cromwell to gain the ear of the king, others
wanted to pay for the lands solicited, others still ask for
the land as a mere favor and promised service like the
one given above.[108]

The newly rich middle class merchant and manufacturer of the towns certainly came in for their share of the confiscated property of the church as aggressively as did the old nobility and gentry of the country. Their greed for land and desire to build up estates had long been in evidence, and the suppression of the monasteries now offered them an unusual opportunity to this end that they were bound to exploit. The influence of these new classes created by the rise and expansion of commerce may be seen in the dismembering of the great estates of the old nobility after the Wars of the Roses.[109] In the pre-Reformation period they must have been a powerful factor in bringing pressure to bear for the suppression of the monasteries and confiscation of the wealth of the clergy as a whole. It fitted in well with the enclosure movement of which there was a sharp revival during this period, and these keen, greedy capitalists had few scruples regarding encroachment on the property of the church. It was a time of building up large estates and the poor yeoman and rich churchman had to suffer for it in an economic way.[110]

This situation may be illustrated by a document dating to the year 1514; which complains of these new middle classes, growing richer and richer, looking about for landed property in which they might invest their surplus money. It ran thus: [111]

> Divers and many Merchant adventurers, Clothmakers, Goldsmiths, Botchers, Tanners, and other artificers and unreasonable coveteous persons, which doth enclose daily many ferms more than they can occupy and mayntayne. . . . Loke at the merchauntes of London and ye shall see when by their honest trade and vocation in merchaundise God hath endowed them with great abundance of ryches, then can they not be content with the prosperous wealth of that vocation

to satisfy them and to help others; but their ryches must abrode in the countrey to bie ferms out of the hands of worshipful gentlemen, honest yeomen, and pore laboring husbandmen.

Thus it was that just as the nobles and country gentry solicited for strips of the suppressed abbey lands, so these new classes begged for their share. In way of illustration there is found in the State Papers the case of a suit presented to Cromwell for the farm of certain abbey lands, mills, waters, etc., of the monastery of Abingdon. The suitor promised to serve the king for this favor with twenty tall men in return. This troop of stalwarts was to be at Cromwell's command. The solicitor was an employer of five hundred wool weavers. He promised Cromwell a remuneration of twenty pounds sterling for his trouble.[112]

What was true of the property of the regular clergy was also the case in regard to the wealth of the secular churchmen. If the property of the latter was not confiscated outrightly like that of the former, it was to say the least brought under the control of the lay powers by a sort of system of pluralism as extensive as that of the old Roman régime. There appeared in 1546 a booklet entitled "A Supplication of the Poor Commons" that gave some insight into the conditions as existing at that time. It was written for the special benefit of the king, and it was meant for a criticism of ecclesiastical tenure. The writer, exaggerating likely for the sake of effect, showed that some of the royal chaplains held so many churches that they sometimes lost track of them. He cited the case of one of these chaplains riding out one day in company with his secretary. In the course of the jaunt they came upon a church beautifully situated and evidently very rich. The property immediately became an object of desire to the greedy chaplain, and he ordered his secretary to make note of it, evidently with the intention of soliciting it for the king. The secretary got out his record and was consulting it carefully when he suddenly exclaimed: "Why Sir, it is your own benefice." Among other things printed in this book the following is significant in regard to the point in question: [113]

> What reason is it that a surveyor of buildings or lands, an alchymist, or a goldsmith shall be rewarded with benefice upon benefice? Which of very reason ought to be committed to none other, but such who by godly learning and conversation were able and would apply themselves to walk amidst the flocks in godly example and purity of life. How great a number is it of them, that in the name of your Chaplains, may dispend yearly benefices, some of C, some CC, some CCC, some CCCC, some CCCCC, yea, some of a thousand marks a year.

VII. The Rise of a New Economic Order

A new economic organization of society based on commerce and industry had long been emerging in Western Europe before the sixteenth century. This new economic order of things had been rapidly supplanting the old feudal régime, based on agriculture, upon which the wealth of the church rested. More subtle forces consequently than the cupidity of a ruling class, the needs of military defense, or the interests of national unity were at work to overthrow the economic power of the clergy. These movements were direct, but the others were indirect. All the movements of change and progress that grew out of the rise of commerce and increase of industry militated against the rigid, static, old order of the church. Such were the growth of nationality and the decay of fedualism;

the increasing prestige of the middle classes and the declining importance of the aristocracy, lay and ecclesiastical; the growth of the town and the decline of the manor; the emerging ideal of mercantilism (statism) and the passing concept of papal cosmopolitanism; an advancing materialistic philosophy of life and a disappearing sense of other-worldliness. In the wake of an expanding commerce came the rise of new institutions and ideals—social, political, economic, intellectual, religious—that tended to displace and discredit the old feudal ecclesiastical scheme of things.

A revived commerce steadily expanding since the tenth century and the crusading activities had suddenly been revolutionized in extent and volume by the discovery of the new ocean routes of DeGama and Magellan. Since manufactured goods were necessary to meet the new and increasing demands of trade, the expansion of commerce was accompanied by the growth of industry. These movements had results, social, political, and economic, of the utmost importance all of which cannot be discussed at this point. In England particularly the new commercialism and industrialism resulted for one thing in an agrarian revolution characterized by the growth of large estates, sheep raising, and the transformation of subsistence farming to commercial agriculture. Favorable conditions and superior methods of breeding in England produced a fleece that gained a reputation abroad in fineness of quality. Trade and industry caused the population to gravitate from the manor to the town, and in the latter sprung up the powerful middle class merchant and manufacturer. The cloth industry in the Low Countries and in England itself increased the demand for wool. Again, labor shortage in the rural districts due to this urban competition and in particular to the ravages of the Black Death coupled with this increased demand for wool brought on the enclosure movement. Common lands and those of the small owner were either seized or bought for sheep runs, and the growth of the large landed estates went on apace. As a result, three middle class groups emerged; the merchant, the manufacturer, and the woolgrower, a new aristocracy of wealth whose interests ran athwart those of the church.

In the late fourteenth century towns like Somerset, Dorchester, Bristol, and Gloucester were already important woolen manufacturing centers. Devonshire and Cornwall were soon added to the group.[114] By the time of Edward IV, the manufacture of cloth in the south of England seems to have been quite general; for there was an insurrection of 4000 wool weavers in Suffolk, and a decided group consciousness had emerged among the industrial classes there.[115] Notice, for instance, the following "poem" written during this reign: [116]

> For the merchants come over our wools for to buy,
> Or else the cloth that is made thereof surely,
> Out of divers lands from beyond the sea,
> To have this merchandise into their own country,
> Therefor let not our wool be sold for nought,
> Neither our cloth, for they mist be sought.
> And in especial restrain straitly the wool,
> That the commons of the land may work to the full.

A very vivid picture of the rural situation portraying the enclosure movement with its evictions, desolation, and oppressive results was given by Sir Thomas More: [117]

> Your shepe that were wont to be so meke and tame, and so small eaters, are now become so great devourers and so wild that they eat up and swallow down the very men themselves. They consume, destroye, and devoure whole fields, howses, and cities. For looke in what

partes of the realme doth growe the fynest and there-
four dearest woll, there noblemen and gentlemen: yea,
and certain Abbotes, not contenting themselves with
the yerely revenues and profytes, that were wont to
grow to their forefathers . . . leave no ground for
tillage. Thei enclose all into pastures, thei throw downe
howses, thei pluck downe townes, and leave nothyng
standyng byt only the churche to be made a shepe-
howse. . . . And as though you loste no small quantity
of grounde by forestes, chases, laundes, and parkes,
those holy men turne all dwellinge places and all glebe
lande into desolation and wilderness. Therefore that
one coveteous and unsatiable cormaraunte and very
plage of his natyve contrey maye compasse aboute and
enclose many thousand akers together within one
hedge or pale, the husbandman be thrust oute of his
owne, or else be coneyne and fraude, or by violent oppression they be put besydes it, or by wronges and injuries thei be so weried that thei be compelled to cell
it al.

Thus by the time of Henry VII and Henry VIII the
spirit of commercialism had taken deep root and trade
and industry were bringing about important changes.
Trade was no longer in the hands of despised foreigners
and the merchant was no longer looked down on. On the
other hand the utmost importance and esteem were attached to such pursuits as may be seen in the Book of
Festivals which makes them a matter of religious concern:
"Ye shall pray for al true shypmen and merchauntes
wheresoever they be, on land or water, that God may
kepe them from peryeles and bryng them home in sauftie
with theyr goodes, shyppes, and merchaundyse to the
helpe, comfort, and profyte of thys realme." [118]
The foreign and domestic policies alike of Henry VII
were planned and prosecuted with a view to the promo-

tion of commerce and industry. Consolidation of the realm and centralization of the administration to insure order within the kingdom was his constant aim. It was for this reason that he set up the special Court of the Star Chamber as a part of the machinery to suppress disorder. A movement toward absolutism was the tendency that characterized his government. His foreign policy also was one of peace and conciliation promoted by marriage alliances and commercial treaties. By means of the latter he not only obtained better understandings in accustomed marts of trade like the Netherlands and Mediterranean cities, but he opened up new areas of trade like in the Baltic.[119]

The program mapped out by the close and careful Henry VII was followed out and enlarged on by the more open handed and presumptuous Henry VIII. The latter resorted to a policy of unrestricted trade in order to give a greater impetus to the expansion of the foreign market. He aimed to bring England into commercial contact with all countries. The Proclamation of Calais issued in 1527 aimed at "extending the wealth, increasing, and enriching of all England." It gave "all liberty and all license to all dealers in all kinds of wares to resort there, to buy, sell, and exchange their goods in any manner they saw fit." Warehouses were to be let to foreigners at reasonable rates; and commercial intercourse was to be conducted in such a manner as to secure the confidence and good will of the alien merchants. The administration of the town was thoroughly reorganized, new fortifications were built, and the harbor was deepened and improved.[120]

In the time of Henry VII the ships of England had already found their way to many parts of the Near East, going as far as Beirut, carrying from English ports kerseys, cotton cloths, calf skins, and woolen goods; they returned laden with silks, rhubarb, wines, olive oil, raw cotton, carpets, and spices.[121] The object of Henry VIII was to stimulate and increase the volume of this trade as well as that of other regions. Portugal had become the center of trade with the East, and England was rapidly being made one of the carriers between Lisbon and the north of Europe. Nothing demonstrates better the growth of English trade and the incidental influences of the middle classes than the development of the English navy. From the small beginnings under Henry VII, the second Tudor expanded a movement that has given him the name of founder of the British navy. By the end of his reign the fleet consisted of fifty-three ships with a gross tonnage of 24,500; one vessel, the Great Harry, being itself a ship of 1000 tons. This navy was manned with 7780 sailors.[122]

The importance of commerce between England and the Continent during this period, and the interlocking interests of manufacturer, trader, and woolgrower in keeping commercial enterprise open may be seen from an incident related by the contemporary writer, Edward Hall. Henry VIII declared a war against Charles V, and the emperor retaliated by declaring an embargo on English goods. The result in England was a serious industrial crisis threatening grave political consequences. The middle classes were so wrought up over the issue that the government took a hand in adjusting inconveniences and compensating for losses involved.[123]

This warre with the Emperor was displeasaunt both to the Merchauntes and Clothiers, for the Merchauntes durst not venture into Spaine, sith Aprill last past, and now was come the xi day of March, wherefore all brode Clothes, Kersies, and Cottons laye on their hands. Insomuch as when the Clothiers of Essex, Kent, Wiltshire, Suffolk, and other shires which use Clothmaking, brought clothes to Blackwell Hall, London, to be sold as thei were wont to do: fewe Merchauntes or none bought any cloth at all. When the Clothiers lacked sale, then they put from them their spinners, carders, thickers, and such others as live by clothwork-yng; which caused the people greatly to murmur, and especially in Suffolk, for yf the Duke of Norfolk had not wisely appeased them, no doubt but that thei had fallen to some riotous act.

In the Low Countries also trade and industry came to a complete standstill, discontent began to brew, and pressure was brought to bear by the middle classes to force a diplomatic understanding: [124]

If this warre was displeasaunt to many in Englande surely it was as muche or more displeasaunt to the tounes of Flaunders, Brabant, Hollonde, and Zelande, and in especial the tounes of Antwerp and Barrow, where the Martes were kept, and where the resort of Englishmen was, for thei sayed that their Martes were undoen, yf the Englishmen came not there, and yf there were no Marte their Shyppes, Hoyes, and Wag-gons might reste, and all Artificers, Hosts, Brokers might slepe, and so the people might fall into miserie and povertie, of these things daily complaints were made to the Lady Margaret, and the Emperor's coun-saile, which wisely pondered the complaints, and after long consultacion had, thei appointed certain ambas-sadors to go to the kynge of Englande, and to entreate for a truce.

VIII. The New Order versus the Old Régime

The result of expanding trade and growing industry was a tendency for the theory of mercantilism to develop and become fixed, and during this period one sees it in its incipiency. The old political and economic theory was the self-sufficiency of the manor—feudalism; the new ideal

was rapidly becoming the self-sufficiency of the nation—
statism. The one had tended to indefinite political disintegration, the other made for political unification. The
theory of mercantilism was to make the state strong by
making it rich; but wealth consisted in money rather
than in commodities. Hence a nation increased in wealth
only in so far as money flowed into it, so that a favorable balance of trade was sought by making exports exceed imports. Money must come into the state rather than
find its way out of the state. One of the outstanding fea-
tures of the mercantilist system was to check the outgo of
money from the realm. Again, mercantilism sought to
make the state strong by making it one. Unification and
centralization were sought. That unity became personi-
fied in the monarch. The stronger the monarch, the more
unified the nation; hence the tendency toward absolutism
made progress. A strong and unified state brought peace
within, which meant prosperity; and it brought protection
abroad, which also meant prosperity and insured foreign
credit. Nothing could aid in the expansion of trade abroad
and the encouragement of industries at home like a strong
monarchy.

Back of these movements tending to absolutism and statism were the new middle classes. The economic interests of
the new aristocracy of wealth made up of merchants, manu-
facturers, and woolgrowers depended on a unified nation
and a highly centralized administration. This alone would
assure them the possibility of establishing remunerative
industries at home, the expansion of commerce abroad,
and security both foreign and domestic. It was the middle classes that were back of the Tudor policy of absolutism in the early sixteenth century because a strong, highly
centralized government best promoted their ends. These
the Tudors soon took into their confidence and shared

the administration; Cromwell, the banker, took the place of Wolsey, the churchman. Any factors within the realm that tended to disintegrate and divide the kingdom would be discountenanced by the middle classes. If the attitude of the clergy threatened the unity of the commonwealth as it seemed to do, the churchmen were discredited. The new middle classes believed in strengthening the national defenses both naval and military, and if the wealth of the church could be used to that end they would approve of its confiscation. Much of the Tudor policy of centralizing the administration, trade expansion, conciliation by commercial treaties and dynastic marriages, and political absolutism may be attributed to the influence of the middle classes created by the rise and expansion of commerce.

The new middle classes not only favored a strong, co-ordinated, central government to protect their business interests at home and abroad, but they demanded a favorable balance of trade. The church and the monasteries were not only a breeding place of disloyalty, anti-nationalism, and divided allegiance, but the channels through which a great deal of money was taken from the realm. In a time of an emerging mercantilism this was resented. Government interference with the free course of trade may be traced back to the reign of Richard II.[125] The protection of the home producer, the increase of exports over imports, the influx and retention of money in the realm, a favorable balance of trade as an economic ideal and principle had already taken deep root on the eve of the Reformation in England. Bacon represented Morton advising Henry VII thus: "That our people be set at work in the arts and handicrafts, and the realm subsist more by itself, that idleness be avoided, and the draining of our treasure for foreign manufactures be stopped. But you are not to stop here only, but to provide further that whatsoever merchandise shall be brought from beyond the seas may be employed for the commodities of the land, whereby the king's stock of treasure may be sure to be kept free from being diminished by any overtrading with the foreigner." [126]

The contemporary historian, Hall, alluding to Henry VIII, said: "The king lyke a politike Prince, perceyved that the Merchaunt strangers, and in especial the Italians, Spaynards, and Portugales, daily brought Oade, Oyle, Sylk, Clothes of Gold, Velvet and other Merchaundise into the Realme, and therefore receyved ready money, which they ever delivered to other merchauntes by exchange and never employed the same monie on the Commodities of this Realme, so that the kyng was hindered in his custom outward, and also the commodities were not uttered, to the great hindrance of his subjectes." [127] Erasmus found out by personal experience how difficult it was to take money out of England. His private purse was closely scrutinized, and the export of any money outside of his immediate expenses was challenged.[128] Under the circumstances the middle classes would resent more and more the fact that vast sums of money were leaving the realm in the form of annates, Peter's pence, funds involved in appeals to Rome, and papal taxes in general.

The rise and growth of commerce and industry with the new and broad contacts they fostered, coupled with the passing of the purely agrarian feudal régime brought in a new philosophy of life as well as a new attitude toward the use of wealth. A materialistic and immediate outlook upon this world took the place of the idealistic clerical concept of a vague other-worldliness. The Renaissance had been teaching men that they were individuals, that they were living in a world to be enjoyed rather than to be endured, that worldly wealth was a means of hap-

piness. The new economic organization based on commerce
and industry had been teaching men wealth was increased only by the proper use of the wealth already acquired. The ideas of the importance of capital, investments,
interest, dividends, personal application, thrift were rapidly taking shape and playing their part in the acquisition
of wealth.

The church as one of the centers and strongholds of
the old type of wealth remained feudal in its economic
organization and failed to adapt itself to the new point of
view. The clash was inevitable. The continuance of ecclesiastical institutions existing largely for non-producing
monks and pilgrims, for the distribution of alms, and for
an outworn feudal system of tenantry was challenged
by men who by thrift, frugality, and industry had made
their way to a place of importance under the newer economic régime. The church fostered elements within itself,
that, so far as the increase of wealth was concerned, were
either non-productive or inefficiently productive. It encouraged idleness by its doles of gratuities to the poor, and
by nourishing monks and pilgrims. The church was failing to pay adequate returns on its investments. "Its splendid empty ceremonies, its broad waste places of ritual,
ceremony, and devotion, its recurring holidays, its galling
system of taxation to subsidize itself were little suited to
the new order of things." The *zeitgeist* was against it.
"The happy-go-lucky pilgrim seeking his holy relics at
healing shrines was being rapidly supplanted in the ideals
of the new utilitarian classes by self-responsible merchants looking for useful commodities to enrich the home
markets. The easy going monk who made productive
labor secondary or spurned it altogether was superseded
by the thrifty manufacturer and the grasping, energetic
landlord." The shifting of industry to town, cottage, and

country estate caused the manor and the monastery to decay. On the whole, the church little adapted itself to the changing circumstances of the times. The new middle classes listened with avidity to proposals for a more beneficial distribution of the property of the church. They began to figure more and more on shifting the burden of taxation from their own shoulders by encouraging the seizure of ecclesiastical endowments. Finally, they developed itching palms to acquire the wealth of the clergy in order to improve their own private fortunes.[129]

In the social, economic, and political upheaval caused by the rise of commerce and the growth of industry, the new middle classes must have wielded a powerful influence in the suppression of the monasteries and in the reorganization of the church as a whole. They rapidly arose in social and economic ascendancy and held important political place. Their influence was not only direct but also indirect. They coveted the wealth of the church and brought pressure to bear in the suppression of the monasteries. They were products of the new régime that for several centuries had been bringing the old order to corrosion and decay. In the Catholic Reformation that followed hard on the Protestant Revolt of the sixteenth century, the church adapted itself spiritually and morally to the spirit of the times by the work of the Council of Trent. At this time it was too late to make a similar adaptation along economic lines because the church had already been spoiled of most of its goods. While a commercial, industrial, and agrarian revolution had been taking place in England, especially in the fourteenth and fifteenth centuries, the church had clung to the old order of things. In the sixteenth century, economically the church ran athwart the new spirit of progress which proved its undoing.

NOTES AND REFERENCES

CHAPTER I

1. Mark x. 14.
2. Acts, iv. 34, 35, 36.
3. But see Vaughan, Life and Opinions of John de Wyclif, London 1831, Vol. I, 28-31.
4. Matthew xxiv. 14; Eusebius, Hist. Eccles., Book III, ch. 39, paragraph 5; Justin Martyr, Tryphone, passim.
5. Edwards, Transition of Early Christianity, p. 42.
6. Ayres, Source Book of Early Church History, p. 283.
7. Ibid. p. 339.
8. Epistle LII, Jerome to Nepotian, Nicene and Post-Nicene Fathers, Series 2, p. 92.
9. Ibid.
10. Matthew of Paris, Chronica Majora, Luard ed., London 1877, Vol. V, pp. 97-8.
11. Arnold, Select English Works of John Wycliffe, London 1869, Vol. III, p. 276.
12. Vaughan, op. cit., I, 32.
13. Legarde, Latin Church in the Middle Ages, New York 1915, p. 303.
14. Dudden, Gregory the Great, New York 1905, Vol. L, p. 296.
15. Ibid., I, 296-320.
16. Adams, Civilization During the Middle Ages, p. 208.
17. Adams, Constitutional History of England, p. 66; Tanner, Notitia Monastica, London 1744, Preface, p. vi.
18. Walsingham, Historia Anglicana, London 1863, Vol. II, p. 205.
19. Stevens, The Royal Treasury of England, London 1725, p. 196.
20. Milman, History of Latin Christianity, New York 1896, Vol. IV, p. 147.
21. Matthew of Paris, Chronicles of England, London 1850, Vol. II, p. 265, III, 213, 230.
22. Froude, History of England, Vol. I, p. 44, London 1890.
23. Roger of Hovedon, Annals, London 1857, Vol. I, p. 186.
24. Matthew of Paris, Chron. Majora V. 98.
25. Heeren strongly defends this view on the thesis that: "Die Kreuzzüge werden eine Hauptquelle der bereicherung, sowohl für den Romischen Hof, als für der Clericus uberhaupt," Werke, II, 149-154; Michaud, on the other hand, seems to think that the clergy had already reached their limit of wealth when the Crusades opened, and during this movement sustained an actual loss due to increased taxation by the papacy collected to carry on the Holy Wars, Crusades, III, 306-308.

26. Trevelyan, England in the Age of Wycliffe, London 1920, 29.
27. Arnold, op. cit., I, 202, 283; II, 180, 288; III, 199, 397.
28. Gregory of Tours, History of the Franks, Brehaut trans. p. 75.
29. Liljegren, Fall of the Monasteries, Leipzig 1924, p. 15.
30. It is impossible to determine the exact territorial area of the knight's fee. It was an agrarian unit of land measurment of which there was no fixed standard. It consisted of a number of hides of land ranging from two to fourteen, though the normal knight's fee embraced five hides of land. At the time of the Conquest and long after, the knight's fee was regarded as an estate worth twenty pounds sterling yearly rental, and consisted of about 120 acres of land stocked with cattle, and equipped with implements. Round, Feudal England, p. 393.
31. Pearson, English History in the Fourteenth Century, London 1878, Vol. II, p. 496.
32. Roger, History of Agriculture and Prices in England, Oxford 1882, Vol. IV, p. 133.
33. Italian Relation in England, Camden Society Publications, p. 38.
34. Milman, op. cit., IV, 364.
35. Herbert, History of England under Henry VIII, London 1872, 563.
36. Ibid., 548.
37. This document may be found in numerous collections and separate editions: Somer, Tracts, London 1809, I, 42; Harleian Miscellany, London 1808, I, 217; Foxe, Acts and Monuments, London 1846; IV, Part II, 659; Furnivall, A Supplication for the Beggars written about the year 1529 by Simon Fish, London 1871; Arber, Simon Fish, A Supplication for the Beggars, London 1878.
38. Foxe. op. cit., IV, Part II, 657.
39. Tanner, op. cit., Preface, p. xxxiii.
40. Calendar of Letters and Papers of Henry VIII, London 1862, Vol. XIII, No. 575; Fiddes, Life of Wolsey, London 1724, p. 100; Strype, Ecclesiastical Memorials, Oxford 1822, Vol. I, pp. 8-9.
41. Italian Relation in England, op. cit., p. 20.
42. Ibid., p. 40.
43. Strype, Memorials of Cranmer, London 1852, I, 51; II, 271.
44. Speed, History of Great Britain, London 1614, p. 778 (100).
45. Yorkshire Archeological Society, Record Series, 1912, Vol. 47, p. 162ff.
46. Ibid., p. 51.
47. Archaelogia Cantiana, Vol. XXIX, pp. 47-84.
48. Calendar of Letters and Papers, op. cit., XIII, No. 394.
49. State Papers of Great Britain, London 1830, Vol. I, Part II, p. 620.
50. Calendar of Letters and Papers, op. cit., XIII, Nos. 779, 764, 1085.
51. Yorkshire Arch. Soc., op. cit., vol. 47, p. 55.
52. This is almost a standardized form used by the commissioners in the suppression of the monasteries. It illustrates vividly the far flung holdings of so many of the abbeys. See: Calendar of Letters and Papers, op. cit., XIII, Nos. 541, 575, 660, 764, 776, 779, 1155, 1222.
53. Gee and Hardy, Documents Illustrative of English Church History, London 1914, p. 320.

54. Matthew, English Works of Wycliff, London 1880, p. 92.

55. Stow, Annales of England, London 1600, p. 964; Speed, op. cit., 778; Herbert of Cherbury, op. cit., 564; Stevens, Royal Treasury, op. cit., 211.

56. Fuller, History of Great Britain, Oxford 1845, Vol. III, 329.

57. Burnet, History of the Reformation in England, 1865, Vol. I, 429.

58. Geikie, English Reformation, New York 1897, p. 262; Gasquet, Henry VIII and the Monasteries, London 1888, II, 348, 533-536.

59. Italian Relation in England, op. cit., p. 20.

60. Ibid., p. 40; Fuller, op. cit., III, p. 322.

61. Stow, op. cit., 694; Herbert of Cherbury, op. cit., 564; Sinclair, History of the Revenue, London 1803, III, p. 182; Stevens, op. cit., p. 213; Fuller, op. cit., III, 374; Tanner, op. cit., passim; Calendar of Letters and Papers, op. cit., X, No. 1238.

62. Stow, op. cit., 964.

63. Hill, English Monasticism, London 1867, pp. 500-501.

64. Calendar of Letters and Papers, op. cit., XIII, Nos. 393, 407, 484, 642; XIV, No. 3; Yorkshire Archeological Society, op. cit., Vol. 48, pp. 41, 45, 47, 48, 53, 56.

65. Speed, op. cit., 787-800.

66. Herbert of Cherbury, op. cit., p. 626.

67. Stevens, op. cit., p. 180; Tanner, op. cit., p. i; Burnet, op. cit., Vol. I, p. 430.

68. Sinclair, op. cit., Vol. I, p. 182.

69. Stevens, op. cit., p. 373; Rogers, op. cit., Vol. IV, p. 29.

70. Stow, op. cit., p. 996.

71. Rogers, op. cit., IV, 20.

72. Gasquet, op. cit., II, 438, 533-535.

73. Speed, op. cit., 802.

74. Ibid., 801.

75. Rogers, op. cit., Vol. IV, p. 89; Gibbins, Industry in England, See map, p. 196; Killburn, Survey of Kent, London 1659, pp. 6-7.

76. Taxatio Ecclesiastica Angliae et Walliae Auctoritate P. Nicholai IV. c. A. D. 1291, London 1882.

77. See Map, Valor Ecclesiasticus, London 1810, Vol. I, front.

78. Ibid., passim., pp. 1-7.

79. Ibid., p. 7.

80. Ibid., pp. 7-16.

81. Ibid., p. 16.

82. Christ's Church Chronicle (1414) gives this as 2467; Speed, 2489; Tanner, 2387; Strype, 2582.

83. Froude, op. cit., Vol. I, p. 46.

84. Powell, East Anglia Rising, Cambridge 1896, pp. 121-5.

85. Rogers, op. cit., IV, 248ff.

86. Stevens, op. cit., 196, 260.

87. Stow, op. cit., p. 94.

88. Latimer, Sermons, p. 40, Arber ed.

89. Valor Eccl., Vol. VI, p. 13.

90. Gibbins, op. cit., p. 196.

CHAPTER II   . . . .

1. Perry, History of the Church of England, London 1890, I, 346f.
2. Roger of Wendover, Rogeri de Wendover Chronica, London 1842, IV, 200; Matthew of Paris, op. cit., IV, 518-538, 554-561, 580-585, 594-600; Matthew of Westminster, Flowers of History, London 1852, II, 275f., 277; Walter of Coventry, Historical Collections, Stubbs ed., London 1872, II, 277-299; Speed, op. cit., 514; Collier, Ecclesiastical History of Great Britain, London 1852, II, 490.
3. Matthew of Paris, op. cit., IV, 539-533, V, 559; M. Westminster, op. cit., II, 196, 226, 283, 284; Perry, op. cit., I, 384f.
4. Walsingham, Historia Anglicana, London 1863, I, 461.
5. Matthew of Paris, op. cit., V, 539; Collier op. cit., II, 463.
6. Matthew of Westminster, op. cit., II, 260; Higden, Polychronicon Monachi Cestrensis, Lumby ed., London 1882, VIII, 190.
7. Matthew of Paris, op. cit., V, 393.
8. Grosseteste, Roberti Grosseteste Epistolae, Luard ed., London 1861, No. 117, p. 338; Collier op. cit., II, 484.
9. Ranke, History of the Popes, London 1891, I, 28; Tout, History of Edward I, London 1901, I, 142.
10. Roger of Wendover, op. cit., IV, 124.
11. Speed, op. cit., p. 514.
12. Gee and Hardy, op. cit., p. 91.
13. Capes, English Church in the 14th and 15th Centuries, London 1900, 85-86, 99.
14. Matthew of Paris, op. cit., III, 328; Fuller, op. cit., II, 167; Collier, op. cit., II, 450.
15. Matthew of Paris, op. cit., III, 332, V, 245, 404.
16. Ibid.
17. Fuller, op. cit., II, 167.
18. Ibid., V, 404; Annales de Burton, Luard ed., London 1864, 251. Roger of Wendover, op. cit., IV, 206.
19. Matthew of Paris, op. cit., V. 532, 558; Fuller, op. cit., II, 168.
20. Matthew of Paris, op. cit., V, 458, 470, 521; Royal and Other Letters of Henry III, Shirley ed., London 1862, No. 331.
21. Matthew of Paris, op. cit., V, 627, 630, 680, 682.
22. Ibid., III, 332; Speed, op. cit., 521.
23. Matthew of Paris, op. cit., V, 404.
24. Ibid., III, 329.
25. Ibid.
26. Ibid.
27. Ibid.
28. Ibid.
29. Ibid., III, 330.
30. Ibid., V, 40, 521.
31. Ibid., III, 332.
32. Ibid., V, 524, 558; Collier, op. cit., II, 450; Perry, op. cit., I, 321.
33. Matthew of Paris, op. cit., III, 331.
34. Ibid.
35. Ibid., 331, V, 245.   ,
36. Ibid., III, 332, V, 245; Speed, op. cit., p. 521.

37. Matthew of Paris, op. cit., III, 334.
38. Ibid., IV, 8, V, 245.
39. Ibid., IV, 441; Annales de Burton, op. cit., 284; Gasquet, Henry III and the Church, London 1905, p. 340.
40. Matthew, English Works of John Wyclif (1880), pp. 22, 64, 66; Arnold, op. cit., III, 397. Speed, op. cit., 525.
41. Matthew of Paris, Chronicles of England, Bohn ed., London 1850, III, 332.
42. Matthew of Paris, Chronica Majora, Luard ed., London 1877, IV, 32, 55, 84, V. 38; Roger of Wendover, op. cit., IV, 230, 232.
43. Matthew of Paris, op. cit., IV, 32.
44. Ibid., IV, 284; Matthew of Westminster, op. cit., II, 223.
45. Matthew of Paris, op. cit., IV, 441.
46. Ibid., V, 355.
47. Grosseteste, op. cit., Epistle No. 131, p. 442; Collier, op. cit., II, 501.
48. Matthew of Paris, op. cit., IV, 441; Matthew of Westminster, op. cit., II, 241.
49. Matthew of Paris, op. cit., V, 544.
50. Matthew of Paris, Chronicles of England, op. cit., III, 332; Matthew of Westminster, op. cit., II, 264.
51. Roger of Wendover, op. cit., IV, 240; Matthew of Paris, Chronica Majora, III, 473-484.
52. Roger of Wendover, op. cit., IV, 228-242; Walter of Coventry, op. cit., 277-299; Collier, op. cit., II, 443.
53. Roger of Wendover, op. cit., IV, 240f.
54. Ibid., IV, 232.
55. Ibid., IV, 232-233.
56. Ibid.
57. Ibid.
58. Ibid., IV, 228f.
59. Ibid.
60. Ibid., IV, 234; Annales de Burton, op. cit., p. 94.
61. Roger of Wendover, op. cit., IV, 228f.
62. Matthew of Paris, Chronica Majora, V, 355.
63. Ibid., IV, 403, 636, V, 36, 545.
64. Matthew of Paris, Chronicles of England, Bohn ed., III, 285-287, 291, 332, 334, 340; Knighton, Chronicon Henrici Knighton, Lumby ed., London 1899, Vol. I, 238; Perry, op. cit., I, 363.
65. Matthew of Paris Chronica Majora, Luard ed., V, 548, 592.
66. Annales de Burton, op. cit., p. 303.
67. Matthew of Paris, Chronica Majora, IV, 403-405; Matthew of Westminster, op. cit., II, 259.
68. Matthew of Paris, Chronica Majora, IV, 404.
69. Ibid., IV, 403, V, 545.
70. Ibid., IV, 636.
71. Cross, History of England and Greater Britain, p. 153.
72. Gee and Hardy, op. cit., p. 178.
73. Matthew of Paris, Chronica Majora, IV, 636.
74. Ibid.
75. Ibid., IV, 636, V, 36.

76. Ibid., V, 37.
77. Ibid., V, 119-124.
78. Ibid., V, 122.
79. Ibid., V, 120
80. Ibid., V, 123.
81. Ibid.
82. Ibid., V, 123f.
83. Ibid.
84. Ibid., V, 125.
85. Roger of Wendover, op. cit., IV, 120f.
86. "Let the zeal of the church universal and of the holy see of Rome move you. Because if all this universal oppression should be imposed, we fear that a general secession would be imminent, which God forbid"—Walter of Coventry, op. cit., II, 277-299; Roger of Wendover, op. cit., IV, 122.
87. Perry, op. cit., I, 343f. (document given).
88. Ibid.
89. Ibid.
90. Matthew of Paris, Chronica Majora, IV, 440-444.
91. Ibid.
92. Ibid.
93. Ibid.
94. Ibid.; Matthew of Westminster, op. cit., II, 246.
95. Matthew of Paris, Chronica Majora, IV, 478.
96. Ibid., IV, 503.
97. Ibid., V, 233.
98. Ibid., V, 393.
99. Ibid., V, 355.
100. Ibid., V, 233.
101. Ibid.
102. Ibid., V, 388; Grosseteste, op. cit., Epistle No. 128, p. 442; Wyclif, De Civili Dominio, Wyclif Society Publications, 1900, Vol. I, p. 348f.; Perry, op. cit., II, 346.
103. Grosseteste, op. cit., Epistle No. 128; Matthew of Paris, op. cit., V, 391, 401; Annales de Burton, op. cit., 312.
104. See Luard, Grosseteste, op. cit., Introduction, passim.
105. Matthew of Paris, op. cit., V, 393.
106. Ibid., V, 405.
107. Ibid.; Grosseteste, op. cit., Epistle No. 131, p. 443.
108. Ibid.
109. Matthew of Paris, op. cit., V, 391; Grosseteste, op. cit., Epistle No. 94, p. 341.
110. Matthew of Paris, op. cit., V, 390f.; Matthew of Westminster, op. cit., II, 261.
111. Matthew of Paris, op. cit., V, 554.
112. Ibid., V, 400-405; Matthew of Westminster, op. cit., II, 275ff.
113. Matthew of Paris, op. cit., V, 97-98.
114. Ibid., V, 405.
115. Knighton, op. cit., I, 230-233.
116. Chronicles of the Reign of Edward I and II, Stubbs ed., London 1882, Vol. I, p. 197.

117. Grosseteste, op. cit., Epistle No. 130, p. 440; Matthew of Paris, op. cit., V, 186.

118. Gesta Mon. S. Albani, I, 309.

119. Matthew of Westminster, op. cit., II, 158ff.

120. Matthew of Paris, op. cit., V, 457, 575, 623.

121. Matthew of Westminster, op. cit., II, 275; Collier, op. cit., II, 498, 602; Perry, op. cit., I, 347, 349.

122. Matthew of Westminster, II, 196, 261; Roger of Wendover, op. cit., IV, 122.

123. Tout, Advanced History of Great Britain, p. 166ff.

124. Matthew of Paris, op. cit., III, 389.

125. Ibid., IV, 100.

126. Matthew of Westminster, op. cit., II, 259-262.

127. Ibid., II, 275, 284.

128. Matthew of Paris, op. cit., III, 482, IV, 420; Matthew of Westminster, op. cit., II, 241; Gesta Mon. S. Albani, I, 384.

129. Annales de Burton, op. cit., 239.

130. Matthew of Paris, op. cit., IV, 420.

131. Roger of Wendover, op. cit., IV, 124.

132. Ibid., IV, 114f.; Matthew of Westminster, op. cit., II, 149; Walter of Coventry, op. cit., II, 275; Perry, op. cit., II, 143.

133. Roger of Wendover, op. cit., IV, 118f.

134. Ibid., Gasquet, Henry III and the Church, op. cit., 80f.; Collier, op. cit., II, 433; Perry, op. cit., II, 318.

135. Roger of Wendover, op. cit., IV, 200f.

136. Ibid., IV, 201.

137. Ibid.

138. Matthew of Paris, Chronica Majora, III, 395.

139. For the accounts of Otho's second visit see Matthew of Paris op. cit., III, 395 to IV, 84; Higden, op. cit., VIII, 211f.; Knighton, op. cit., I, 227f.; Annales de Burton, op. cit., 107f.

140. Matthew of Paris, op. cit., III, 483.

141. Ibid., IV, 414.

142. Ibid., III, 413, 568.

143. Ibid., IV, 84.

144. Ibid., IV, 10.

145. Ibid., IV, 6, 9.

146. Ibid., IV, 84.

147. Ibid., IV, 5.

148. Ibid., IV, 29ff.

149. Matthew of Paris, op. cit., IV, 38.

150. Ibid., IV, 39.

151. Ibid., III, 397, 486, 526, IV, 30, 82, 84.

152. Ibid., IV, 42, 60.

153. Ibid., IV, 137, 160.

154. Ibid., IV, 440f., 526-538.

155. Ibid., IV, 284, 368f.; Matthew of Westminster, op. cit., II, 222.

156. Matthew of Paris, op. cit., IV, 368-369.

157. Ibid., IV, 379, 416.

158. Ibid., IV, 379.

159. Ibid., IV, 419, 440f., 478, 504.

160. Ibid., IV, 311-316, 418f., 440f., 504, 526f., 554-559, 580-585, 594-598, 617-623.

161. Speed, op. cit., p. 538 (73).

162. Matthew of Paris, op. cit., IV, 312, 590.

163. Ibid., IV, 419f., 534, 554, 560.

164. Ibid., IV, 419.

165. Ibid., IV, 420.

166. Ibid., IV, 422.

167. Ibid.

168. Ibid., IV, 554, 558.

169. Ibid., IV, 552, 561; Matthew of Westminster, op. cit., II, 260.

170. Matthew of Paris, op. cit., IV, 10, 15, 19, 580, 595; Annales de Burton, op. cit., 68, 73.

171. Matthew of Paris, op. cit., V, 184.

172. Matthew of Westminster, II, 283.

173. Matthew of Paris, op. cit., IV, 526ff.

174. Ibid., IV, 536.

175. Ibid., IV, 526f.; Annales de Burton, op. cit., p. 265.

176. Matthew of Paris, op. cit., IV, 526

177. Matthew of Westminster, op. cit., II, 284.

178. Matthew of Paris, op. cit., IV, 536.

179. Ibid., IV, 534.

180. Ibid., IV, 532.

181. Ibid., IV, 530.

182. Ibid., IV, 531.

183. Matthew of Paris, op. cit., IV, 591.

184. Ibid., IV, 591-595.

185. Ibid.

186. Ibid., IV, 561; Matthew of Westminster, op. cit., II, 264-5.

187. Ibid., IV, 526, 538, 554, 561.   ?

188. Ibid., IV, 561; Matthew of Westminster, op. cit., II, 264.

189. Annales de Burton, op. cit., p. 298; Matthew of Paris, op. cit., IV, 274, 282.

190. Ibid., IV, 324f.

191. Ibid., V, 373f.

192. Ibid., V, 457, 470; Annales de Burton, op. cit., p. 339.

193. Annales de Burton, p. 349; Matthew of Paris, V, 457, 470; Gesta Mon. S. Albani, p. 380.

194. Matthew of Paris, op. cit., V, 470.

195. Ibid., V, 458.

196. Ibid. V, 473, 498, 531.

197. Ibid., V, 515.

198. Ibid., V, 524f.

199. Ibid., V, 526; Annales de Burton, op. cit., 387-390.

200. Matthew of Paris, op. cit., V, 520ff.

201. Ibid., V, 623f.; The Annals of Burton gives this amount as 135,000 marks, op. cit., p. 390; the Gesta Monachi S. Albani places it at 250,000 pounds sterling, op. cit., I, 383.

202. Matthew of Paris, op. cit., V, 595; Gesta Monachi S. Albani, I, 383.

203. Matthew of Paris, op. cit., V, 623.
204. Ibid., V, 627.

CHAPTER III

1. See Chap. I, p. 3-4.
2. Jerome, op. cit., Epistle No. 31.
3. Ammianus Marcellinus, History, Book XXVII, p. 441, Bohn ed.
4. Adams, Civilization During the Middle Ages, p. 205.
5. Knighton, Chronicon Henrici Knighton, London 1899, I, 232.
6. Paradiso, XX, 19; Inferno, XIX, 115.
7. Sabatier, Saint Francis of Assisi, p. 29.
8. Arnold, Select English Works of John Wycliffe, 1869, III, 514.
9. See Knighton, op. cit., I, 346-7; Peckham, Registrum Epistolarum, Vol. II, 635, 638; Annales de Burton, op. cit., p. 422; Tanner, op. cit., p. xxxiv.
10. Matthew of Paris, Chronicles of England, Bohn ed., II, 153.
11. See document in Collier, op. cit., II, 126f.; note articles, 18, 13, 14, 15, 19, 20.
12. Annales de Burton, op. cit., p. 422.
13. Adams and Stevens, Select Documents of English Constitutional History, New York 1901, p. 66.
14. Tout, History of Edward I, London 1901, p. 57; Tanner, op. cit., p. ix; Bede, History, Stevenson ed., p. 659.
15. Adams and Stevens, op. cit., pp. 68-96; Tout, op. cit., 121-134.
16. Cunningham, Growth of English Industry and Commerce, 5th ed. 1910, Vol. I, 270-298; Stubbs, Constitutional History of England, 4th ed., 1896, Vol. II, 164, 201, 398, 431.
17. Stubbs, op. cit., II, 200-201.
18. Peckham, op. cit., Preface, Vol. I, Introd. lxi, 635, 638.
19. Knighton, op. cit., I, 346.
20. Ibid., I, 347.
21. Ibid., I, 227-229.
22. Arnold, op. cit., III, 514.
23. Traill, Social England, London 1902, Vol. II, p. 235.
24. Knighton, op. cit., II, 2; Geraldi Cambrensis, Opera, London 1867, Vol. IV, pp. 30-32; Patent Rolls 1414, 283, 294, 1413, 23, 73; New, History of the Alien Priories in England, University of Chicago Press, 1914, p. 85.
25. New, op. cit., 53, 56; Speed, op. cit., 628.
26. New, op. cit., 75, 76, 77.
27. New, op. cit., 58.
28. Ibid., 9.
29. Ibid., 45-46.
30. Matthew of Paris, Chronica Majora, IV, 288.
31. Patent Rolls 1395, 5.
32. New, op. cit., 55.
33. Ibid., 67.
34. Ibid., 76.
35. Taswell-Langmead, Constitutional Hist. of England, 325; Froude, History of England, London 1890, Vol. II, pp. 12-15.

36. Walsingham, Historia Anglicana, London 1863, II, 4; Cheney, Readings in English History, New York 1908, 260; Speed, op. cit., 595 (19).

37 Walsingham, op. cit., 275, 320; Collier, op. cit., III, 148.

38. Lechler, John Wycliffe and his English Precursors, London 1878, Vol. II, p. 225.

39. Walsingham, op. cit., I, 322, 469ff., II, 1-11; Knighton, op. cit., II, 141; Powell, Rising in East Anglia in 1381, Cambridge Univ. Press, 1896, pp. 11, 34; Speed, op. cit., 295; Capes, English Church in the 14th and 15th Centuries, London 1900, p. 134.

40. English Historical Review, Vol. XI (1896), p. 319.

41. Walsingham, op. cit., 321; Capes, op. cit., 136; Taswell-Langmead, op. cit., 326; Knighton, op. cit., II, 151; Lechler, op. cit., II, 225.

42. Stubbs, op. cit., II, 460.

43. Wyclif, Dominio Divino, Wyclif Society Publications, 1896, Ch. II, pp. 8-15; Wyclif, De Civili Dominio, Wyclif Society Publications, 1890, Vol. I, Ch. 1, pp. 1-8.

44. Matthew, English Works of John Wyclif Hitherto Unprinted, London 1880, pp. 282-296.

45. Arnold, op. cit., III, 341.

46. The Scriptural passages used against the idea of endowment are usually the three following: Numbers xviii. 20; Deuteronomy xviii. 3; Ezekiel xliii. 28.

47. Wyclif, Tractatus de Ecclesia, Wyclif Society Publications, 1886, pp. 359ff.; Arnold, op. cit., III, 340.

48. Ibid.

49. Wyclif, De Ecclesia, op. cit., 177, 191, 251, 290ff.

50. Matthew, op. cit., pp. 282-296.

51. Ibid.,

52. Ibid., pp. 359ff.

53. Wyclif, Dialogus, sive speculum Ecclesia Militantis, Wyclif Society Publications, 1896, pp. 1-4.

54. Ibid., pp. 7-11.

55. Ibid., p. 16.

56. Ibid., pp. 11-19.

57. Ibid., pp. 19-31.

58. Ibid., pp. 33-34.

59. Ibid., pp. 34-48.

60. Ibid., pp. 51-62.

61. Ibid., pp. 62-63.

62. Ibid., pp. 84-85.

63. Arnold, op. cit., I, 87, 308; Matthew, op. cit., pp. 164-179; De Simonia, Wyclif Society Publications, 1898, p. 70; Opera Minora, Wyclif Society Publications, 1913, p. 51.

64. Matthew, op. cit., pp. 168-177; Arnold, op. cit., I, 75, 446.

65. Matthew, op. cit., p. 176.

66. Ibid., pp. 62, 72, 97, 184, 237, 249, 435.

67. Matthew, op. cit., 168-177; De Civili Dominio, op. cit., II, 1-26; De Ecclesia, op. cit., 169, 189f., 384.

68. Matthew, op. cit., 164f.; Arnold, op. cit., III, 282, 292.

69. Arnold, op. cit., III, 283.

70. Ibid., III, 289.
71. De Simonia, op. cit., 70-84.
72. Ibid., p. 78; Arnold, op. cit., III, 283.
73. Ibid.
74. Matthew, op. cit., 33, 35, 276, 280, 213, 496.
75. Ibid., 62, 184.
76. Ibid.
77. Ibid., 63.
78. Ibid., 62.
79. Ibid., 171; Arnold, op. cit., III, 282.
80. Ibid.
81. Ibid., III, 287-288.
82. De Simonia, op. cited, passim; see also, Matthew, op. cit., 237-245.
83. De Simonia, op. cit., 2.
84. Ibid., p. 16.
85. De Simonia, op. cit., pp. 5, 8, 37, 38, 44, 82; De Ecclesia, op. cit., 192.
86. Arnold, op. cit., 226, 278, 488; Matthew, op. cit., 377; De Simonia, op. cit., p. 4.
87. De Simonia, op. cit., 27-37, 40-45, 62-70; Matthew, op. cit., p. 62.
88. Arnold, op. cit., III, 226.
89. Ibid., III, 276.
90. Ibid., III, 277; Matthew, op. cit., p. 129.
91. Arnold, op. cit., III, 255, 299, 366, 400; Matthew, op. cit., pp. 1-27.
92. Arnold, op. cit., III, 299, 384f.
93. Ibid., III, 300.
94. Ibid., III, 299.
95. Wyclif, De Civili Dominio, Wyclif Society Publications, 1900, 4 volumes.
96. Ibid., Vol. II, pp. 14-15.
97. Arnold, op. cit., III, 297ff.
98. Ibid., III, 298, 301.
99. Matthew, op. cit., pp. 116-133.
100. Arnold, op. cit., III, pp. 213-218.
101. Ibid., III, 216.
102. De Civili Dominio, op. cit., II, 26-58.
103. Ibid., I, 96-103.
104. Ibid., II, 26-58; De Ecclesia, op. cit., 69-82; Dialogus, op. cit., 68 De Officio Regis, Wyclif Society Publications, 1887, pp. 1-90.
105. Walsingham, Ypodigma Neustriae, London 1876, p. 324.
106. Dialogus, op. cit., p. 65.
107. Ibid., p. 72.
108. Ibid., 67-78.
109. Matthew, op. cit., pp. 276-280.
110. De Simonia, op. cit., pp. 8-9, 27-28, 40-45, 54-70.
111. Matthew, op. cit., 62, 82.
112. Ibid., 167, 389; Arnold, op. cit., I, 141, 199; Vaughan, op. cit., II, 248, 252ff.
113. De Simonia, op. cit., 44-45; De Ecclesia, op. cit., 328-359.

"Sed longe melius est quod rex et regnum aufferat bonum suum quod spoliant tam multipliciter depauperantes regnum." Wyclif, De Officio Regis, op. cit., p. 164.

Anyone who is able may piously do away with the whole system of endowment of the clergy, and the king of England, as not subject to Caesar ought to take it upon himself to correct the abuses of endowment by restoring the church to its primitive purity foolishly forsaken by the clergy of an earlier age. Ibid., 211ff.

The heirs of those who made endowments should be interested in the proper uses of such endowments. Christ drove the worldly merchants from the temple. This should serve as an example to the king. The greater part of endowments should be forfeited to the crown which has power over the clergy and its wealth. Old Testament kings were known to have deposed priests, as Solomon did Abiather the high priest, because the stability of the kingdom demanded it. The church has so declined because of its wealth that the penalty of withdrawing endowments would not be too heavy a one. It is the duty of the king to take the initiative in this procedure. Wyclif, De Civili Dominio, op. cit., IV, 454ff.

114. Matthew, op. cit., 121, 132-139, 286f.; Arnold op. cit., III, 216, 297f., 301, 303, 397, 400.

115. Walsingham, Historia Anglicana, op. cit., II, 32, 53.

116. Ibid., II, 65, 108, 157.

117. Tyrell, History of England, III, 497.

118. Walsingham, op. cit., II, 51, 53, 55, 56, 216, 299, 317.

119. Knighton, op. cit., II, 175, 177, 190, 282; Adam of Usk, Chronicon Adae de Usk, 1307-1421, London 1904, p. 141; Henry, History of Great Britain, 1800, Vol. VIII, pp. 72-79.

120. Knighton, op. cit., II, 183, 260; Adam of Usk, op. cit., 140; Collier, op. cit., III, 298; Speed, op. cit., 615 (23).

121 Adam of Usk, op. cit., p. 141.

122. Collier, op. cit., 294-298.

123. Walsingham, op. cit., II, 244, 247, 299, 282.

124. Tyrell, op. cit., III, 1050.

125. Ibid., III, 1056; Knighton, op. cit., II, 264.

126. Walsingham, op. cit., II, 159, 216, 291;

127. Wyclif, De Civili Dominio, op. cit., II, 7; Stubbs, op. cit., II, 440; Capes, op. cit., p. 97.

128. Walsingham, Historia Anglicana, II, 139f.; Walsingham, Ypodigma Neustriae, p. 367f.

129. Walsingham, Historia Anglicana, II, 109, 141.

130. Ibid., II, 215-217; Walsingham, Ypodigma Neustriae, 267.

131. Walsingham, Historia Anglicana, II, 216-217.

132. Walsingham, Ypodigma Neustriae, 391; Gee and Hardy, op. cit., p. 133.

133. Walsingham, Historia Anglicana, II, 259, 265; Ypodigma Neustriae, 403, 409.

134. Walsingham, Historia Anglicana, II, 265-267; Sinclair, op. cit., I, 140; Speed, op. cit., 619 (42); Collier, III, 265.

135. Walsingham, Historia Anglicana, II, 282-283; Capes, op. cit., p. 182.

136. Blunt, Reformation of the Church of England, London 1874, Vol. I, 284 (note).

137. Speed, op. cit., 619 (42).

138. Ibid., 626 (18); Collier, op. cit., III, 303.

139. Quoted by Speed, op. cit., 626 (18).

140. Collier, op. cit., III, 302.

141. Walsingham, Historia Anglicana, II, 291, 298-9, 326.

142. Strype, Ecclesiastical Memorials relating to Religion under Henry VIII, Oxford, 1822, Vol. I, 212, II, 188-193.

143. Fuller, op. cit., II, 390; Summers, Lollards of Chiltern Hills, London 1906, p. 65.

144. Summers, op. cit., 65.

145. Fuller, op. cit., II, 469.

146. Ibid., II, 452; Collier, op. cit., III, 388; Summers, op. cit., 62.

147. See Henry, History of Great Britain, 3rd ed., 1900, Vol. X, Book V, section 2 entire.

148. Peacock, Repressor of Overmuch Blaming of the Clergy, Babington ed., London 1860, Vol. II, pp. 320f., 334-347, 350-366; Ibid., Introduction; Perry, op. cit., II, 471-483; Collier, op. cit., III, 388f.

149. Peacock, op. cit., Part III, entire.

150. Ibid., Introduction p. xx; Collier, op. cit., III, 393.

151. Peacock, op. cit., Introduction, note 6.

152. Ibid., I, 127.

153. Ibid.

154. Ibid., I, 1-4.

155. Ibid., I, 275ff.

156. Ibid., II. 371

157 Summers, op. cit., 74-159; Trevelyan, England in the Age of Wycliffe, London 1920, p. 347f.; Vaughan, op. cit., II, 348f.; Strype, op. cit. I, pp. 1ff.

158. Foxe, Acts and Monuments, London 1846, IV, 209-215.

160. Ibid., IV, 241.

161. Strype, op. cit., 113-133; II, 50-65.

162. Calendar of Letters and Papers, Henry VIII, op. cit., Vol. I, 3289, p. 373.

163. Strype, op. cit., I, 247ff.

164. Ibid., II, 182.

CHAPTER IV

1. Gee and Hardy, Documents Illustrative of English Church History, London 1914, pp. 149, 179, 201.

2. Ibid., p. 148.

3. Ibid., 146-148.

4. Lagarde, Latin Church in the Middle Ages, New York 1915, 304-318.

5. Ibid., 304-344.

6. Ibid., 343.

7. Ranke, History of the Popes, London 1891, Vol. I, p. 306.

8. Lagarde, op. cit., 343; Milman, History of Latin Christianity, New York 1896, p. 51.

9. Matthew of Paris, Chronicles of England, Bohn ed., III, 101.

10. Chronicles of the Reigns of Edward I and Edward II, Stubbs ed., London 1882, Vol. II, pp. 197-199.

11. Legarde, op. cit., 343.

12. Roger of Hovedon, Annals, Bohn ed., London 1857, Vol. II, 337; Matthew of Paris, op. cit., II, 240; Matthew of Westminster, Flowers of History, London 1852, p. 226; Strype, Ecclesiastical Memorials relating to Religion under Henry VIII, Oxford 1888, Vol. II, p. 161; Ranke, op. cit., I, 43f.; Milman, op. cit., IV, 48.

13. Herrick, History of Commerce and Industry, 1917, p. 97.

15. Gee and Hardy, op. cit., 178, 210.

16. Ibid., 210.

17. Ibid., 178.

18. See above, Chap. II.

19. Walsingham, Historia Anglicana, 1863, Vol. I, pp. 230, 259; Knighton, Chronicon Henrici Knighton, London 1889, Vol. II, p. 28; Collier, Ecclesiastical History of Great Britain, London 1852, Vol. II, pp. 487, 598; Perry, History of the Church of England, London 1895, Vol. I, pp. 404, 419, 473.

20. Lagarde, op. cit., p. 331.

21. Ibid.

22. Matthew of Paris, op. cit., II, 282.

23. Holinshed, Chronicle, II, 348.

24. Ibid., II, 542.

25. Lagarde, op. cit., 326.

26. Ibid., 338.

27. Gee and Hardy, op. cit., 148.

28. Vision of Piers the Plowman, Skeats ed., Passus I, 6f., 55-65.

29. Wright, Political Poems and Songs, London 1869, Vol. II, 333.

30. Matthew, English Works of John Wyclif Hitherto Unprinted, London 1880, pp. 164, 166, 167, 184.

31. Ibid., 393; Arnold, Select English Works of John Wycliffe, London 1869, Vol. III, pp. 278-291.

32. Matthew, op. cit., p. 393.

33. Ibid., 173.

34. Devon, Issues of the Exchequer, Vol. III, p. 513.

35. Ibid., III, 406.

36. Calendar of Letters and Papers of Henry VIII, London 1862, Vol. I, Part II, p. 1.

37. Ibid., Vol. X, p. 15.

38. Lagarde, op. cit., 336.

39. Matthew of Paris, op. cit., II, 259, 261.

40. Lagarde, op. cit., 337.

41. Ibid.

42. Foxe, Acts and Monuments, London 1846, Vol. V, p. 190.

43. Lagarde, op. cit., 339; Chronicles of Edward I and II, op. cit., II, 197.

44. Lea, History of the Inquisition, II, 64, III, 427.

45. Lagarde, op. cit., 333.

46. Gee and Hardy, op. cit., 145-231, quotation p. 148.

47. "In the giving of tithes of trade, all, both male and female, of the

parish of Dunstable shall give oblation instead of tithe, of all their trade made in parts cismarine and transmarine, on every Sunday before the end of high mass at the convent, what they think proper, on the altar of St. Peter in Dunstable, and if they be absent on one Sunday or more, they shall offer in the said place, on the first Sunday on their return, the tithe which has fallen due during their absence. If one man has many dwellings, he shall pay according to the time that he has dwelt there the tithes of trade, provided he does not move with intent to defraud the church of Dunstable; but if in the Lent next following, his conscience tells anyone that he has offered less than his due tithe at the altar, he shall offer all the rest on the eve of Easter, and discharge himself thereof, as he would that of the Sacrament or penance enjoined may profit him, and as he would avoid damnation at the Last Judgment." Selden Society Publications, Borough Customs, Vol. II, pp. 207f.

48. "Since it is doubtful what and how much should be given for tithes when there are so few cows and sheep that no cheese can be made from the milk, or in like manner when there are so few calves, lambs, kids, chickens, piglings, geese, or fleeces to be divided by ten; therefore it is our will to hand down a certain rule in these matters; for in leaving them to local customs we should rather increase than remove the cause of quarrels. We therefore decree that one farthing should be given as tithe for each lamb, kid, or pigling below the number of seven. If there be seven, let one be given in tithe, the next year, whatever is lacking from the number of ten shall be allowed for tithing. For the milk of each cow, let a penny be given; for each milch ewe, a farthing; for each goat, a half penny, etc." Exeter Constitutions, Wilkins, Concilia, Vol. II, 158f.

49. Foxe, op. cit., IV, 307.

50. Ibid., IV, 258.

51. Strype, op. cit., I, 71-74; II, 25-27.

52. Gee and Hardy, op. cit., 141f.

53. Ibid., 144.

54. Seebohm, Oxford Reformers, 1914, pp. 230-247.

55. Blunt, Reformation of the Church of England, London 1874, pp. 11-12.

56. Seebohm, op. cit., pp. 40, 86f., 247.

57. Ibid., 222; Foxe, op. cit., IV, 230, 246, 247.

58. Seebohm, op. cit., 148f.

59. Erasmus, Praise of Folly, Holbein ed., 258.

60. Ibid., 263.

61. Ibid., 269.

62. Ibid.

63. Ibid., 270.

64. Foxe, Acts and Monuments, IV, 657.

65. Simon Fish, A Supplication for the Beggars, Arber ed., 1878, Introd., p. vi.

66. Ibid., pp. 1-2.

67. Ibid., pp. 4, 5, 9.

68. Ibid., p. 6.

69. Ibid., p. 7.

70. Simon Fish, op. cit., p. 9.

71. Ibid., p. 1.

72. Ibid., p. 17.

73. Hall, History of Henry VIII, London 1901, Vol. II, p. 165.

74. Ibid., II, 167.

75. Wright, Political Poems and Songs, op. cit., I, 333.

76. Arnold, op. cit., III, 305.

77. Gibson, Codex juris ecclesiastic Anglicani, London 1713, Vol. II, 580.

78. "Whereas the ministers of bishops, and other ordinaries of holy church take of the people grievous and outrageous fines for the probating of wills, and for making of acquittances thereof, the king hath charged the archbishop of Canterbury and the other bishops, that they cause the same to be amended." Gibson, op. cit., II, 580.

79. Ibid.

80. Ibid., I, 181.

81. Hall, op. cit., II, 166; Strype, op. cit., I, 112; Calendar of Letters and Papers, op. cit., Vol. IV, No. 6043.

82. Gee and Hardy, op. cit., 149; see also Strype, op. cit., I, 192.

83. Coulton, Medieval Studies, No. 8, Series I, London 1915, p. 5.

84. Burnet, History of the Reformation in England, Clarendon Press, 1865, Vol. I, p. 41; Foxe, op. cit., IV, 183f.; Selden Society Publications, Borough Customs, op. cit., II, 211.

85. Notice the account of receipts for mortuaries in the Church of St. Mary's, Ottery, for the years 1437-1438: "He accounteth for 9 s. for an ox, mortuary of the wife of Thomas Glade, and sold to the said Thomas—6 s. for a cow, the mortuary of John Harbelyn's wife, and sold to the said John—6 d. for a ewe, the mortuary of Matilda Byre, and sold to John-at-the-Well—12 d. for a pig, the mortuary of John Benyne, and sold to the widow of the said John, etc., etc." Oliver, Monasticon Dioecesis Oxoniensis, London 1846, p. 282.

86. Gibson, op. cit., II, 744.

87. Ibid.

88. Selden Society Publications, Borough Customs, op. cit., II, 211; Coulton, op. cit., p. 6.

89. Burnet, op. cit., I, 41; Foxe, op. cit., IV, 183ff.

90. Gibson, op. cit., II, 727, 795.

91. Hall, op. cit., II, 16.

92. Ibid.

93. Strype, op. cit., I, 606.

94. Burnet, op. cit., IV, 192f.

95. Strype, op. cit., I, 606f.

96. Matthew of Paris, op. cit., II, 44, 60, 406.

97. Gibson, op. cit., II, 921f.

98. Matthew of Paris, op. cit., III, 7.

99. Hume, History of England, II, I, 251.

100. Collier, op. cit., III, 126.

101. Capes, op. cit., 22; Collier, op. cit., II, 560.

102. Gibson, op. cit., II, 923-926, 945-947.

103. Hall, op. cit., II, 167, 170.

104. Cromwell, Life and Letters of Thomas Cromwell, Merriman ed., Clarendon Press, 1902, Vol. I, 96, 105; Gee and Hardy, op. cit., 145.

105. Strype, op. cit., I, 75, 112.
106. Hall, op. cit., II, 273. This was in 1537, but it was equally true earlier in this period.
107. Calendar of Letters and Papers, op. cit., V, No. 886.
108. Ibid., IV, Part III, No. 49.
109. Gee and Hardy, op. cit., 145-15.
110. Phillimore, Ecclesiastical Laws of the Church of England, London 1895, Vol. II, passim; Gibson, op. cit., II, 1120-1133.
111. Hook, Lives of the Archbishops of Canterbury, London 1865, Vol. III, p. 29f.
112. Perry, op. cit., II, 25-26; Strype, op. cit., I, 112, 198.
113. Hook, op. cit., III, 31f.
114. Ibid., III, 34.
115. Gee and Hardy, op. cit., 147.
116. Ibid., 146.
117. Ibid., 148.
118. Stubbs, Constitutional History of England, 1896. Vol. II, 439.
119. Perry, op. cit., II, 25.
120. Hook, op. cit., III, 30.
121. Gee and Hardy, op. cit., 148-153.
122. Gee and Hardy, op. cit., 178, 201.
123. Hook, op. cit., IV, 380; Lagarde, op. cit., 312-314; Matthew of Paris, op. cit., 131f; Adams and Stevens, op. cit., p. 13, article 12.
124. Lagarde, op. cit., 315; Stubbs, op. cit., III, 338; Collier, op. cit., III, 13; Strype, op. cit., I, 168; Burnet, op. cit., I, 250; Perry, op. cit., II, 78; Calendar of Letters and Papers, op. cit., V, No. 886.
125. Collier, op. cit., III, 597; Stubbs, op. cit., III, 338.
126. Walsingham, Historia Anglicana, op. cit., I, 323.
127. Ibid.
128. Wyclif, De Simonia, op. cit., pp. 54-62.
129. Gibson, op. cit., II, 870.
130. Strype, op. cit., I, 222; II, 158; Blunt, op. cit., L, 252f.
131. Ibid.
132. Ibid., I, 257.
133. Gee and Hardy, op. cit., 178-180; Hall, op. cit., II, 204.
134. Strype, op. cit., I, 326.
135. Fuller, op. cit., III, 97.
136. Gee and Hardy, op. cit., 179-180.
137. Calendar of Letters and Papers, op. cit., V, No. 886.
138. Strype, op. cit., II, 158.
139. Calander of Letters and Papers, op. cit., Vol. V, No. 722 (6).
140. Gibson, Codex, op. cit., I, 125; Gee and Hardy, op. cit., 180; Strype, op. cit., I, 168.
141. Lagarde, op. cit., 315; Henry, History of England, VIII, 62.
142. Gee and Hardy, op. cit., 179.
143. Burnet, op. cit., I, 366.
144. Calendar of Letters and Papers, op. cit., VII, Nos. 1377, 1380, 1381, 1482.
145. Gee and Hardy, op. cit., 187, 195.
146. Ibid., 188, 189.
147. Ibid., 188.

148. Ibid., 210.
149. Matthew, op. cit., p. 22.
150. Gee and Hardy, op. cit., 218.
151. Lagarde, op. cit., p. 305; Coulton, Social Life in England, Cam-bridge 1918, p. 195.
152. Low and Pulling, Dictionary of English History, p. 891.
153. Royal Historical Society, Transactions, Vol. XV, p. 174; Lagarde, op. cit., 305.
154. Cunningham, Growth of English Industry and Commerce, 1910, I, 272.
155. Royal Historical Society, Transactions, XV, 191.
156. Lagarde, op. cit., 305.
157. Royal Historical Society, Transactions, XV, 106.
158. Ibid., XV, 185.
159. Collier, op. cit., III, 596: Gotlob, Aus der Kamera, p. 215.
160. Royal Historical Society, Transactions, XV, 183, 196-198.
161. Stubbs, op. cit., II, 475.
162. Lagarde, op. cit., 308.
163. Ibid., 308-312.
164. Gee and Hardy, op. cit., 210.
165. Ibid.

CHAPTER V

1. Calendar of Letters and Papers of Henry VIII, London 1862, Vol. IV, Introd., p. 651.
2. Latimer, Seven Sermons Preached before Edward VI, Arber ed., 1869, p. 40.
3. Calendar of Letters and Papers, op. cit., VIII, No. 609; IX, Nos. 1064, 1065, 1066; Wriothesley, Chronicle of England, 1485-1539, Cam-den Society Publications, 1875, pp. 27, 57.
4. Gee and Hardy, Documents Illustrative of English Church History, London 1914, p. 244.
5. Ibid., 251.
6. Strype, Ecclesiastical Memorials Relating chiefly to Religion under Henry VIII, Oxford, 1882, Vol. I, p. 222; II, p. 158f.; Blunt, Reforma-tion of the Church of England, London 1874, Vol. I, p. 252f.
7. Strype, op. cit., I, 244f.
8. Calendar of Letters and Papers, op. cit., IX, No. 1065.
9. Strype, op. cit., I, 206.
10. Cavendish, Life of Wolsey, London 1827, Singer ed., 88-96. Fiddis, Life of Wolsey, London 1827, 100, 187.
11. Calendar of Letters and Papers, op. cit., VI, No. 1164; Bayne, Life of Fisher, London 1921, p. 78.
12. Ibid.
13. Herbert of Cherbury, History of England under Henry VIII, Lon-don 1872, p. 548.
14. Cromwell, Life and Letters of Thomas Cromwell, Merriman ed., 1902, Vol. I, p. 47.
15. Hall, History of Henry VIII, London 1901, Vol. II, p. 210; Foxe Acts and Monuments, London 1846, Vol. V, p. 58f.
16. Hall, op. cit., II, 210.

17. Foxe, op. cit., V, 384-404.
18. Ibid., V, 507.
19. Hall, op. cit., 201; Foxe, op. cit., V, 268.
20. Strype, op. cit., I, 198; Hall, op. cit., II, 183, 200.
21. Hall, op. cit., II, 165, 211; Foxe, op. cit., V, 59.
22. Hall, op. cit., II, 212.
23. Hall, op. cit., II, 165, 211; Foxe, op. cit., V, 56-57.
24. Strype, op. cit., I, 535; Strype, Memorials of Thomas Cranmer, London 1852, Vol. I, p. 50.
25. Herbert of Cherbury, op. cit., p. 548.
26. Speed, History of Great Britain, London 1614, p. 778 (100).
27. Tanner, Notitia Monastica, London 1744, Preface, p. xxxvi.
28. Calendar of Letters and Papers, op. cit., VIII, Nos. 297, 560, 565, 566, 609, 623, 661, 666, 736, 838, 895; IX, Nos. 100, 167, 186, 491, 789, 790, 846, 986, 1064, 1066, 1150; X, Nos. 49, 99.
29. Hall, op. cit., II, 28of.: Gasquet, Henry VIII and the Monasteries, London 1888, Vol. II, Chs. 5, 6.
30. Calendar of Letters and Papers, op. cit., XI, Nos. 768 (2), 828 (6); XII, Nos. 70 (11); XIV, No. 186; Hall, op. cit., II, 270; Speed, op. cit., 774 (96).
31. Strype, Eccles. Mem., op. cit., I, 532; Suppression of the Monasteries, Yorkshire Archeological Society, Record Series, Vol. 47, 1912, p. vii; Gibbins, Industry in England, 1903, p. 204.
32. Hall, op. cit., II, 226, 270; Strype, Eccles. Mem., op. cit., I, 296-298; II, Nos. 52, 74.
33. Strype, Eccles. Mem., op. cit., I, 245.
34. Hall, op. cit., II, 275; Tanner, op. cit., Preface, p. xxxix.
35. Hall, op. cit., II, 271f.; Strype, Eccles. Mem., op. cit., II, 266f.
36. Wriothesley, op. cit., p. 57
37. Calendar of Letters and Papers, op. cit., XI, Nos. 714, 828 (5); XII, Nos. 6, 29, 380, 481, 533; Suppression of the Monasteries, op. cit., pp. 31, 38, 41, 47.
38. Stow, Annales of England, London 1600, pp., 968, 969, 973; Speed, op. cit., p. 778 (99).
39. Strype, Eccles. Mem., op. cit., I, 294; Herbert of Cherbury, op. cit., p. 598; Wriothesley, op. cit., 57, 63; Wright, Suppression of the Monasteries, Camden Society Publications, 1842, p. 95; Complaint of Roderyck, Early English Texts Society, Vol. 31, pp. 115, 117.
40. Strype, op. cit., 58; Speed op. cit. p. 773 (96).
41. Strype, op. cit., I, 471; Speed, op. cit., 773f.
42. Calendar of Letters and Papers, op. cit., VIII, No. 609.
43. Venice Archives, Calendar of State Papers and Manuscripts relating to English Affairs, London 1867, Year 1535, No. 54.
44. Cromwell, op. cit., II, No. 174.
45. Ibid.
46. Ibid.
47. Ibid., II, No. 169.
48. Gee and Hardy, op. cit., 394.
49. Foxe, op. cit., V, 367.
50. Herbert of Cherbury, op. cit., 563.
51. Cromwell, op. cit., I, pp. 40, 90, 109, 112, 123; Strype, op. cit.,

I, 173; Burnet, qp. cit., Records Part II, No. 14; Calendar of Letters and Papers, op. cit., XIII, No. 120 (1).

52. Gee and Hardy, op. cit., 394.

53. Foxe, op. cit., V, 377.

54. Wyclif, De Officio Regis, Wyclif Society Publications, 1857, p. 185.

55. Arnold, English Works of John Wycliffe, London 1869, III, 216.

56. Foxe, op. cit., II, 500, 786.

57. Somer, Collection of Scarce and Valuable Tracts, London 1809, Vol. I, 42f.

58. Traill, Social England, London 1902, Vol. III, 77f.

59. Gibson, Codex Juris Ecclesiastici Anglicani, London 1713, II, 872.

60. Gasquet, op. cit., I, 318.

61. Herbert of Cherbury, op. cit., 624f., 630; Strype, op. cit., I, 522f.

62. Dixon, History of the Church of England, I, 105.

63. Innis, History of England and the British Empire, New York 1913, Vol. II, 103; Cromwell, op. cit., I, 178; Burnet, op. cit., I, 294; Williamson, Maritime Enterprise, 1913, 124f.

64. Hall, op. cit., II, 286; Strype, op cit., I, 476; Herbert of Cherbury, 620, 625, 630; Cromwell, op. cit., Nos. 174, 187, 189, 216-218, 300, 301, 310.

65. Cromwell, op. cit., No. 300.

66. Ibid., No. 301.

67. Hall, op. cit., II, 286.

68. Ibid., II, 286-287.

69. Herbert of Cherbury, op. cit., 624-626.

70. Ibid., p. 563.

71. Gasquet, op. cit., I, 317-321; Burnet, op. cit., I, 430; Dixon, op. cit., I, 101.

72. Strype, op. cit., I, 422f.

73. Herbert of Cherbury, op. cit., 549.

74. Ibid., 563.

75. Strype, op. cit., I, 425.

76. Strype, Eccles. Mem., op. cit., I, 533.

77. Ibid., I, 422f.; Wright, Suppression of the Monasteries, op. cit., p. 262.

78. Strype, op. cit., I, 417-421.

79. Wright, Suppression of the Monasteries, op. cit., p. 112, No. 49.

80. Burnet, op. cit., I, 431.

81. Ibid.

82. Gee and Hardy, op. cit., 150.

83. Blunt, op. cit., I, 488.

84. Traill, op. cit., III, 66.

85. Calendar of Letters and Papers, op. cit., VIII, Nos. 258, 294; IX, No. 13; X, Nos. 531, 599, 601, 613, 621, 654, 552, 557, 567, 563, 572, 717, 800, 825, 1233; XIII Part I, Nos. 49, 406, 524, 547, 605, 642; Wright, Suppression of the Monasteries, op. cit., Nos. 39, 52, 53, 54, 65, 77, see also note p. 116; Strype, op. cit., I, 405f.; Yorkshire Archeological Society, Suppression of the Monasteries, op. cit., pp. 4, 24, 36, 58-78; Oliver, op. cit., pp. 23, 26, 36, 104, 112; Tanner, op. cit., Preface, xxiv.

86. Cunningham, op. cit., I, 489, Gibbins, op. cit., 204; Innis, op. cit., II, 95; Cromwell, op. cit., I, 179; Froude, op. cit., III, 206; Taswell-Lang-

mead, Constitutional History of England, 346f.; Foxe, op. cit., V, 180;
Brewer, in his Introduction to Calendar of Letters and Papers, op. cit.,
I, 555-556.
87. Calander of Letters and Papers, op. cit., IX, No. 1066; VIII, No.
609.
88. Venetian State Papers, op. cit., 1532, No. 753.
89. Calendar of Letters and Papers, op. cit., XIV, Pt. I, No. 186.
90. Ibid., IV, No. 89.
91. Cromwell, op. cit., I, 166.
92. Gee and Hardy, op. cit., 257f.; Strype, op. cit., I, 385; Gibbins,
op. cit., 203.
93. Gee and Hardy, op. cit., 257.
94. Somer, Tracts, op. cit., I, 40.
95. Calendar of Letters and Papers, op. cit., VII, Nos. 552, 1355, 1482;
Nichols, Narratives of the Days of the Reformation, Camden Society Publications, 1859, 280.
96. Sinclair, History of the Public Revenue, London 1803, Vol. 1, 183.
97. Calendar of Letters and Papers, op. cit., X, Nos. 450, 956, 922.
98. Ibid., X, Nos. 831, 922, 956; Cromwell, op. cit., Nos. 136, 137, 147,
149, 173; Burnet op. cit., I, 327.
99. Gasquet, op. cit., II, 3; See Liljegren, Fall of the Monasteries, Leipzig 1924, pp. 19ff.
100. See note 85.
101. Calendar of Letters and Papers, op. cit., X, 601, also 599.
102. Strype, op. cit., I, 405f.; See Wright, Suppression of the Monasteries, op. cit., p. 116.
103. Calendar of Letters and Papers, op. cit., IX, No. 850.
104. Ibid., X, No. 599.
105. Ibid., X, No. 572.
106. Ibid.
107. Wright, Suppression of the Monasteries, op. cit., No. 54, p. 121.
108. Burnet, op. cit., I, 430; Strype, op. cit., I, 615.
109. Curtler, The Enclosure and Redistribution of Our Land, 1920,
p. 70f.
110. Strype, op. cit., I, 608-622.
111. Curtler, op. cit., p. 73.
112. Calendar of Letters and Papers, op. cit., XIII, No. 315.
113. Strype, op. cit., I, 415.
114. Smith, Chronicon Rusticum Commerciale, or Memoir of Wool,
London 1803, pp. 54, 59.
115. Ibid., 80.
116. Wright, Political Poems and Songs, 1859, II, 282.
117 More, Utopia, Arber ed., 1869, p. 40f.
118. Strype, op. cit., II, 147.
119. Busch, England Under the Tudors, London 1895, I, 68-82, 141-
147; Temperly, Henry VII, p. 16of.; Traill, op. cit., II, 550; Williamson,
op. cit., 1-30, 120f.
120. Chronicle of Calais, Camden Society Publications, p. 100f.
121. Traill, op. cit., III, 83.
122. Lindsay, History of Merchant Shipping, London 1874, II, 88,
95, 561-562, Appendix 5; Williamson, op. cit., 372-406.

123. Hall, op. cit., II, 129.

124. Ibid., II, 130.

125. Ibid., II, 197; Cromwell, op. cit., II, No. 107, 270.

126. Bacon, History of the Reign of Henry VII, 1889, p. 79.

127. Hall, op. cit., II, 196.

128. Erasmus, Letters, Nichols ed., No. 110, p. 227.

129. Brewer, Introduction to Letters and Papers of Henry VIII, op. cit., p. dclvii; Blunt, op. cit., I, 19; Strype, op. cit., II, Nos. 27, 34, 43, 47, 51, 52, 53, 54, 56.

BIBLIOGRAPHY

Abrams, A., English Life and Manners in the Middle Ages, London 1913.

Adam of Usk, Chronicon Adae de Usk, 1347-1421, London 1904.

Adams, G. B., and Stevens, H. M., Select Documents of English Constitutional History, New York 1901.

Addy, S. O., Church and Manor, A Study of English Economic History, London 1913.

Andrews, J. P., A History of Great Britain from Henry VIII to James I, London 1806.

Annales de Burton, Annales Monastici, Luard ed., London 1864.

Arber, E., Simon Fish, A Supplication for the Beggars, London 1878.

Arnold, Thomas, Select English Works of John Wycliffe, 3 vols., London 1869.

Ashley, W. J., Edward III and His Wars, Extracts from English Sources, London 1887.

Bacon, Sir Francis, History of the Reign of Henry VII, Lumby ed., Cambridge University Press, 1889.

Barnes, Joshua, The History of Edward III, Cambridge 1668.

Bateson, M., Borough Customs, Selden Society Publications, 2 vols., 1904.

Bayne, Ronald, Life of John Fisher, Bishop of Rochester, London 1921.

Bewsher, F. W., Reformation and Renaissance, 1485-1547, London 1916.

Bland, A., Brown, P. A., and Tawney, B. A., Select Documents of English Economic History, London 1914.

Brinkelow, H., The Complaynt of Roderyck, Early English Texts Society Publications, London, 1874.

Bliss, W. H., Calendar of Entries in the Papal Registers Relating to Great Britain, 11 vols., London 1893.

Blunt, J. H., The Reformation of the Church of England, Its History, Principles, and Results, 2 vols., London 1874.

Brewer, J. S., The Reign of Henry VIII to the Death of Wolsey, Gairdiner ed., London 1884.

————Calendar of Letters and Papers of Henry VIII, Foreign and Domestic, 21 vols., London 1862.

Brown, F., Calendar of Venice State Papers and Manuscripts relating to English Affairs, 5 vols., London 1867.

Burnet, G., The History of the Reformation in England, Pocock ed., 7 vols., Clarendon Press, 1865.

Busch, W., England Under the Tudors, 2 vols., London 1895.

Calvin, D. S., Wyclif and His Place in the Reformation Movement, University of Chicago Press, 1899.

Campbell, Wm., Materials for the History of the Reign of Henry VII, 2 vols., London 1873.

Cannon, Henry L., The Poor Priest, a Study of the Rise of English Lollardry, American Historical Association Reports, Vol. I, p. 451f.

Capes, W. W., The English Church in the Fourteenth and Fifteenth Centuries, London 1900.

Cavendish, Geo., Life of Cardinal Wolsey, London 1827.

Cheney, Edw. P., Readings in English History Drawn from the Original Sources, New York 1908.

Chronicon Angliae, ob anno domini 1328 usque ad annum 1388, 2 vols., London 1874.

Clay, R. M., The Medieval Hospital in England, London 1909.

Collier, Jeremy, An Ecclesiastical History of Great Britain to the Reign of Charles II, London 1852, 9 vols.

Commin, J. O., An Old Exeter Manuscript . . . a Writ of Proclamation against the Lollards in the time of Henry IV, Exeter 1907.

Corson, L., A Finding List of Political Poems Referring to English Affairs in the XII and XIV Centuries, Philadelphia 1910.

Coulton, G. G., Social Life in Britain, Cambridge 1911.

———— Priests and People before the Reformation, Medieval Studies, No. 8, London 1915.

Cromwell, Thomas, Life and Letters of Thomas Cromwell, Merriman ed., 2 vols., Clarendon Press, 1902.

Cross, H. L., A Shorter History of England and Greater Britain, New York 1912.

Cunningham, Wm., Growth of English Industry and Commerce, 5th ed., Cambridge 1910.

Curtler, W. R. H., The Enclosure and Redistribution of Our Land, Oxford 1920.

Dart, J., History and Antiquities of the Cathedral Church of Canterbury, London 1726.

Day, Clive, History of Commerce, New York 1917.

Dearmer, P., Religious Pamphlets, New York 1898.

Danton, Wm., A History of England in the Fifteenth Century, London 1888.

Dietz, F. C., History of English Finance, 1485-1588, University of Illinois, 1921.

Dodds, R. and E., The Pilgrimage of Grace, 1536-1537, 2 vols., Cambridge University Press, 1915.

Dowell, S., A History of Taxation in England, 4 vols., London 1884.

Dudden, F. H., Gregory the Great, His Place in Thought and History, 2 vols., New York 1905.

Dugdale, Sir Wm., Monasticum Anglicorum, London 1846.

Durham, F., The Denarius Sancti Petri in England, Royal Historical Society Transactions, Vol. XV.

———— English History Illustrated from the Sources, London 1902.

Dymnok, R., Rogeri Dymnok Liber contra XII errores et haereses Lollardorum, London 1922.

Edward I, Chronicle of the Reigns of Edward I and II, 2 vols., Stubbs ed., London 1882.

Einstein, L. D., Tudor Ideals, New York 1921.

Ellis, Sir Henry, Original Letters Illustrative of English History, 3 vols., London 1825.

Fabre, P., Etude sur le Liber Censuum de l'Eglise romaine, Paris 1892.

Fabre, P. et Duchesne, L., Censius Liber Censuum de l'Eglise romaine, Paris 1910.

Fabyan, R., New Chronicles of England and France, London 1911.

Fiddis, Richard, Life of Cardinal Wolsey, London 1827.

Fish, Simon, A Supplication for the Beggars, Furnivall ed., London 1878.

Fish, Simon, A Supplication for the Beggars, Arber ed., London 1871.

Fisher, H. A. L., A History of England from Henry VII to the Death of Henry VIII, London 1906.

Floyer, J. K., Studies in the History of English Church Endowment, 1917.

Fletcher, J. S., The Reformation in Northern England, London 1925.

Foxe, John, Acts and Monuments, 8 vols., London 1846.

Frazer, N. L., English History Illustrated from the Original Sources, 1307-1399, London 1901.

Froissart, Sir John, Chronicles of England, France and Spain, 1906.

Froude, J. A., A History of England from the Fall of Wolsey to the Death of Elizabeth, 10 vols., London 1890.

Fuller, Thos., A History of the Church of England to 1648, Brewer ed., 6 vols., Oxford 1845.

Furnivall, F. J., A Supplication for the Beggars written about the year 1529 by Simon Fish, London 1871.

Gairdiner, Jas., A History of the English Church in the Sixteenth Century, London 1902.

—— Letters and Papers Illustrative of the Reigns of Richard III and Henry VII, London 1861.

——Lollardry and the Reformation in England, A Historical Survey, 4 vols., London 1908.

Garrison, W. E., Preparation for the Reformation in England before Wycliff, University of Chicago, 1897.

Gasquet, F. A., The Eve of the Reformation in England, London 1905.

—— Henry VIII and the English Monasteries, London 1888.

—— Henry III and the Church, London 1905.

Gee, H. and Hardy, W. H., Documents Illustrative of English Church History, London 1914.

Geike, J. C., The English Reformation, How It Came About, New York 1897.

Gerald of Cambridge, Opera Geraldi Cambrensis, Dimock ed., 7 vols., London 1867.

Gibbs, W. J. R., Exercises and Problems in English History, 1485 to 1820, Cambridge 1913.

Gibson, Edmund, Codex juris ecclesiastici Anglicani, 2 vols., London 1713.

Gierke, G., Political Theories in the Middle Ages, Cambridge University Press, 1900.

Gilpin, W., The Lives of Wycliff and Lord Cobham, London 1765.

Gottinger, R., Wyclif's Theory of Church and State, University of Chicago, 1906.

Godwyn, Morgan, Annales of England containing the reigns of Henry VIII, Edward VI, and Mary, London 1630.

Göller, E., Der Liber taxarum der papstlichen Kammer, Rome 1905.

Gottlob, A., Die Servitientaxen in 13 Jahrhundert, Stuttgart 1901.

Grafton, R., Grafton's Chronicle: or the History of England from 1189-1558, 2 vols., London 1809.

Great Britain State Papers, Published under authority of His Majesty's Commission, London 1830.

Great Britain Record Commission, Valor Ecclesiasticus of Henry VIII, 6 vols., London 1810.

Hadden, A. W., and Stubbs, Wm., Councils and Ecclesiastical Documents relating to Ireland and Great Britain, 3 vols., Oxford 1849.

Haller, J., Papsttum und Kirchenreform, Berlin 1903.

Hall, Edward, History of Henry VIII, London 1904.

Hall, Edward, Hall's Chronicle containing the History of England from Henry IV to Henry VIII, London 1809.

Hannick, E. A., Reginald Peacock, Churchman and Man of Letters, Washington 1922. (Ph.D. Thesis, Cath. Univ. of America.)

Hardwicke, P. Y., Miscellaneous State Papers, 1501-1726, London 1778.

Hardyng, J., The Chronicle of John Hardyng, with a continuation by Richard Grafton, London 1812.

Harleian Miscellany, A Collection of Scarce and Curious Tracts, 10 vols., London 1808.

Harpsfield, N., Le premier divorce de Henri VIII et le schisme d'Angleterre, Champion ed., Paris 1917.

Haweis, J. O. W., Sketches of the Reformation and the Age of Elizabeth taken from contemporary sources, London 1844.

Heeren, A. H. L., Vermishte Historische Werke, 5 vols., Göttingen 1821.

Henry III, Royal and Other Historical Letters of Henry III, Shirley ed., 2 vols., London 1862.

Henry VIII, Calendar of Letters and Papers of Henry VIII, Foreign and Domestic, Brewer ed., 21 vols., London 1862.

Herbert, Edward, Lord of Cherbury, The History of England under Henry VIII, London 1872.

Henry, R., The History of Great Britain, 8 vols., London 1800.

Herrick, C. A., A History of Commerce and Industry, 1917.

Heylyn, P., Ecclesia Restuarata, A History of the Reformation in England, Robertson ed., Cambridge 1849.

Higden, R., Polychronicon R. Higden Monachi Cestrensis, Lumby ed., 8 vols., London 1882.

Hill, O. T., English Monasticism, Its Rise and Influence, London 1867.

Hoff, J. H., The Pilgrimage of Grace, University of Chicago, 1917.

Holinshed, R., The Chronicles of England, Scotland, and Ireland, 6 vols., London 1807.

Hook, W. F., The Lives of the Archbishops of Canterbury, 6 vols., London 1865.

Hovedon, Roger, The Annals of Roger of Hovedon, Bohn ed., London 1857.

Hutton, W. H., The Misrule of Henry III, Extracts from the Original Sources, London 1887.

——— Simon de Montfort and his Cause, Extracts from the Original Sources, London 1909.

Hyland, S. K., A Century of Persecution under Tudor and Stuart Sovereigns from Contemporary Records, New York 1920.

Innis, A. D., England Under the Tudors, London 1905.

——— A History of England and the British Empire, 4 vols., New York 1923.

Knighton, Henry, Chronicon Henrici Knighton Monachi Leycestrensis, 2 vols., London 1889.

Kennedy, W. M. P., Studies in Tudor History, London 1916.

Lagarde, A., The Latin Church in the Middle Ages, New York 1915.

Langtoft, P., Chronicle of Peter Langtoft, Hearne ed., 2 vols., Oxford 1725.

Latimer, Hugh, Seven Sermons preached before King Edward VI, Arber ed., Birmingham 1869.

Le Bas, C. W., The Life of John Wyclif, London 1832.

Lechler, G. V., John Wycliffe and his English Precursors, Lorimer translation, 2 vols., London 1878.

Lewis, J., The Life of Doctor John Fisher, with appendix of original documents, London 1855.

Leibermann, F., Peterspence and the Population of England about 1164, English Historical Review, 1896, pp. 744f.

Lindsay, W. S., A History of Merchant Shipping and Ancient Commerce, 4 vols., London 1874.

Lindwood, G., Provinciale . . . Constitutiones Angliae, Oxford 1689.

Locke, A., War and Misrule, 1307-1399, London 1913.

Longman, Wm., The History of the Life and Times of Edward III, London 1869.

Loserth, L., Johannis Wyclif Tractatus de Ecclesia, London 1896.

Luard, H. R., Roberti Grosseteste Epistolae, 2 vols., London 1861.

Luard, H. R., Matthaii Parisiensis Chronica Majora, 7 vols., London 1877.

Luard, H. R., On the Relations between England and Rome during the earlier part of the reign of Henry VIII, Cambridge 1877.

Lumby, J. R., Chronicon Henrici Knighton Monachi Leycestrensis, 2 vols., London 1899.

Liljegren, S. B., The Fall of the Monasteries and Social Changes in England, Leipzig 1924.

Madden, Sir F., Matthaii Parisiensis Monachi S. Albani Historia Anglorum, 3 vols., London 1866.

Maitland, S. R., Essays on Subjects concerning the Reformation in England, London 1849.

Matthew, F. D., The English Works of Wyclif Hitherto Unprinted, London 1880.

Matthew of Paris, Matthaii Parisiensis Chronica Majora, 7 vols., London 1877.

Matthew of Paris, Chronicles of England, Bohn ed., London 1850.

Matthew of Westminster, Flowers of History, 2 vols., London 1852.

Merriman, R. S., The Life and Letters of Thomas Cromwell to 1535, 2 vols., Clarendon Press, 1902.

Michaud, J. F., History of the Crusades, 3 vols., New York 1863.

Milman, H. H., A History of Latin Christianity, 8 vols., 1906.

Moberly, C. E., The Early Tudors, Henry VII and Henry VIII, 1890.

Montalembert, Count de, The Monks of the West from St. Benedict to St. Bernard, 6 vols., London 1894.

More, Sir Thomas, Utopia, Robinson translation, Arber ed., 1869.

Morris, Wm., The Dream of John Ball, London 1888.

New, C. W., History of the Alien Priories in England to the Confiscation of Henry V, University of Chicago Press, 1914.

Nicholas, IV, Pope, Taxatio Ecclesiastica Angliae et Walliae Auctoriatate P. Nicholai IV. c. A.D. 1291, London 1802.

Nichols, J. G., Narratives of the Days of the Reformation, Camden Society Publications, 1859.

Norgate, Kate, The Minority of Henry III, London 1912.

Oliver, Geo., Monasticon Diocesis Oxoniensis, London 1846.

Oman, C. W. C., A History of England from Richard II to Richard III, London 1906.

Page, Wm., The Victorian History of the Counties of England, London 1907.

Papal Registers, Calendar of Entries in the Papal Registers relative to Great Britain and Ireland, 11 vols., London 1892.

Peacock, Reginald, The Repressor of Overmuch Blaming of the Clergy, Babington ed., London, 1860.

Pearson, C. H., English History in the Fourteenth Century, 2 vols., London 1876.

Peckham, J., Registrum Epistolarum Fratris Johannis Peckham, 2 vols., Martin ed., London 1882.

Perry, G. C., A History of the Reformation in England, 2 vols., London 1895.

——— A History of the Church of England, 3 vols., London 1890.

Phillimore, Sir R., Ecclesiastical Laws of the Church of England, London 1895.

Pocock, N., Records of the Reformation, 1527-1533, 2 vols., Oxford 1880.

Pollard, A. F., Tudor Tracts, 1532-1588, Westminster 1903.

——— The Reign of Henry VII from the Original Sources, 3 vols., London 1914.

——— The Reign of Henry VIII, London 1905.

Poole, R. L., Wycliffe and the Movement for Reform, London 1889.

Powell, E., The Rising in East Anglia in 1381, Cambridge 1896.

Prothero, G. W., The Life of Simon de Montfort, London 1877.

Prynne, G., Antiquae Constitutiones Regni Angliae, London 1672.

Ranke, L. von, The History of the Popes in the Sixteenth Century, 3 vols., London 1891.

Rishinger, Wm., Chronicle of William Rishinger, Camden Society Publications, London 1840.

Riley, H. T., Johannis de Trokelowe . . . Chronica et Annales, 1259-1406, London 1866.

——— Willemi Rishinger Chronica et Annales, London, 1865.

Roger of Wendover, Rogeri de Wendover Liber qui Dicatur Flores Historiarum, Hewlitt ed., 3 vols., London 1886.

Rogers, J. E. T., A History of Agriculture and Prices in England, 1259-1793, 6 vols., Oxford 1882.

Rutland, J. M. H., Rutland Papers, Original Documents illustrative of the reigns of Henry VII and VIII, Camden Society Publications, 1842.

Sanders, N., De origine ac progresev schismatis anglicani libri tres, Romae 1586.

Seebohm, F., The Oxford Reformers, London 1914.

Shadwell, L. L., Enactments in Parliament, Oxford Historical Society Publications, 4 vols., 1912.

Sheppard, A., Christ Church Letters, Camden Society Publications, Vol. 19, p. 10f.

Shirley, W. W., Fasciculi Zizanorum Magistri Johannis Wyclif cum Tritico, London 1858.

—— Royal and Other Historical Letters illustrative of the reign of Henry III, London 1862.

Sinclair, Sir John, A History of the Public Revenue of the British Empire, 3 vols., London 1803.

Smith, John, Chronicon Rusticum Commerciale, or Memoir of Wool, A Summary of Statutes relating to Wool, London, 1747.

Snell, F. C., The Customs of England, London 1911.

Somers Tracts, A Collection of Scarce and Valuable Tracts relating to England, 13 vols., London 1809.

Speed, Sir John, The History of Great Britain, London 1614.

Spelman, Sir John, Councils and Ecclesiastical Documents relating to the Church of Great Britain, Oxford 1869.

Stevens, J., The Royal Treasury of England, London 1725.

Stow, John, The Annales of England, London 1600.

Strype, John, Memorials of Thomas Cranmer, 2 vols., London 1852.

—— Ecclesiastical Memorials relating chiefly to Religion under Henry VIII, 2 vols., London 1822.

Stubbs, Wm., Seventeen Lectures on the Study of Medieval and Modern History, Clarendon Press, 1887.

—— Constitutional History of England in Its Origin and Development, Oxford 1896.

—— Memoriale Fratris Walteri de Coventria, 2 vols., London 1873.

—— Chronicles of the Reigns of Edward I and Edward II, 2 vols., London 1882.

Summers, W. H., The Lollards of Chiltern Hills, London 1906.

—— Our Lollard Ancestors, London 1906.

Tanner, J. R., Tudor Constitutional Documents, 1485-1603, Cambridge University Press, 1922.

Tanner, Thos., Notitia Monastica, London 1744.

Thomas, F. S., Historical Notes, 1509-1714, London 1856.

Thompson, E. M., Chronicon Angliae ab anno 1326 usque ad annum 1388, 2 vols., London 1874.

Touchet, Geo., Historical Collections, Dublin 1784.

Tout, T. F., A History of Edward I, London 1901.

––––––– An Advanced History of England, London 1920.

Traill, H. D., Social England, A Record of Progress of the People, 6 vols., London 1902.

Transactions of the Royal Historical Society, Vols. VI and VII and X, New Series, London 1901.

Trevelyan, Geo., England in the Age of Wycliffe, London 1920.

Turner, Sharon, A History of the Reign of Henry VIII, London 1827.

Usher, R. G., The Reconstruction of the English Church, 2 vols., New York 1910.

Valor Ecclesiasticus of Henry VIII, Great Britain Record Commission, London 1810.

Vaughan, R., Life and Opinions of John de Wycliffe, London 1831.

Venice Archives, Calendar of State Papers and Manuscripts Relating to English Affairs, London 1867.

Vinogradoff, P., Oxford Studies in Social and Legal History, London, 1914.

Vergilius, Polydore, Three Books of History containing the reigns of Henry VI to Richard III, Camden Society Publications, London 1844.

Walter of Coventry, The Historical Collections of Walter of Coventry, Stubbs ed., 2 vols., London 1872.

Walsingham, Thos., Chronica Monasterii S. Albanii regnante Ricardo II, London 1867.

––––––– Historia Anglicana, 2 vols., London 1863.

––––––– Ypodigma Neustriae, London 1876.

Walsh, W., England's Fight with the Papacy, London 1912.

Weingarten, H., Die Revolutionskirchen Englands, Liepzig 1868.

Williamson, J. A., Maritime Enterprise, 1485-1588, Clarendon Press, 1913.

Wilson, J. E., John Wycliffe, Patriot and Reformer, New York 1884.

Wishart, A. F., A Short History of Monks and Monasteries, London 1902.

Wright, Thos., Political Poems and Songs relating to English History, 2 vols., London 1859.

—— Three Chapters of Letters relating to the Suppression of the Monasteries, Camden Society Publications, 1842.

—— The Metrical Chronicle of Robert of Gloucester, 2 vols., London, 1887.

—— Chronicle of Pierre de Langtoft to the death of Edward I, 2 vols., London 1868.

Wriothesley, C., A Chronicle of England, 1485 to 1539, Camden Society Publications, 1875.

Wyclif, John, Latin Works of John Wyclif, Wyclif Society Publications, 1883-1913.

—— Tractatus de Ecclesia, Loserth ed., 1886.

—— Opera Minor, Loserth ed., 1913.

—— Polemical Works, Buddinsieg ed., 1883.

—— Dialogus, sive speculum Ecclesia Militantis, Pollard ed., 1886.

—— De Civili Dominio, Loserth ed., 4 vols., 1900.

—— De Dominio Divino, Libre tres, Poole ed., 1890.

—— De Apostasia, Dziewicki ed., 1889.

—— De Blasphemia, Dziewicki ed., 1893.

—— De Simonia, Herzber-Fräncke ed., 1898.

—— De Officio Regis, Pollard-Sayle ed., 1887.

Wycliffe, John, An Apology for Lollard Doctrine, Camden Society Publications, London 1842.

Wylie, J. H., The Reign of Henry V, 2 vols., Cambridge University Press, 1914.

Yorkshire Archeological Society, Record Series, Suppression of the Monasteries, Vol. 47, 1912.

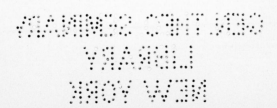
COLUMBIA UNIVERSITY
LIBRARY
NEW YORK